WHERE THE CROSS STANDS

The Last Chance To Reclaim America

Michael Harold Brown

Spirit Daily Publishing
www.spiritdaily.com
11 Walter Place
Palm Coast, Florida 32164

The publisher recognizes and accepts that the final authority regarding the apparitions in the Catholic Church rests with the Holy See of Rome, to whose judgment we willingly submit.

—*The Publisher*

Where the Cross Stands by Michael Harold Brown

Copyright © 2017 Michael H. Brown

Published by Spirit Daily Publishing

All rights reserved. No part of this book may be reproduced or transmitted in any form whatsoever without the written permission of the publisher.

For additional copies, write:
Spirit Daily Publishing
11 Walter Place
Palm Coast, Florida 32164

or contact: www.spiritdaily.com

ISBN 978-0-692-83525-8

Printed in the United States of America First Edition

For Our Lady of La Leche

"But realize this, that in the last days difficult times will come. For men will be lovers of self, lovers of money, boastful, arrogant, revilers, disobedient to parents, ungrateful, unholy, unloving, irreconcilable, malicious gossips, without self-control, brutal, haters of good, treacherous, reckless, conceited, lovers of pleasure rather than lovers of God, holding to a form of godliness, although they have denied its power; Avoid such men as these. For among them are those who enter into households and captivate weak women weighed down with sins, led on by various impulses, always learning and never able to come to the knowledge of the truth. Just as Jannes and Jambres opposed Moses, so these men also oppose the truth, men of depraved mind, rejected in regard to the faith. But they will not make further progress; for their folly will be obvious to all . . ." (2 Timothy 3)

Chapter 1

In the oldest city in the United States is the tallest known Cross in the world. It stands on the Matanzas Bay where boats head out into the Atlantic, and it can be seen from miles out to sea. It marks the spot where the first documented Catholic Mass in the U.S. took place.

Surely there had been earlier Masses, explorers in previous years who were known to have priests aboard: adventurers who had reached places such as southwestern and northwestern Florida.

But this is the official spot where—for all intents and purposes—Catholicism entered America.

It stands two hundred and eight feet tall, does the Cross, erected there in 1966 as if to offset—or war against—the evil which entered the country that decade and especially that *year*. (More on this shortly.) To kayak under this Cross, which is located at the oldest Marian shrine on the continent, is to feel Grace. I have done this numerous times, praying under its umbrella of protection.

Some day in the future—perhaps the not so distant future—this Cross and this area will play a role in the spiritual and temporal survival and revival of America.

Remember these words: "*. . . I have ordained as a beacon of light . . . the place near the water where the Cross stands.*"

When I first moved to Florida, I was not aware of that mysterious prophecy, nor, for years after, was I at all focused on this Cross, despite its prominence, twenty-five miles from my home, in the skyline of St. Augustine. I knew there was a special feeling of Grace in this city as well as the quaint feel of Europe: brick streets, preserved Colonial buildings, cobblestone, and carriage rides. I also knew that the shrine, a gorgeous little spot just north of a Ponce de Leon tourist attraction (supposedly the "fountain of youth"), was very old, dating back to the sixteenth century (long before Williamsburg, Virginia, as well as before that first official "thanksgiving" at Plymouth Rock). A unique, vine-covered chapel is dedicated there to Our Lady of La Leche, or "Our Lady of the Milk," showing the Blessed Mother nursing her Child. Pregnant women come here to ask for safe deliveries, as do women seeking to become fertile, often finding those prayers answered.

I have been to many shrines around the world, and few are as beautiful.

There are egrets, and roseate spoonbills ("miniature flamingos"). Fish jump in the pools of water from the inlet. Just out a bit, dolphins surface, chuffing air. And just south are white-sand beaches and the soothing sound of surf, overseen by fishermen on a pier and flapping pelicans.

For now, it is a quiet place.

Some day, it will be busier.

This is my own little "prophecy."

Some day, it will explain what has happened to the United States and what will occur, in the future—the near future—if trends continue, if there is not a dramatic turnaround.

I wrote a book in 1992 called *The Final Hour*, and that hour, though dwindling—despite the sand moving through the hourglass—has not yet concluded.

We have time.

We have minutes.

We as a society—and as a Church—can still rebound.

We can still recover America.

We can stave off "chastisements."

We can turn morals around.

We can prevent the unraveling of society.

With prayer and fasting, we can stop war; we can suspend the laws of nature.

With hope, we can succeed despite indications to the contrary—despite compelling facts indicating that the country has gone around the bend, that it over the top, that it has passed the point of no return. There is still a chance. It is a prayer to say beneath this Cross. It is a prayer for anywhere.

But time is short, and in the near-distance, a trumpet sounds.

Chapter 2

Our story begins in ancient Rome during the most nefarious time—at least as far as we know—since Jesus.

It's not to say that Roman times were the worst in history. It behooves us to recall how quickly people were beheaded or otherwise slain in ancient Israel for what today would not even get a person jail time, or the simple immorality during the time of Noah. Look how frequently war was waged, how populations suffered massive casualties, throughout the Old Testament. In Egypt were the pharaohs with their slaves, concubines, and paganism (occult). There was Cleopatra. There were temple prostitutes! There was Sodom. There was *Babylon* (the "whore" of *Revelation*). In the holy city of Jerusalem was King David, a man who had killed and committed adultery. In ancient Ireland, druids (the forerunners of witches). In Greece, sorcerers. There was Herod. There was the head of John the Baptist. In China, murderous tyrants. Humans have always sinned.

But Rome was a special case, and in many ways it compares to modern America.

As in our era, there was gluttony. There was rampant consumption. There was partying—feast after feast, at least among nobility. Materialism was on display everywhere, as now. When Mount Vesuvius erupted in 79 A.D., many died because they tried to save their jewels, caskets of gold, and silver dishes as the bowels of hell opened, as stones rained from the sky, as the sun darkened and the moon had declined to shed its light (see *Matthew* 24:29).

There was the smell of sulfur.

A historian named Pliny the Younger wrote that during this eruption the sea had shrunken "as if withdrawn by the tremors of the earth," beaching sea creatures—while in another direction "loomed a horrible black cloud ripped by sudden bursts of fire, writhing snakelike and revealing sudden flashes larger than lightning."

Men had lived solely for the flesh. In one doomed, soot-covered room in Pompeii, south of Rome, where there were three days of smoke and darkness, archeologists would find the graffiti of someone who had been repulsed by the decadence. On a blackened wall were scratched the words, "Sodom, Gomorrah."

There had been perversion. There was infanticide: babies left for the wolves, if the parents didn't want another, or if they were seen as unfit, as we have partial-birth abortion. There had been the occult: temples dedicated to Jupiter and Saturn and Hercules and Diana. The Roman Empire was befallen by this disaster after an unusual appearance of Halley's Comet, which hung like a sword.

Nation had risen against nation.

There had been civil uprisings.

Food shortages led to famine.

Another conflagration erupted, destroying the Temple of Jupiter. "No one could have supposed that the great triple shrine on the hill towards which the company moved would [in 69 A.D.] sink into ashes and rubble, a symbol no longer of Rome's eternity but of its seemingly imminent extinction," wrote Kenneth Wellesley, "that Italy should be twice invaded by storm, that three successive emperors should die by assassination, suicide or lynching, and that the whole empire, from Wales to Assouan and from Caucasus to Morocco, should be convulsed and disarrayed."

It was a long series of unrelenting punishment—chastisements—that stretched from about 60 A.D through the sixth century.

Invasions, uprising.

They were men, the barbarians, armed with clubs, bows, battle axes, and swords, set on total ruin. It was an apocalyptical and terrifying time, as they assaulted Rome and assaulted again, pillaging the city. In Milan a bishop named Ambrose believed the world was coming to an end, and if that was a recurrent, errant prophecy, something prophesied since the Montanists in the second century—a premature, false notion, overly dramatic—it *did* seem like a day of judgment and it *was* a day of judgment as Goths were joined by clans known as Vandals, who spilled over the borders or arrived in slashing raids.

Rome had invited it. She had laid out a red carpet. Through idolatry, her citizens had invoked demons for centuries, and now here were barbarians from the north—from those regions that would form the rootstock of Russia and Germany. Warrior types. It was the end of the Classical Period and beginning of the Dark Ages. The city was sacked not only by the Goths but also a yet more barbarous horde known as Hunnica or "Huns"—an Asian tribe identified curiously with Scythian werewolves. They were accused of drinking blood, cannibalizing the young, and destroying so many towns no one could number the dead or the pillaged churches.

They were said to come with flames and again the smell of sulfur, attacking with deafening howls, presaged, when they attacked Constantinople, by a great quake. Before them the earth trembled.

Even as such vicious attacks continued, plague returned at regular intervals and when it struck Italy between 588 and 591, it even claimed the life of Pope Pelagius II. Rampant fever and swelling called "buboes" (thus the term bubonic) only added to the woe, as did a flooding of the Tiber. The scourges caused the new Pope, Gregory, one day to be known as "the Great," to wonder if mankind was approaching the Final Judgment.

In a letter to King Ethelbert of Kent, he speculated that "the unending kingdom of the saints is approaching" and predicted there would be many "unusual" signs, including "climatic changes, terrors from heaven, unseasonable tempests, wars, famines, pestilences, and earthquakes," if not just then, soon in subsequent years. "Everywhere death, everywhere mourning, everywhere desolation!" wrote this Pontiff, also known as Gregory the Dialoguist for his many writings (including on mysticism and near-death experiences).

"Cities are destroyed, armed camps overturned, districts emptied of peoples, the earth reduced to solitude. Not a native remains in the countryside, nor scarcely an inhabitant in the cities; nevertheless, these small remains of humankind are still being slaughtered daily and without cease. The scourges of Heavenly justice have no end because even in their midst there is no correction of the faults of our actions."

Chapter 3

Although no one can be certain of dates so far back, some record January 590 as the month Pope Gregory led a three-day procession through the streets of Rome in a desperate bid to call down intervention.

The processionists carried that statue made, it was said, by the apostle Luke and kept at Mary Major Basilica—where Pope Francis currently seeks aid before trips abroad, and which Mary had once designated as the spot for a church in a dream to another Pontiff. The statue was fashioned in unstained wood and showed Mary with the Christ Child. It was believed to have special power as a palladium (relic against evil)—a belief the Holy Father obviously shared and was carried with solemnity past the flooded homes, the shops and consular offices closed because of the plague, past the old pagan strongholds and the destructions caused by barbarians, past the baths of the Emperor Diocletian, so infamous for his persecution of Christians, past people falling and dying, exorcising a city where Christians had been killed for refusing to eat meat which had been offered to a goat's head, the time-honored symbol of Satan, and now suffered disease. "Lord have mercy!" shouted the processionists.

"Kyrie eleison!"

That's when it had happened. As the procession crossed an old stone-arched bridge over the Tiber and arrived at the mouth of Via Conciliazone near St. Peter's, the devout caught glimpse, they insisted, of a mirage above an old rotund funerary: the incredible sight of an angel identified as Michael putting away his sword and marking the end of God's justice, just as many centuries later the third secret of Fatima would include the image of an angel with a flaming torch, ready to scorch the earth, but the flames drowned out with a light coming from the Virgin.

It was an apparition atop what is today called Castel Sant'Angelo, and almost immediately the sickness, the series of centuries-long punishments, ended.

Such was not superstition. When northern Spain encountered similar oppression, in this case by invading Muslims, Pope Gregory gave the miraculous statue to the bishop of Seville, who became Saint Leander.

It was credited with turning back Islam but buried during subsequent Muslim takeovers.

Centuries later, to get to the heart of this little historical excursion, in the hilly terrain southwest of Madrid, a humble cowherd—*so often is a shepherd!*—was searching for a lost cow. His name was Gil Cordero (of Cáceres) and the year was 1326. Thirsty and fatigued and heading toward the sound of a stream (he'd been searching for three days), Cordero spotted the missing animal laying on a mound of stones, motionless. Figuring the animal to be dead, the cowherd pulled out a knife and prepared to take the animal's hide, which he could then sell. As was customary, in these parts, where Christianity was unabashed, he made the initial incision in the form of a Cross on the cow's breast.

Suddenly, the animal moved—not just flinched, not just budged, but sprang up on its hooves, restored to life. The "dead" cow was standing!

At the same moment, Gil spotted something or someone coming from the woods—a woman, but no normal woman. That was obvious immediately. There *were* no normal women out this way, in the lonely, untrammeled wilderness. It was a female "of marvelous beauty," say historical accounts (at the Marian Library in Dayton, Ohio) and she *said, "Have no fear, for I am the Mother of God, by whom the human race achieved redemption. Go to your home and tell the clergy and other people to come to this place and dig here, where they will find a statue."* She also asked for a chapel to be built there.

Although Cordero was initially mocked, officials knew that many relics had been buried during the horrible Muslim invasions and the bishop led the entire village—knights, noblemen, and priests, as well as average folks—to the spot Cordero indicated, pushing aside stones and boulders and digging into the earth until it collapsed into a small cave.

Inside was just what the apparition promised: a statue (along with an ancient bell). As a document buried with it explained, *it was the image of Mary that Pope Gregory the Great had paraded a thousand years before in Rome.*

The unstained, oriental wood seemed in perfect condition despite six centuries in the earth—coming out of seclusion at a time when the last Muslim holdouts were being expelled. (Such had been the Muslim or "Moor" dominance that to the west, in Portugal, a hamlet had been named after one of Mohammed's daughters, whose name had been Fatima.)

Here we get to the most amazing part of it. For the area where Cordero and fellow villagers found the statue was known as "Hidden Channel," after a waterway that apparently narrows and was obscured by woods. It may have been the water Gil had heard, for all we know, in 1326.

What we know for sure is that in the local dialect, "Hidden Channel" was translated as *"Guadalupe."*

Chapter 4

That was two full centuries before the far more famous Guadalupe appearances in Mexico.

Incredibly, the site of this apparition became a major pilgrim spot and—more incredibly, more providentially yet—replicas of the statue, the palladium used by Pope Gregory, spread far and wide.

One of the pilgrims known to have frequented the shrine and carry a replica was a Spanish explorer (of Italian birth) named Cristóbo Colón, or Christopher Columbus. The replica went with him on his voyages to the new world.

Here we come to America.

It was at the monastery housing this effigy, in Extremadura, by Guadalupe River, that the Spanish monarchs, Isabella and Ferdinand, in fact had signed documents authorizing that first voyage of Columbus.

"Isabella had prayed at the foot of the Black Madonna for guidance on whether to finance Columbus's journey," notes an historical account. "Columbus went to the monastery to pray for a safe voyage. When he returned to Spain, he traveled to the monastery to thank the Virgin for her help and protection."

This gets us into the nitty-gritty of it and also takes us to what is not recorded in history textbooks.

For Christopher Columbus was not only a devout Catholic, but—like other explorers who would follow in his wake—a missionary.

He considered the evangelization of the New World his *primary* goal.

If his devotion was not obvious enough in the names of his key ship, the *Santa Maria* (named for the image at Guadalupe), it was there during the first voyage as the crew recited the Hail Mary daily and upon landing at spots along the way, in the Caribbean, prayed the *Salve Regina*.

One such island Columbus named Guadeloupe.

Others were called by names such as San Salvador (for the Savior).

In fact, Columbus, I came to learn, was a third-order Franciscan who when possible attended daily Mass, including a liturgy as well as Confession before setting out on his dangerous, remarkable, history-making exploration.

Fair of complexion, with freckles and an aquiline nose, neither pudgy nor rail-thin, with grey hair, on the muscular side, high of cheekbone, somewhat taller than average, with the carriage of an aristocrat, yet the sensibilities of a crewman, Columbus often had a monk's cord around his waist and sometimes—not aboard, that anyone has reported, but after his famous expeditions—was seen in a monk's robe, entertaining thoughts, at one point, of entering a monastery.

This was one very Catholic man, which goes a ways toward explaining the resistance to him, the attempts by secularists to downplay his role in the very establishment of a hemisphere—not just North America, but the Latino regions as well—and eliminate a day that on the American calendar was dedicated to him. His goal was not just discovery, as one writer noted, but "bringing the remote and unknown regions of the earth into communion with Christian Europe; carrying the light of the true Faith into benighted and pagan lands and gathering their countless nations under the holy dominion of the Church."

This is hidden history.

This I never learned in history class.

As it turns out, there is much hidden in the establishment of America.

On the *Santa Maria*, the standard of the Cross was raised, and the explorer carried a picture of Jesus Crucified. Some believe they sang "Star of the Sea" on the way across the often foreboding Atlantic—these waters so prone to tropical storms, even category-five ones.

Concerned about direction, and anxious to spot land, Columbus and his crew at one point spotted a strange light that to this day has not been explained definitively. This was on October 11, 1492, and was described, in his own journal, as "a small wax candle that rose and lifted up, which to few seemed to be an indication of land." Academics have come up with various potential explanations: that it was tar torches carried by natives, or the bioluminescence of protozoa along the rock (this latter explanation discarded due to Columbus's depiction of it as from a point source, and also the timing: such protozoa only radiate lights after a full moon; this was near the first quarter). Whatever it was, the worried crew soon caught sight of land.

Upon landing, Columbus immediately planted the standard of the Cross and prostrated himself three times in thanksgiving, according to biographer George Barton, kissing with teary eyes "the soil to which he was conducted by the Divine Goodness," while the others "participating in his emotions and kneeling as he did, elevated a Crucifix in the air.

"Raising his grateful hands and thanking from the bottom of his heart his Heavenly Father, Columbus found in the effusions of his loving gratitude, an admirable prayer, the first accents of which are preserved by history: *'Lord Eternal and Almighty God, Who by Thy Sacred Word hast created the heavens, the earth, and the seas, may Thy Name be blessed and glorified forever. May Thy Majesty be exalted who hast deigned to permit that, by Thy humble servant, Thy Sacred Name should be made part of the world.'*"

Christopher Columbus was declaring half of the world—a hemisphere stretching, as it turned out, more than twenty thousand miles, from Chile to Alaska, from Vancouver to Puerto Rico—for Christianity, for Catholicism, for Jesus.

No wonder later scholars would later seek to besmirch him!

No wonder his name is being eradicated!

How many secularists—atheists—would want it known that the discovery of America was a Christian moment and that the first thanksgiving was Catholic?

San Salvador means "Holy Savior."

Academics wanted it to be "Watlings Island."

It was here, on this island in the Caribbean, that Columbus ordered two large pieces of wood cut and formed into a crude Cross, raised on the spot where first he had planted that banner.

Soon after, they discovered an island he called "Santa Maria de la Conception," once more betraying not only his deep and ardent Catholicity but his devotion to Mary.

Had she sent him that "candle"?

A large Cross was planted here also, in the center of the island.

Miracles of healing were soon associated with the Cross.

Fevers vanished.

And according to lore, the Cross survived attempts by the Indians—unnerved by its fame—to destroy it.

Said Barton, "They came to it in large force and tried with all their might to pull it down. The Cross remained unmovable, defying their strength. Mortified at this failure, they tried to destroy it by fire.

"Having collected a lot of dry brushwood, they came at night and surrounding the Cross with inflammable fagots to a considerable height, set fire to them. The Cross soon disappeared in the flames and smoke. The idolaters went away satisfied, but the next morning they perceived the Cross, subsisting entirely and perfectly preserved, amid the smoking cinders. Its natural color was not even altered, except that at the foot there appeared a little dark spot as if someone had approached it with a lighted candle."

Chapter 5

In gratitude for the historic voyage—and saving his crew from a storm on the way back—Columbus returned on pilgrimage to Guadalupe in Extremadura, venerating the dark two-foot-tall Romanesque Madonna, which was clothed in extravagant vestments added a few decades after its discovery, the underlying statue rarely seen in the form it was when Cordero discovered it but—when first unearthed—decidedly more humble of dress. Her face nearly black, she held a scepter, the Christ Child on her lap. Power emanated to such an extent that King Alfonso XI attributed defeat of Muslim invaders and the Christian retaking of Spain to the relic.

(Would this one day be a message for America?)

Again, this long before Guadalupe in Mexico.

In 1928, the Spanish Guadalupe image was formally crowned—ironically, on October 12, the anniversary for Columbus' discovery of America.

Several Native Americans brought back to Spain by Columbus were baptized at the shrine.

Meanwhile, crosses had now been erected in the New World. In Cuba, one stood by a river. And clerics, who had joined Columbus on subsequent voyages—Franciscans, Dominicans, Augustinians—were soon aboard the ships of other explorers, including Ponce de Léon, who discovered Florida around Easter in 1513, according to many accounts, and hence the name *La Florida* in recognition both of the verdant landscape and Paschal flowers (though still others say the arrival took place in April).

Upon landing (wherever in Florida he may have set anchor), Ponce recited the same solemn prayer Columbus had:

"Almighty and Eternal Lord God, Who by Thy Sacred Word has created heaven, earth, and sea, blessed and glorified be Thy humble servant and praised be Thy Majesty, and grant that through Thy humble servant Thy Sacred Name may be known and preached in this other part of the world. Amen."

This trip had no priest and so there was no Mass—yet—on what would be the mainland of North America. That would soon change. There are legends that Saint Brendan of Ireland landed in Greenland long before and that here had been a liturgy involved around 1112 A.D. (Greenland is technically part of North America), and there are legends of Vikings setting foot as far south as Newfoundland and even Maine. At Kensington, Minnesota, a slab of soft calcite some believe was put there in the 1300s bore mysterious runic markings. If not a hoax, it meant that a century before Columbus (who during his second voyage had Mass celebrated at La Isabela west of the Dominican Republic), Vikings had etched the following:

"Eight Goths and 22 Norwegians on an exploring journey from Vinland very far west. We had camp by two skerries, one day's journey north from this stone. We were fishing one day when we returned home and found ten men red with blood and dead. AVM [Ave Virgin Mary] save us from this evil. We have

ten men by the sea to look after our vessel forty-one days' journey from this island. Year 1362."

If true, the Virgin had been invoked seven centuries ago in what is now the U.S.

What we do know is that by 1521, De Léon, accompanied by at least one priest, had landed in Puerto Rico and then near Naples, Florida, where he was mortally wounded by hostile Indians. As pointed out by Michael V. Gannon, an eminent historian, "Catholic priests sailed with Ponce de Léon in 1521 on his second voyage to the land that Ponce had discovered and named; and on six subsequent Spanish explorations to the Florida shoreline from 1521 to 1565, priests of the Church were here to raise the Cross in the sand, and to offer unnumbered Masses on wilderness altars. In the striking phrase of the nineteenth-century historian John Gilmary Shea, 'The altar was older than the hearth.'"

Four years after De Leon was in Puerto Rico, two Dominican priests were *known* to have been part of the attempt at a settlement somewhere just north of Florida. It is believed these priests were by Cape Fear near Wilmington, North Carolina before venturing elsewhere and establishing a small settlement called San Miguel de Gualdape, where, it is believed, Mass was celebrated in the summer or autumn of 1526.

By some accounts they landed in South Carolina on the Feast of the Archangels. The explorer they were with, who made various voyages, sent one of his expeditions as far north as Delaware Bay.

But where was San Miguel de Gualdape?

Was it in South Carolina, Georgia?

Some believe they may also have had a temporary settlement at what is now Jamestown, Virginia.

Was the first U.S. Mass said *there*?

In 1528, on Good Friday, a landing party led by another Spanish explorer put shore at what is now Stump Pass near Englewood on the Gulf side of Florida and was there at least until Easter Sunday, by which time it is virtually assured the Franciscan priest with them, Father Juan Suarez, celebrated the liturgy—raised the Host, offered up the chalice, invoking Christ in the most powerful prayer known to man.

On Holy Saturday, the commander, Pánfilo de Narváez, delivered a formal declaration (to Indians hiding in the brush) requiring them to "recognize the Church as mistress and superior of the universe, and the Supreme Pontiff, called Pope . . . and that you consent and give opportunity that these fathers and religious men may declare and preach these things to you."

So it was that the Spanish explorers, funded by royalty who instructed them to evangelize the natives (not harm but convert them), had established not just a Christian nation but a *Catholic* one by 1528—almost a century before Jamestown.

Moreover, this occurred just before an event momentous not only in the way of Catholicism and the Western Hemisphere, but in the way of any religion in the entire world.

That was Mary's appearance at that second and vastly more famous "Guadalupe" near Mexico City, where a dozen years after Ponce de Léon's first landing, another peasant, Juan Diego, very much like Cordero, witnessed the Blessed Virgin on a hill called Tepeyac above a temple dedicated to a goddess and not far from where Aztecs at pyramids were conducting horrendous blood sacrifices. Soon, a Christian temple would replace—banish—the pagan one. Soon, the Indians would halt the sacrifices.

So many know the story: how she appeared on a hill to Diego, who had been converted by the Spanish, and left her image—still extant, still inexplicable, with hues and coloring that scientists cannot identify—on the burlap-like sisal agave cactus cloak or "tilma" he wore, an image still readily available to visitors at the massive shrine that has hosted royalty and Popes and, with up to twenty million visitors a year, became the most visited Catholic place in the world (with more than double the visitors at Lourdes, and also more than the Vatican; more even than make the annual Hajj pilgrimage to Mecca). The eyes of the image, on material that has never disintegrated (despite a normal longevity of just a few decades), refract light like human ones and has been discovered upon magnification to have the distinct silhouettes of human figures—including Diego—in her pupils or irises: *human images* resembling those involved in the case (Juan, the bishop, and witnesses), as if to photograph the moment that occurred five centuries ago. This was all located in parts of the eye that were close in size to a millionth of a yard.

Not in those centuries has the cactus burlap disintegrated—despite the acidic, saline air of Mexico City and despite the normal longevity of such material for just a few decades.

Replicas on the same material lasted but thirty years.

Five hundred years after first materializing, it looks freshly painted (as I can attest, visiting it most recently in 2016). The "paint" in the image has never faded, cracked, or peeled, as images just half a century old would do, and up close, within centimeters, it seems colorless; on my first visit I witnessed how her aspects shift according to distance from it, as if alive.

Even if the tilma hadn't lasted, even if there weren't those inexplicable images in the eyes, even if scientists could determine what kind of pigments or oils or minerals were used in the "paint," there would be the irrefragable mystery of how anyone could have painted with such intricacy on such a surface. There is no under-sketching, and even if there was, the pocks and spaces in such a weave would prohibit any form of refined painting. The tone on the image's skin—the gray and caked-looking white pigment of the hands or face—combine with the rough surface of the cloak to "collect" and diffract light.

This isn't what pigments in artwork do; this is what the surface "sculpturing" of a butterfly scale or bird feather does.

Like Guadalupe in Spain, she has dark myrtle olive-green skin, reminding one of Queen Esther in the Old Testament (of whom it was written, in a Babylonian text, "Her skin was greenish, like the skin of a myrtle"). She wears clothes common to both Mexico and Palestine.

It was a year, 1531, of Halley's Comet.

As an early account put it, "Our Lady descended to Tepeyac; at the same time, there came a smoking star."

The Indians had part of the truth, but they were lacking what the Virgin now came to give them: Jesus.

In fact, the day of "resurrection" on the Aztec calendar (their "Easter," if you will) was December 12.

That was the date, of course, on which Mary first appeared at Guadalupe, a date later changed with institution of the Gregorian calendar to December 24.

The Aztecs "Easter" was joined to what we celebrate as Christmas while the Guadalupe image presented a woman was pregnant!

No human could have designed this.

More, between eight and twelve million Mexicans all but immediately converted to Christianity.

And it all occurred as more explorers—more *Catholics*—were sailing to the New World, specifically attempting to settle and evangelize that land of Paschal flowers known as *La Florida*.

Chapter 6

If the picture wasn't intriguing enough, Dominican priests with a commander named Don Tristán de Luna y Arellano landed somewhere on the northern shore of the Gulf of Mexico, perhaps near what is now Pensacola or not too far from there at Pascagoula, Mississippi. The date: August 15, 1559.

The Pensacola settlement, marked to this day by a Cross, lasted just a year or so before it was devastated by a hurricane.

But wherever the historian's eye was cast, Gannon pointed out, there stood an altar and surmounting Cross.

Something big, something spiritual and intense, was afoot in this wonderland of white sand and crystal springs. There was a mystical character, an afflatus that arched into the soul as one ventured into a wilderness of burnished palmettos (roamed by stealth panthers), of drifting manatees and grazing prairie buffalo, of tea-dark creeks spotted by the gliding, scanning browridges of alligators (which may have been more than twenty feet in length and weighed perhaps a thousand or more pounds).

As the first priests arrived, egrets waded, redfish schooled, dolphins leapt.

Across this array of wilderness had also ventured Hernando De Soto. Had his crew partaken in the first Florida Mass back in 1526—when, in the footsteps of De Leon, they set about claiming the vast territory, traveling from Tampa up north toward Tallahassee before entering what is now Georgia and the western Carolinas and circling back to Louisiana and crossing the Mississippi?

There is no doubt that Masses, perhaps the first in the U.S., were said when De Soto arrived, for among his six hundred men were twelve priests, most of whom died as De Soto's crew was decimated by disease and hostile Indians.

A fierce battle with Indians occurred near the Alabama River on October 15, 1540, and herein is proof that the Body and Blood of Christ were raised above this mysterious land that one day would be called the U.S. and stand as the most unique nation in world history (and now stands as one tragically endangered). During the battle, wrote Gannon, "all the vestments, chalices, patens, altar furnishings, and wheat and wine needed for Mass were destroyed." This was more than two years after De Soto landed and all but proves the liturgy had been celebrated from what is now Tampa up through Tallahassee and points north, west, and east around the time of Guadalupe.

A later chronicler, Garcilaso de la Vega, recorded the effect of the Indian destructions, saying, "Thereafter, an altar was erected and decorated on Sundays and Holy Days of obligation. Standing at the altar, a priest, vested in a buckskin chasuble, said the *Confiteor*, the introit of the Mass, and the oration, Epistle, and the Gospel, and all the rest up to the end of Mass without consecrating. The Spaniards call this the 'Dry Mass,' and the one who said the Mass, or another priest, read the Gospel and delivered a sermon on it. From this they derived consolation in the distress they felt at not being able to adore Our Lord and Redeemer Jesus Christ under the sacramental species. This lasted for almost three years, until they left Florida for [Mexico], the land of the Christians."

Jesus had been elevated above the sand, above those palmettos, near the springs De Leon may have sought, in a land Columbus had never reached, a land so many had died yearning to conquer.

And it had experienced this Catholic sanctification nearly six decades before Jamestown and *eighty years before the Puritans* at Plymouth Rock.

That De Soto had a profound affinity for Christianity is seen in the name he had given the bay he entered: *Espirítu Santu*, the "Bay of the Holy Spirit."

We know it today as Tampa Bay. (So too erased was the "Bay of Saint Mary," now called the Chesapeake, the "Lake of the Blessed Sacrament," now Lake George, the "Village of Mary," now Montreal, and the mighty "River of the Immaculate Conception," now called the Mississippi.)

Bear with me for a bit more history.

Despite awaiting Indians, one priest from Saragossa on a ship called the *Santa María de la Encina* was so determined he waded ashore and was clubbed to death, kneeling with a small Crucifix, uttering a final prayer.

Priests died, settlements failed. Food gave out and waves from fierce cyclones battered decks, snapped anchor cables, and sent storm surges that caused those who had made shore to flee inland for their lives.

This was an era during which hurricanes may have been much more intense than in recent centuries, for the world was just now coming out of global warming—the Medieval Warmth—that according to one scientist I interviewed, Dr. Kam-biu Liu of Louisiana State University, may have caused "mega-hurricanes" all the way up to New England: above category-five in intensity. In the Gulf were what researchers call "warm core rings"—pockets of unusually warm water that cause explosive barometric deepening, made all the worse by higher global temperatures (ones similar to what the earth is currently approaching).

That warming was fading but may still have been in place at the time of these Spanish expeditions.

One official at the Dade County emergency management office claimed the fiercest systems may have had winds of up to two-hundred-and-fifty miles an hour and sixty-foot storm surges—in effect, tsunamis—that lashed Marco Island near Naples where explorers so often tried to land and where he believed was evidence Colusa Indian settlements had been buried by sand hurled in gigantic ocean surges (others disputed this).

Whatever the details of historic "mega-storms," it was beyond dispute that settlers were far less prepared than modern man for the eventualities of even a tropical storm, not to mention one with tornadic winds. They were thrashed, drowned, or forced ashore by leaking wallboards. There were food shortages that had reduced sailors and priests alike to eating horse meat and chewing on the hide. Tensions led to dissension—outbursts of violent anger. Many vanished during inland expeditions. Divine help was an urgent necessity. The liturgy was an obvious answer. If, by overwhelming implication, Mass was celebrated during the De Soto mission, there is no doubt whatsoever it also occurred during the De Luna expeditions that stretched into the 1560s, for it is recorded that during the offering of Mass at the beachhead near Pensacola (noted Gannon), one of the priests, Father Domingo de la Anunciación, suddenly turned with the Sacred Host in his hands and addressing De Luna—questioning the leader's faith—"risked a prophecy," telling the governor "that if he would become reconciled with the captains and repent his sin in causing dissension and suffering among the people, before three days a ship would arrive in port with help to relieve the hunger of the colony." (The governor did, and a supply ship arrived the following day!)

Chapter 7

But eventually they fled to Mexico. Another attempt at permanently establishing European rule—and Christianity—had failed.

And now we get into the thick of it. We come to the north-central part of Florida, where Christianity in the U.S.—and arguably America itself, as we know it—were founded.

I am speaking here of the general area around what is now St. Augustine, which some historians believe may have been the first place De Leon actually landed in Florida before venturing south and into the Gulf (or, at least, somewhere betwixt Cape Canaveral and Jacksonville).

It was in this area that a man who was an evangelical and determined in his Catholicism as Columbus succeeded in what had eluded, what had frustrated, so many before him: established the first permanent European settlement in mainland North America.

This is so well recorded that it is beyond dispute: there was a Mass in 1565—again, decades before Jamestown, Williamsburg, Plymouth, or Santa Fe—after extraordinary, supernatural occurrences.

Mary was involved. There was no question about this.

It involved Admiral Pedro Menéndez de Avilés, who like De Luca had been tasked by the king of Spain specifically "to instruct the Indians," relating to them gently so that they "might more easily be taught our Holy Catholic Faith and be led to good practices and customs and to perfect behavior," which to Europeans meant shedding their pagan beliefs in earth spirits. That also had been the instruction to De Luca: not to antagonize the Indians but to "settle by good example, with good works and with presents, to bring them to a knowledge of Our Holy Faith and Catholic Truth."

If, up to now, no one could say with official certainty if, when, and where the explorers held liturgies, it was indisputable that Mass was celebrated on U.S. soil at St. Augustine on September 8, 1565, Mary's official birthday.

The oldest city in the United States is thus also the place of the first formally verified elevation of the Host on the U.S. mainland—this massive territory (from Atlantic to Pacific) that soon would no longer all be lumped together as "Florida" but would become forty-eight states and the most advanced and powerful nation in the history of the world, outdistancing the Roman Empire.

Catholics were first to settle the United States and did so specifically and beyond question to establish Christianity.

How many modern classrooms would dare to teach *this?*

If men like Columbus and De Soto were obvious in their affinity for Christ (and the Blessed Mother), it was also the case with Menéndez and of course the four priests he brought in a large fleet of nineteen ships and 1,500 soldiers, sailors, millers, sheepshearers, hunters, and farmers.

The chaplain of the fleet, which was to be followed, soon, by a thousand more soldiers, was Father Francisco López de Mendoza Grajales.

As Gannon put it, in these men "lay the Church's hope of planting the Cross permanently in Florida's sands."

A Cross near the water.

Were there problems?

There were problems: storms again. In the rollicking sea, only five ships remained together. The flagship had broken away from the rest, never to be seen again, and another hobbled toward land with severe leaks. One ship lost its way, and another sprung a leak.

The five vessels fared well until they ran into another tempest, this one, in the words of Menendez's brother-in-law, Gonzalo Solís de Merás, "the most frightful hurricane one could imagine.

"The sea, which rose to the very clouds, seemed about to swallow us up alive, and such was the fear and apprehension of the pilot and other sailors that I pushed myself hard in exhorting my brethren and companions to repentance."

Crewmen tossed supplies and equipment overboard to lighten the ship as waves crashed over. It was a storm that would terrify them for several days, such that, in Father Lopez's words, "we thought surely we would perish, and during the whole night I preached to the crew, and exhorted them to put their trust in God."

It wasn't clear what "category" this storm rated, but obviously it was one with unusual potency. These were seasoned seamen. They had seen gales. They had been in tropical storms. Had the devil, prince of the power of the air, conjured the storm to resist them? (Indian for hurricane was *hurucan*, which meant evil spirit.)

Winds pummeled the crew as they scrambled on a rolling deck, withdrawing masts, overwashed, the ship feeling at times as if it would turn on its side, or—tossed by an avalanche of sea, by a tsunami, cresting high above—would capsize altogether. The sounds of straining floor-boards and mast posts, of groaning side planks, was enough to unnerve the most intrepid ship hand, these waves that during day had turned from turbid to frothing, boiling gray, below a sky piled with puffy cumulus as the system had approached, then mountainous black ones shooting lighting from all sides as the center approached. Prayer was the only recourse as crewmen felt their way along gunwales, reaching for rope or deck rails. Once it hit, thunder was barely audible in the roar of the wind, the plummeting clouds, the sky melding with waves.

Even ships as large as these tossed and then bobbed at the bottom of troughs, before the next wave lifted them like driftwood. Rain came sideways. There was spindrift. And the spray from the waves would have been blinding, if it was a cyclone. Waves one after another, from beneath, from the sides, the ocean moving more like a river, crew shifting cargo for better ballast, the ship taller than wide, the hull slamming in troughs, battering itself, keeling from thirty degrees on one side to thirty degrees on the other, the weight at the bottom their salvation, along with Mary.

This went on, from what I can tell, for the better part of two days.

Finally, on August 5, the ship with Menendez and Father Lopez had made it to Dominica (where there were rumors of Indians who practiced cannibalism), and then on to Puerto Rico, where they were reunited with two other vessels and the lost flagship.

It was a miracle. No one was sure how it happened. After taking on new supplies, and additional men, the expedition, still missing two-thirds of its force, set forth (on

August 15) and headed toward the favored, if treacherous, trade routes of the Bahama Channel.

But it was here, on August 27, according to Father Lopez's own diary, that a marvel factored into the picture.

It came at nine that evening when a comet suddenly blazed through the dark directly above the ship. According to Father Lopez, all were astounded, for it gave "so much light that it might have been taken for the sun. It went toward west—that is, toward Florida, and its brightness lasted long enough to repeat two *Credos*."

God, he wrote, "showed to us a miracle from Heaven."

Chapter 8

The priest took it for what it was: an omen, reassurance from Heaven, from Mary, *Estrella del Mar* (the "Star of the Sea"), that despite their fears, despite the tempests, despite surges of ocean in an era when surges from the sea may have been more than what modern seamen witness, God was with them; His Son was watching.

It was the next day—the feast day of Saint Augustine, August 28—that, in the words of Father Lopez, "we soon had the pleasure of seeing land, and found ourselves actually in Florida."

And so it was that the first permanent settlement in what within a century would be the United States of America was established by a devout admiral and a cadre of missionary priests.

Did they teach this at Harvard? Was it part of "common core" curricula? Did even students at Christian schools—Catholic and otherwise—know of these events?

After sailing along the coast (first Cape Canaveral, then north, past Daytona Beach, in search of a harbor they could use for the big ships), scouts were sent ashore and encountered deeply spiritual Timucuan Indians who were friendly and even provided shelter for them. From there Menéndez headed for a French fort in Jacksonville to halt France from taking over the new land, and after a brief skirmish, moved south again and moored the vessel at what would become known as St. Augustine. Two companies and infantry, along with Father Lopez, disembarked and crossed the white sands, widened at low tide (this spot known as "River of the Dolphins," which still frequent it) on September 7.

The plans specifically were to proclaim the land under the "Name of God."

Menéndez chose to wait for the Virgin's official birthday to himself set foot on the sands of this dazzling, dangerous place, this shore of sultry winds, sable palms, and gently swaying oaks—gentle now that the tempest had passed. On spots in the distance were the fuliginous updrafts of small wildfires, and on tufts of island, may have been the remarkable rookeries known to these parts: spoonbills and egrets and great herons and anhinga, wings spread to dry.

Above: a tern, or a parade of pelicans, a hawk kiting, perhaps an eagle, the bird that would become this nation's symbol, nesting as they did a short way inland.

When he disembarked, the admiral was met by Father Lopez, who was carrying a Cross and singing *Te Deum Laudamus* ("To God Be Praise").

Cannons fired. Flags undulated in the breeze. Noted Father Lopez, "The general, followed by all those who accompanied him, marched up to the Cross, knelt, and kissed it. A large number of Indians watched these proceedings and imitated all they saw done."

A solemn Mass was then said in honor of the Virgin's Nativity and a royal envoy had rations served to the Indians, and the Timucuans themselves contributed food, as they all dined together.

This—not the Puritans, not Plymouth Plantation—was the first "thanksgiving."

The menu was a stew of salted pork and garbanzo beans, accompanied with ship's bread and red wine. Some speculate the Indians brought mullet, crab, oysters, and other local seafood, perhaps even cured alligator and venison, possibly wild turkey.

Not for another forty-two years would Jamestown be established, while the Plymouth thanksgiving came fifty-years after.

More to the point: after Mass, Holy Water drawn from the brine inlet was used to christen this first permanent American settlement, Nombre de Dios (Name of God).

As at other places in Florida and spots discovered elsewhere—in the Caribbean, in Mexico—a Cross was planted in the sand.

Chapter 9

Aside from everything else, it was also the very beginning, as Gannon phrased it, "of the parish of St. Augustine and of the permanent service of the Catholic Church in what is now the United States."

A mission was established to service the Indians.

It was the first Catholic church on the continent.

Official records unmistakably label it as where "the first Mass was said on September 8, 1565 . . . and afterwards, an Indian village was built there, with a chapel in which was placed an image of *María Santísima de la Leche*" (or "Our Lady of the Milk": after an image in a grotto at Bethany near Bethlehem of Mary nursing the Child, a grotto where there is also what tradition holds to be a sample of the Virgin's milk).

In 1965, a two-hundred-and-eight-foot Cross was erected at this spot on the inlet and is visible for miles out in the Atlantic, as much a marker, a beacon, as a lighthouse.

I have sat and prayed there. I've kayaked the inlet. I have felt the unusual Grace.

This place may figure into the future of America.

When I spoke briefly with Gannon, a professor emeritus at the University of Florida and once director of the mission, now ninety, he explained that the Cross—at minimum the highest free-standing Cross in the hemisphere, believed by most to be tallest in the *world*—was put where it is through study of an old map citing the vicinity of Menéndez's landing. "Nobody knows exactly where the Mass took place," Gannon told me. "It could be a hundred yards this way or a hundred yards that way. We picked out the general area and engineers chose the spot." Two-thirds the length of a football field, the Cross was fashioned with stainless-steel plates brought down in sections from "somewhere up north," according to Gannon; assembled in St. Augustine; and then set on a granite slab. Nearby is a bronze statue of Father López, arms raised in praise, in thanksgiving. The massive structure, notes the diocese, "stands as a sentinel over the Mission and a 'Beacon of Faith' for all who pass this way."

Chapter 10

And so the tallest known Cross was in place at that spot, *Nombre de Dios*, from which Christianity fanned out to the rest of Florida, then north as far as Virginia, west to Texas. The dedication: September 8, 1965, in the midst of the tumultuous, revolutionary, and ultimately devastating "Sixties." Few even heard of this construction --lost as it was in news about the Beatles (who released four albums that year), a war in Viet Nam (which was worsening), and riots in places like Los Angeles (which grabbed headlines with the looting and arson). There were the sirens, the winds of war, the drumbeat of rock, and it pounded at the American psyche. Signs? On Palm Sunday, tornadoes swept across six states. There was also a massive blackout in the Northeast: darkness from Western New York to Boston, D.C., and Manhattan.

The St. Louis Arch opened that year and got the attention; not the Cross.

Science was quickly becoming the new religion. Who cared about a Cross in some small Florida city? It was a nation mesmerized by the Gemini space program, launched from the very land, Canaveral, that Menéndez had skirted.

But there it was, in St. Augustine, the Cross by the water, silent, towering over the inlet, marked the first Christianity in America.

And that very September in 1965 was another comet, ringing back memories of Father López.

This was "Ikeya-Seki" (named for its discoverers) and it was so bright that even by day it was visible to the naked eye, the brightest such celestial object in a thousand years, to be labeled by astronomers as "the Great Comet of 1965."

It is thought to have been part of a family of comets called the "Kreutz sungrazers," which date back many centuries.

Might a member of this family—or, improbable though it may seem, *Ikeya-Seki* itself—have been what Father Lopez also had witnessed five centuries before? "It came out of nowhere," said one 1965 report, "and was described by some as being ten times brighter than the full moon." There, smack in the middle of the raucous, life-changing, country altering 1960s, the month of the Cross, was the comet. One could at least furrow the brow.

The comet was part of the debris, apparently, of a much larger comet—hundreds of comets were thought to have been spawned—that some estimated as coming around every five hundred or so years (five hundred not so far away from 1565) and however unlikely, that it was the same bolide, its brightness called to mind the good Father Lopez ("so much light that it might have been taken for the sun") and played into the notion, from ancient times, that comets bore mystical significance.

Was there something apocalyptic about the founding of America?

There in a new hemisphere, under what was clearly the sure Hand of Christ, a new land was opened up to the rest of the world, a wondrous, primeval place; not only the site of the first parish Mass, but "the first authenticated instance of a Roman Catholic community gathering together on the Eastern Seaboard to celebrate the rites of Christian worship," as another historian ably phrased it. "Due to its significance, the site of the first Holy Mass in the United States has become known in modern times as 'America's Most Sacred Acre.'"

Great was the prophetic current during the foundation of America. Many rushed here believing (as historians put it) "that their actions might hasten the Second Coming of Christ" and Columbus himself guessed that the world had one hundred and fifty years before its end.

Europe was recovering from the "Black Death," during which visions had risen on all sides, including those of a Franciscan friar, Roger Bacon, who alluded to a "great Western Ocean" and the impending threat of the antichrist. Columbus was among his adherents.

Did this explain the zeal of explorers to expand Christianity to the ends of the earth (see *Matthew* 24:14)?

Before the great bubonic outbreak, society had swerved onto the wrong course—had taken a truly disastrous turn, to fashion and commercialism—and though it wasn't The End, seers had sensed something coming.

Now, they were feeling the same about exploration of distant lands.

"The discovery of the New World promoted end-time fantasies of cataclysmic ends, temple rebuilding, and crusading," noted historians Timothy J. Johnson and Gert Melville. "Seeking an understanding of the origins of the Native Americans, some concluded that they had in fact descended from the lost ten tribes of Israel destined to be convert to Christianity in the last days. Indeed, the discovery of the New World brought together a collection of beliefs or signs of the impending end."

Such facts are why one must be discerning when it comes to predictions.

Yet certain things could not be discounted, such as the Battle of Lepanto, shortly after the landing at St. Augustine, during which Muslim invaders were dramatically defeated by a Christian armada. There was a massive Rosary procession from the minute the expedition had started, and as Pope Pius V fervently prayed and as cardinals gave Communion, the allied fleet boldly positioned its forces under the command of Admiral Giovanni Andrea Doria—who like Columbus had a devotion to Mary and carried an oil-painted copy of the Mexican Guadalupe, the same one that had vanquished the false Aztec gods with him. The battle was engaged on October 7, 1571 and as it raged, Doria retired to his cabin, knelt before the image, and implored her help.

By nightfall, the momentum began to miraculously change. A Turkish squadron was captured and a sudden wind drove the smoke of combat in the faces of Muslims, who panicked. In one of the great maritime victories, the Christian fleet captured 117 galleys, liberated fifteen thousand enslaved Christians, and sank or burned about fifty Turkish galleys while losing only twelve itself—even for rationalists, impossible odds.

At the very hour of triumph Pope Pius, conversing with some of his cardinals, suddenly turned from them, opened a window, and as if approached by an invisible messenger remained standing for a long while, eyes toward the sky. Closing the window, he pivoted back to the cardinals and said, "This is not a moment in which we talk about business. Let us give thanks to God for the victory He has granted to the arms of the Christians"—a prophecy of what was occurring out there—near far-off Corinth—with Doria.

That there was a Mass in 1565—if I may repeat, decades before Williamsburg, before Santa Fe, before Plymouth Rock, after extraordinary, supernatural occurrences—is beyond dispute.

Mary was involved. No questioning this.

The oldest city in the United States was thus also the place of the first provable Eucharist on the mainland—this territory that soon would be the most advanced, powerful nation in the history of the world.

Establishment of a Christian nation had not only been a goal of Menendez's but his central one.

It came at a price.

Just a year after Saint Augustine was settled, Jesuits were killed on what is now Amelia Island. According to survivors, a missionary was strangled underwater and beaten to death while reciting a litany of the saints and clutching a rosary. So intense was some of the violence that soon the order pulled out of the state, leaving evangelical work to Franciscans, one of whom was slain at the foot of a mission altar, beheaded by natives who carried the severed trophy atop a high post and pillaged four other missions. It was said that the Indian uprisings—which erupted periodically—were due to the "browbeating" of Timucuans when it came to issues such as polygamy, trial marriage, burials (the Timucuans revered ancestors; missionaries ordered their remains burned), and native dress, all against doctrine. There was also human sacrifice. When a leader ("cacique") died, children were sometimes killed and buried alongside him (or her, for their were female chiefs). At the same time, natives suffered greatly from the Spanish, their population plummeting from an estimated 770,000 to 150,000 in just five decades, mainly due to disease brought by the Europeans but also as a result of plundering and brutality, for

Spaniards were known to take Indians as slaves and kidnap chiefs for ransom. Gold and sugar were often behind the conquests. Timucuans were tortured or hunted down and torn asunder by bloodhounds.

But they would find common good—the Timucuans and Europeans, astonishingly—in Catholicism. It was natives who composed the majority of congregants in the first parish (*Nombre de Dios*, where the Cross was planted), and in less than a century, twenty to thirty thousand were baptized at dozens of churches. Between that landing at St. Augustine—since the comet—and the beginning of the 1700s, a hundred and forty churches and mission centers were established in Florida alone, converting, educating, and baptizing eleven different tribes. Sadly, attacks by pirates and later the British would soon destroy those missions and schools and convents to the last one, and Indians would continue to see their numbers plummet as a result of diseases brought over from Europe, viruses against which their immune systems were unfamiliar.

But Catholicism had touched the soil of America, had been planted, with that Cross, and a spiritual bond with the natives was forged, shown in the impressive spiritual sensitivity of Timucuan. The Virgin Mary was especially popular among them. "To question whether the converted Indians showed themselves to be true Christians, and not just savages over whom had been placed a thin veneer of the white man's religion, Fray Francisco Parejo [of Auñon, Spain] answered that many of the men and women were so fervent in their new beliefs, and so well instructed, that they catechized other Indians," wrote Gannon. "The baptized Indians regularly assisted at Mass on Sundays and feast days, 'in which they take part and sing.' From the *visitas*, or mission stations, the outlying tribes came to the *doctrinas* to hear the *Salve Regina* sung on Saturdays, then stayed overnight for Mass the next morning. The Indians were also regular in the recitation of morning and evening prayers, and showed a consoling initiative in things spiritual. Whenever a missionary left the *doctrina* for an extended journey, it was not unusual for the men and women to approach him for Confession first, saying, 'perhaps I shall die before your reverence returns.'"

By March 25, 1606, the first Confirmation known to have occurred in the U.S. took place at the church in St. Augustine, which has the oldest parish records in America and which would also host the first ordination.

Images of saints graced the Indian churches, particularly the Blessed Mother.

Chapter 11

I had no idea of this history before moving to the area.

Looking for what fit my family best in the state, on impulse I had gotten off an exit for the city of St. Augustine, which I had never visited before, and to my befuddlement, felt a wave of Grace.

Before the trip, I didn't even know exactly where the city was located, let alone about its intense history.

I had no clue it was the place of the first official liturgy, the first parish; no clue about all the historic struggles and the Catholic favor of America's very discovery and foundation.

There was simply a special, magnetic feeling.

We did not end up in the city (we located a ways south), but still can feel it when we visit: the Blessed Mother, Saint Augustine. Jesus. He was present even to those Timucuans, *especially* to the Indians, who had a natural spiritual proclivity, one that searches for God in its own way, sometimes—like anyone, like other approaches to the spiritual - diverging onto wrong paths but longing for God.

How brave were all these explorers—Catholic or Indian or Protestant, operating on faith in the face of dangers at every turn. It was wild territory. It shows how blind faith bears greatest fruit. One can summarize the struggle by imagining the difficulties of encountering diamondbacks and coral snakes, then the vicious thunderstorms and floods and long dry seasons—wildfires—and alligators, and if not reptiles, sharks in the inlets, and mosquitoes from all corners; and poisonous plants inland; even charging buffalo roamed the prairies; even panthers.

In New Mexico, which was settled soon after Florida, had been the parched mesas, mountain lions, and more Indians.

It was also in New Mexico that the oldest still-standing church would be built and dedicated to the Archangel Michael in Santa Fe forty years before Jamestown.

I can attest to a special feeling here also. Spirits roam. They are everywhere there have been people and there had been paleo-Indians in America for at least eleven thousand years. In 1539, a missionary named Marcos de Niza proclaimed the entire region as the "New Kingdom of Saint Francis" and planted a Cross as other Catholics played their part, perhaps mystically, including Maria of Agreda. Wearing a sky-blue cape (perhaps to ward off evil) over her cream-and-brown habit with black veil, the Franciscan Conceptionist nun reportedly bilocated in the early seventeenth century from her cloistered convent in Spain, allegedly appearing to the Jumano Indians in what we now call Texas and New Mexico. "She is said to have visited them over five hundred times, most frequently from 1620 to 1623, walking among them through the land and conversing with them in her own tongue," writes author Marilyn H. Fedewa. "According to accounts in historical documents, the 'flying nun' taught the Indians about Christianity and prepared them for Baptism."

After Florida, Catholicism touched the Carolinas, Texas, and New Mexico. The same was true of Virginia, where even *here* were found Crucifixes, Rosary beads, and medals (in the remains of a fort that *preceded* Jamestown). In Jamestown itself (where Protestants too had planted a Cross), a silver Catholic reliquary was unearthed from the grave of an early Jamestown leader, Gabriel Archer. "Some have suggested that Archer might not just have been a secret Catholic, *but a secret Catholic priest,*" noted *Christianity Today* after archeological finds in 2015 (*my italics*).

Far to the north, near Lake Huron, the Madonna appeared to a Jesuit named Jean de Brebeuf and a dozen years after that to a couple of Huron Indians who had been imprisoned by Iroquois (helping the Hurons, who were converted, to escape).

Was this in history class—*any* history class—at a single college or university in the United States, including Catholic ones?

The important point is that Christianity had set foot in a big way in what would become America. It was like the Virgin of Guadalupe was giving marching orders. Two who visited her shrine in Mexico City, Padre Eusebio Kino and Fra Junipero Serra, then fanned up into Arizona, New Mexico, and California.

In Upstate New York, there was also the saintly Mohawk, Kateri Tekakwitha, while in Ossernenon, three Jesuit missionaries died by the hands of Mohawks as they sought, as did so many settlers (Catholic or Protestant), to claim pagan grounds for Jesus—seeing their mission not just as stepping onto a new continent but as planting the Cross and raising the Chalice to defeat the devil, who hid behind arcane ritualism. As one of the martyrs, Saint Isaac Jogues, said (in 1643): "How often on the stately trees of the forests did I carve the most sacred name of Jesus, so that, seeing it, the demons might fly, who tremble when they hear it! How often, too, did I strip off the bark to form the most Holy Cross of the Lord, so that the foe might fly before it; and that by it, Thou, O Lord, my King, 'might reign in the midst of thy enemies' (*Psalm* 109:2), the enemies of thy Cross (*Philippians* 3:18), the misbeliever and the pagan who dwell in that land, and the demons who rule so fearfully there!"

Not to be denied was the absence of Christ and that pagan rites had charged the soil.

There are "territorial" spirits" and they gain power through what humans have done below, with rituals, with "sacrifices," with the idolatry of gods or goddesses—including those of the earth, wind, fire, air, and water. These forces were what Jesus came to break and that were now battled by great saints like Serra as he traveled from Guadalupe across Mexico and up through California by foot—on painful, swollen feet—carrying a heavy wooden Cross as he established missions from what is now San Diego up to San Francisco in the interesting year of 1776, as a nation was born.

Chapter 12

In the mix—from the West Coast to the East—was invisible turbulence. Goodness adheres to goodness; badness collects around what is occult. In Moodus, Connecticut, strange rumblings were heard by Indians who believed there was a "god" in the area who got angered at local witches and caused a wind that echoed and blew witches from their caves. ("Thought to be a sign of the god's anger, local Native American tribes would offer sacrifices to appease his wrath," said an article.)

In Salem, Massachusetts, where an Indian village had stood, horrid trials for witchcraft were held when the daughter and a niece of a Puritan minister, aged nine and eleven, started having "fits" (that is, seizures, which are often suspect as having a spiritual root). As the Smithsonian magazine put it, the girls "screamed, threw things, uttered peculiar sounds and contorted themselves into strange positions, and a local doctor blamed the supernatural." Another girl, Ann Putnam, age 11, experienced similar episodes, blaming three women, including a Caribbean slave named Tituba, who, said Smithsonian, confessed that "the Devil came to me and bid me serve him" and described "elaborate images of black dogs, red cats, yellow birds and a 'black man' who wanted her to sign his book. She admitted that she signed the book and said there were several other witches looking to destroy the Puritans."

That "spiritual forces in high places" (see *Ephesians* 6) cling to vicinities was seen too in the heartland of the new nation, in Ohio, where massive tornadoes strike a town called Xenia with a frequency that has no known meteorological reason (the Indians referred to it as the "place of the evil wind"), while in Upstate New York (straddling old Seneca grounds) was a bizarre magnetism, and it erupted in the centuries after the nation's founding. It was along this stretch (known now as the "psychic highway") that "prophet" Joseph Smith first had his visions. Noted an author named Mitch Horowitz, "Stretching from Albany to Buffalo, it was the Mt. Sinai of American mysticism, giving birth to new religions such as Mormonism and Seventh-Day Adventism, and also to Spiritualism, mediumship, table-rapping, séances, and other occult sensations—many of which mirrored, and aided, the rise of Suffragism and related progressive movements. The nation's occult culture gave women their first opportunity to openly serve as religious leaders—in this case as spirit mediums, seers, and channelers. America's social and spiritual radicals were becoming joined, and the partnership would never fade. Indeed, the robust growth of occult and mystical movements in nineteenth-century America—aided by the influence of Freemasonry and Transcendentalism—helped transform the young nation into a laboratory for religious experiments and a launching pad for the revolutions in alternative and New Age spirituality that eventually swept the globe. In the early twentieth century, the new spiritual therapies—from meditation to mind-body healing to motivational thinking—began revolutionizing how religion was understood in contemporary times: not only as a source of salvation but as a means of healing. In this sense, occult America had changed our world."

As he and others pointed out, in 1774, the woman now called Mother Ann sailed from Liverpool to New York with eight followers. As the legend goes, the ship almost capsized in a storm. But Ann, in a state of eerie calm as waves crashed over the bow, told the captain that no harm would befall them. She reported seeing "two bright angels of God" on the mast. The ship survived. After toiling at menial labor in New York City, the pilgrims—now twelve, minus Ann's husband, it is further reported—scraped together enough resources to form a tiny colony in the knotty, marshy fields of Niskayuna, near Albany in New York's Hudson Valley in 1776. The twelve apostles, as they saw themselves, anointed the place "Wisdom's Valley."

"Throughout the first decades of the nineteenth century, itinerant ministers continually traveled the newly settled region, crisscrossing its hills and valleys with news of the Holy Spirit. The circuit-riding preachers and their tent revival meetings often left the area in a torrent of religious passion. For days afterward, without the prompting of ministers or revivalists, men and women would speak in tongues and writhe in religious ecstasy. Many would report visitations from angels or spirits. Folklore told of the area once being home to a mysterious tribe—older than the oldest of Indian tribes, maybe even a lost tribe of Israel. These ancient beings, so the story went, had been wiped out in a confrontation with the Native Americans. Some believed their ghosts and messengers still walked, composing a world within a world amid the daily 'goings-on.'"

Across the "new" land, the nascent nation, was the spiritual dimension.

In Niagara Falls was a spot in the gorge downstream from the famous cataracts known as "Devil's Hole" due to its dark past, including a massacre. The Indians believed that a giant snake representing evil resided in a twenty-foot cavern hard by the river and one explorer, Francis de la Salle—who encountered Devil's Hole and ignored the legend—was soon after murdered by members of his expedition.

That had been in 1687.

Seven decades later was the massacre in which more than eighty British were scalped or otherwise wounded and then thrown by the Senecas into the turbulent gorge. A creek there was known as "Bloody Run," and centuries later, would become famous for its toxic contamination (as the white man brought his own evil). "Violent deaths at this most baleful location have been attributed to suicide, murder and the occasional slip-and-fall 'accident,' and not a year goes by without another victim being claimed by Devil's Hole," noted a local newspaper. "Visitors tell of hearing strange, mournful voices and sighting mysterious lights in the vicinity, called by one visiting writer a place 'cursed by an aura of sheer bad luck.'"

There was a spiritual battle in place: no question. Some said they saw the Face of Christ in the mist that rises at the base of the famous falls; on the dark side, others cited numerous suicides, and in olden times, the Indian maidens who were sent over the brink in an annual sacrifice.

Both Augustine and Thomas Aquinas spoke of spirits that can infest places.

Was this not true across the "new" American landscape?

Down in Florida (along I-4, near Orlando) were old Seminole burial grounds and in this area would rise a hamlet of mediums, psychics, and fortune-tellers (as was also true in western Upstate New York).

In that hamlet, called Cassadaga today, statues of Indians today adorn drooping landscapes.

(Just to the west of Cassadaga are Orlando and its famous attractions, now including a theme park dedicated to Harry Potter.)

Other mounds could be found near or under New Orleans, Louisiana, and Savannah, Georgia.

In San Francisco the natives referred to some in their tribes as "two-spirited" (or *berdache*: known for homosexuality).

And so as the nation formed, so were there struggles, spiritual and temporal.

According to lore, George Washington had an apparition of a woman at Valley Forge who showed him the darkness as well as the future of the republic. Although it has been discredited—the account was penned by Charles Wesley Alexander, a Philadelphia journalist who published fictional visions and dream pieces in a periodical for Union veterans of the Civil War, under the pseudonym "Wesley Bradshaw"—there can be truth in fiction, in this case of "a dark, shadowy being as an angel standing, or rather floating, in mid-air between Europe and America," and also an "ill-omened specter" from Africa (slavery?).

Battling darkness was the influx of Christianity.

In 1776, all European Americans save for 2,500 Jews identified themselves as Christian, according to the Heritage Foundation: ninety-eight percent of the colonists were Protestant and a remaining 1.9 percent Catholic (as what had started with Columbus, De Leon, and Menéndez took a back seat).

But the point is *Christianity.*

Benjamin Franklin, Ethan Allen, Thomas Jefferson, John Adams, and Thomas Paine, if not overly devout, were greatly influenced by their Christianity.

So were Samuel Adams, Patrick Henry, John Jay, and Roger Sherman (all embracing it).

When there was reference to "a shining city upon a hill," in the writing of John Winthrop, it wasn't something secular; it was from *Matthew* 5:14.

In fact, Virginia's first legal code mentioned a "sacred cause"; mandated regular church attendance; and even proclaimed "that anyone who speaks impiously against the Trinity or who blasphemes God's name will be put to death."

Biblical texts were incorporated wholesale into documents such as the Mayflower Compact.

If, at St. Augustine, Catholics had planted the first Cross, Protestants were codifying it.

Swearing, cursing, lying, drunkenness, obscene words, and sodomy were punishable.

While Thomas Jefferson was certainly not a Christian in the strict biblical sense (editing out parts he thought were fable), and while, also no doubt, Masonry was involved in the nation's early days, and even the design of the capital, Jefferson declared himself as "a disciple of the doctrines of Jesus" and the Declaration of Independence—the most famous document produced by the Continental Congress during the Revolutionary War—proclaimed that: "We hold these truths to be self-evident: that all men are created equal; that they are endowed by their Creator with certain unalienable rights; that among these are life, liberty and the pursuit of happiness"; referred to "the laws of nature and of nature's God"; and closed by "appealing to the Supreme Judge of the world," noting the signers' "reliance on the protection of divine Providence."

As governor, Jefferson issued calls for prayer and fasting.

A Christian nation?

No doubt.

"By almost any measure, colonists of European descent who settled in the New World were serious Christians whose constitutions, laws, and practices reflected the influence of Christianity," said the Heritage Foundation.

America was supposed to be a nation founded on the New Testament.

It was Christianity that formed the very concept of liberty.

In law lectures back then, it was almost as if they were quoting Aquinas.

Would you know that now? Would modern politicians, media, judges, and educators act like it was Christian? Or were they distorting its past to extinguish its religion?

Moreover, "separation of Church and state" wasn't to halt religion from influencing government but government from controlling religion.

When there were arguments that involved religion, it was usually about *how government could best serve the Christian faith.*

Religious liberty was a right that was "unalienable."

In his famous Thanksgiving Day Proclamation (in 1789), Washington, for his part, said it was "the duty of all nations to acknowledge the providence of Almighty God, to obey His Will, to be grateful for His benefits, and humbly to implore His protection and favor," and recommended "the People of these States to the service of that great and glorious Being, Who is the beneficent Author of all the good that was, that is, or that will be . . ."

How could this now be taken from us?

"Almost without exception," said Heritage, "they agreed that civic authorities could promote and encourage Christianity and that it was appropriate for elected officials to make religious arguments in the public square. There was virtually no support for contemporary visions of a separation of church and state that would have political leaders avoid religious language and require public spaces to be stripped of religious symbols."

The first communities in the Northeast were Bible-based commonwealths.

The constitution in South Carolina even proclaimed the Old and New Testaments to be of Divine origin.

Maryland was a haven for Catholics fleeing persecution by the English government. (Virginia-Maryland: Virgin-Mary.)

In 1777, the Continental Congress voted to spend $300,000 to purchase bibles that were to be distributed throughout the thirteen colonies.

And in 1782, the United States Congress declared: "The Congress of the United States recommends and approves the Holy Bible for use in all schools."

On November 20, 1798, in his Last Will and Testament, Patrick Henry wrote: "This is all the inheritance I give to my dear family. The religion of Christ will give them one which will make them rich indeed."

"Give me liberty or give me death," he also had said.

Said the Bible (*2 Corinthians* 3:17: ". . . where the Spirit of the Lord is, there is liberty."

It was James Madison who said, "We have staked the future of all of our political institutions upon the capacity of mankind for self-government . . . according to the Ten Commandments . . ."

All but two of the first one hundred and eight universities were Christian (including Yale and Harvard).

Signers of the Declaration, writers of the Constitution, and those who penned the Bill of Rights were men who were not just Christians but Christians who loudly proclaimed it.

On his very day of Inauguration, after a swearing in on an open Bible—which he kissed—President George Washington gathered Congress and his first Cabinet at the Chapel of St. Paul in Lower Manhattan and consecrated the United States under the protection of the Almighty. The U.S. was consecrated, Christian-style, by its first and most famous president.

A chief justice in the Supreme Court, John Marshall, would write (in 1833) that "the American population is entirely Christian, and with us Christianity and Religion are identified. It would be strange indeed, if with such a people, our institutions did not presuppose Christianity, and did not often refer to it, and exhibit relations with it." And as Abraham Lincoln would later remark, "Our fathers established these great self-evident truths that posterity might look again to the Declaration of Independence, and take courage to renew the battle which their fathers began, so that Truth and Christian virtues might not be extinguished from the land."

Yet, this was to be taken from us. This was to be stripped. This was to be whitewashed for future generations, for schoolchildren—indoctrinated as they would be in a public system that sought to stamp out the religious roots.

This "roots" saga we never hear about; we never see made into a TV series.

"Then my eyes beheld a fearful scene," wrote Alexander. "From each of these countries arose thick black clouds that were soon joined into one; and throughout this mass there gleamed a dark red light behind which I saw hordes of armed men, who, moving with the cloud, marched by land and sailed by sea to America, which country was enveloped in the volume of cloud.

"And I dimly saw these vast armies devastate the whole country and burn the villages, towns, and cities that I had beheld springing up."

Chapter 13

Fiction as prophecy.

It was dangerous stuff. It was perilous stuff. One day, America would head down a path that had never been recorded in its previous history: not even close, not even, perhaps, in ancient Rome.

Nations that had been Christian were allowing—had bequeathed the right—to end the lives of babies even just weeks or days away from birth—and if the abortionist somehow didn't fully succeed, to leave the child on a cold sterile stainless-steel table, unwrapped, to die alone, wailing to no one's ears.

In Canada, Christianity—Catholicism—had arrived just five years after Columbus, in 1497, when, as Wikipedia recounts, in 1497 "John Cabot landed on Newfoundland, raised the Venetian and Papal banners and claimed the land for his sponsor King Henry VII of England, while recognizing the religious authority of the Roman Catholic Church. A letter of John Day states that Cabot landed on 24 June 1497 and 'went ashore with a Crucifix and raised banners bearing the arms of the Holy Father.' In 1608, Samuel de Champlain founded the first Catholic colony in Quebec City. In 1611, he established a fur trading post on the Island of Montreal, which later became a Catholic colony for trade and missionary activity."

Around this same time, a shrine to honor Saint Anne was constructed in Montreal and became a site of miracles.

But the modern spirit was wiggling in the womb. There would be the French Revolution—during which Reason was proclaimed a goddess and man began to worship his own intellect.

This was "enlightenment." This was "progress." And it quickly spread across the nations. The sciences began a takeover. The brain was to be exalted, not the monstrance. The same France that had sent over Christian explorers who had settled Quebec and instilled devotions such as that of Saint Anne—who had given devout names to towns and rivers—turned secular and "rationalistic" and began to drag America, at first, mainly its academia, into the same orbit.

Around this time Masons, who embraced the new French philosophies, began not just spreading the "enlightenment," but influencing the very nature of America's capital, with a number of the "Founding Fathers," starting with George Washington himself, belonged to Lodges (though they were also Christian).

We see the remarkable struggle here, a confusion (the hallmark of evil), a jostling between God and His adversary (just as was seen in the confused spirituality of Indians).

One could debate what was intentional and what was not—what was clever design and what was in the imagination of those seeking conspiracy (what even tends to paranoia)—but without question Masons built the White House (laid its cornerstone) as well as the Capitol, and *if* there were intentional symbols, imbued (in the Masonic tradition), with occult power, then there was a potential curse (or at least influence).

On October 13, 1792, a parade of Freemasons assembled at the Fountain Inn in Georgetown with architect James

Hoban (a Mason and Catholic) and proceeded to the site of the excavation for what was then called the "President's House."

Though the White House would eventually be destroyed by seizing British (during the war of 1812), the point was that the original house for U.S. presidents had an occultic taint. One could add that a Masonic French architect, Pierre Charles L'Enfant, designed the streets of D.C. to form Masonic symbols. Did such symbols actually transmit power? Did they hold a sway that was not detectable? For that matter, what was one to make of the dollar bill with an all-seeing eye atop a pyramid and underneath the word *Novus Ordo Seclorum* (New World Order)?

Hoban was a member of Georgetown Lodge Number 9 despite an encyclical issued by Pope Clement XII fifty years before threatening Catholics who became Masons with excommunication.

(Did he even know this encyclical? Do current-day Catholics?)

While Washington wasn't at the excavation, by all accounts he was present at (and presided over) a Masonic ritual during which the cornerstone was laid for the Capitol (or as it was known then, the "Congress House").

The date was September 18, 1793, and Washington (a good—a great—man) crossed the Potomac and first stopped at the site for the future White House before moving on with members of three Masonic lodges to the site for the Capitol, marching "in the greatest solemn dignity, with music playing, drums beating, colors flying and spectators rejoicing" up a rudimentary dirt road that one day would be Pennsylvania Avenue.

Occultists in Europe—the lodges there—believed that the new land would be the top rung of a new world order, a new Atlantis, and some believed that from it would come the antichrist.

Chapter 14

Was this why Columbus and his followers mentioned the end times? Is this why—besides the lure of gold or sugar—they were in such a rush: the belief that an antichrist would be spawned in the New World? Was there a chance they were in a race to spread Catholicism and stop that?

It was an uproarious time, and at turns may have seemed apocalyptic. Duels. The wild west. Virtual eradication of Indians (many peace-loving). Along the Mississippi, a fantastic series of quakes—the most powerful on record in the lower forty-eight—rocked farms and towns from Missouri to Boston (where church bells were set ringing). In one stretch of the mighty river, at one point, the water, tsunami-like, moved *backwards*. This was from 1811 to 1812 and they were up to "eight" in magnitude—far more powerful than any recorded on the San Andreas. The ground itself rolled like waves, with fissures unleashing geysers of mud, sand, and water. Nor was nature the only source of turbulence: the year after the quakes, Washington D.C. was burned to the ground by the British.

If the Indians had their paganism, and violence, but also their great spiritual sensitivity, and if the Spaniards had carried the banner of Catholicism, but often fell into greed, as well as brutality, if the Founders were Christian but also, in some cases, Masonic, so it was that good and evil, truth and deception, showed themselves in the establishment of America.

For every Elizabeth Anne Seton, for every John Neumann, for every Mother Cabrini, there were dozens of plantation owners, lumber magnates, and soon oil barons. In a word: secularism. Worried about this, nuns in Louisiana belonging to the Ursuline order sent President Thomas Jefferson a letter asking if their property rights would be honored by the new government. His response, which I have seen, is still kept encased at the convent. "I have received, holy sisters, the letter you have written me wherein you express anxiety for the property vested in your institutions by the former governments of Louisiana," wrote Jefferson. "The principles of the Constitution and government of the United States are a sure guarantee to you that it will be preserved to you sacred and inviolate, and that your institution will be permitted to govern itself according to its own voluntary rules, without interference from the civil authority . . . Be assured it will meet all the protection which my office can give it."

It was a historic statement but it didn't end the Ursulines' worries. There were other problems. They were short staffed. The work was overwhelming. And things got nearly desperate when a mainstay of the community, Mother St. Xavier Farjon, died in 1810. That caused another nun, Sister St. Andre Madier, to appeal to a cousin of hers back in France. The cousin was named Mother St. Michel Gensoul. Sister Andre asked her to come to the U.S. and help the struggling Ursulines. The details are relevant: Mother St. Michel had escaped the deadly wrath of the French Revolution and had much work to do in her own land. France was a mess. Religious communities still had been under the duress of Napoleon. But Mother St. Michel also realized that the Ursulines in the United States might cease to exist without her help. Inspired by the Holy Spirit, she went to Bishop Fournier of Montpelier and requested leave.

One can imagine the bishop's reaction. He needed Mother St. Michel where she was. He couldn't afford to lose another nun. So many had died in the revolution or fled. "The Pope alone can give this authorization," he told Mother St. Michel. "The Pope alone!"

That was tantamount to refusal, for it was virtually impossible at that time to communicate with the Pope, who was under house arrest by Napoleon. Not only was he in the distant city of Rome and not only was mail far less than what it is in our day, but Pius VII had been cut off from the world by the emperor's men, who held him in custody as they waited to transport him to Fontainebleau. We don't need too much history here. We need only know that secularism raged—chalices, monstrances, and statues had been destroyed; churches turned into museums; Mary replaced by the Goddess of Reason—and the Pope's jailers had received strict instructions not to allow communication. Thus, writing to him was, at best, a waste of time.

But that didn't stop Mother St. Michel. She knew the Virgin Mary and she knew that if it was God's Will, Our Blessed Mother could do anything. With that trust did she pen a letter to the pontiff on December 15, 1808, setting forth the reason why she wanted to aid her sister nuns in America. "Most Holy Father," she wrote, "I appeal to your apostolic tribunal. I am ready to submit to your decision. Speak. Faith teaches me that you are the voice of the Lord. I await your orders. From your holiness, 'Go' or 'Stay' will be the same to me." When no opportunity arose for getting the letter out of France, Mother St. Michel prayed before a statue of the Blessed Virgin. "O Most Holy Virgin Mary," she said, "if you obtain a prompt and favorable answer to my letter, I promise to have you honored in New Orleans under the title of 'Our Lady of Prompt Succor.'"

It wouldn't be the first time Mary was known as Our Lady of Perpetual Succor. There was an ancient, miraculous painting under that title on the island of Crete. Like Our Lady of Good Counsel, as well as the statue revered by Columbus, this one had moved to Rome during Moslem invasions. There its great and quick powers were noted when a paralyzed man was healed immediately after the image was processed near his home. Countless other miracles were attributed to it. The image was also known as "Our Lady of Never-Failing Help" and "Our Lady of Ever-Enduring Succor" and it showed Mary holding her Child, the Madonna styled in the Byzantine fashion and gazing at those who looked upon her and Jesus.

But now there was a new title, and a new series of miracles.

Soon after her prayer, Mother St. Michel's letter left Montpelier—finally.

The date was March 19, 1809.

And somehow it got to the Pope—who despite the dire need for nuns in France granted Mother St. Michel's request.

Just over a month after the letter was mailed, Pius had a response sent to Mother St. Michel, saying, "Madame, I am charged by Our Holy Father, Pope Pius VII, to answer in his name. His Holiness cannot do otherwise than approve of the esteem and attachment you have fostered for the religious state . . . His Holiness approves of your placing yourself at the head of your religious aspirants, to serve as their guide during the long and difficult voyage you are about to undertake."

The prayers had worked and they had been astonishingly prompt. Mother St. Michel ordered a statue carved and Bishop Fournier, overwhelmed by the miracle, requested the honor of blessing it.

The statue of "Our Lady of Prompt Succor" arrived in Louisiana with Mother St. Michel in 1810.

And nearly immediately there were two momentous miracles.

The first occurred in 1812, when a terrible fire erupted in New Orleans, devastating what is now the French Quarter. That was where the convent was and the fire was a true holocaust—propelled by the wind, it headed right for the convent.

That was when one of the nuns placed a small statue of the Virgin on a window facing the fire and Mother St. Michel again began to implore the Virgin. "Our Lady of Prompt Succor, we are lost unless you hasten to our aid!"

It is said that the wind instantly shifted, driving the fire away.

The Ursuline convent was one of the few buildings spared destruction!

Such events show us that nothing is beyond the reach of prayer, no problem, no disaster.

It was not without significance as far as the establishment of America.

Three years after the hellish fire, in 1815, yet more trouble haunted New Orleans during the war between the American and British. Louisiana was a part of the United States but England was looking to confiscate the former territory and its troops arrived near New Orleans on the plains of Chalmette to square off against General Andrew Jackson.

This too was an amazing and well-documented miracle. For there was no way the Americans could win. The British had fifteen thousand troops. The American force was six thousand. It looked like the Americans—and the city of New Orleans—were doomed.

The night of January 7 the Ursuline sisters went before the Blessed Sacrament and stayed through the night. Others joined them in the chapel, praying and weeping before Mary. On the morning of January 8 the vicar general offered Mass at the main altar, above which the statue had been placed. The prayers were said in special earnest, for the thundering of cannons had been heard by all in the chapel.

During Communion—at the very moment of the Eucharist—a courier rushed into the chapel to inform all present that the British had been miraculously defeated.

They had been confused by a fog and had wandered into a swamp, in full view of the waiting Americans, who fired upon them from unseen positions.

About 2,600 British were lost while the Americans suffered very few casualties.

It was not Our Blessed Mother who killed the British. It was not Mary who initiated battle. But it was the Blessed Virgin who came to the aid of the just who implored her. "The result seems almost miraculous," admitted the New Orleans *Picayune*. "It was a remarkable victory, and it can never fail to hold an illustrious place in our national history." General Jackson himself went to the convent to thank the nuns for their prayers. "By the blessing of Heaven, directing the valor of the troops under my command, one of the most brilliant victories in the annals of war was obtained," he proclaimed to his troops, describing the victory in a letter to the vicar as a "signal interposition of Heaven."

The old convent remains the oldest building in the Mississippi valley but no longer houses the statue or convent, which are now located on State Street. But the feeling around the statue, which I have visited several times, is tangible. Graces still flow. Favors are granted. We see in this case the powerful way the Virgin can operate when pious people come to her in faith. The great 1815 victory came after a night in front of the Blessed Sacrament and then was announced during holy Communion, leaving us no doubt as to the source, the wellspring, of Mary's miracles (Jesus).

How different it was back then.

Oh Mary, you have come so many times through history to aid your children. Come now to our aid. Come to the prompt aid of our families. Come to the aid of the United States, which has sunken into materialism and unholiness and darkness.

And let us remember the words of Jefferson:

"I have received, holy sisters, the letter you have written me wherein you express anxiety for the property vested in your institutions by the former governments of Louisiana. The principles of the Constitution and government of the United States are a sure guarantee to you that it will be preserved to you sacred and inviolate, and that your institution will be permitted to govern itself according to its own voluntary rules, without interference from the civil authority . . . Be assured it will meet all the protection which my office can give it."

Chapter 15

How far the U.S. would stray: from open acknowledgment not just of the Divinity but of Mary's intercession, by no less than Andrew Jackson (arguably as famous a general as has existed, soon to be president), to where we are now.

Jackson was a first-hand witness to spiritual warfare when the homestead of three brothers in Tennessee who'd fought for him in the Battle of New Orleans (John, Jesse, and Drewry Bell) was plagued by a poltergeist that became infamous as the "Bell Witch." Strange bangs were heard at night and sheets yanked from the beds.

In 1819, when Jackson decided to visit the farm to see what all the talk was about, horses pulling the wagon with his entourage halted suddenly as they approached the property and could go no further.

When Jackson proclaimed that it must be the rumored witch, he was said to have heard a disembodied female voice telling him to proceed, which Jackson and his men did, discussing the Indians and other topics as they waited to see if the supposed entity would manifest. When, after several hours, it did not, one of the men, claiming to be a "witch tamer" (with a silver bullet), boasted that the spirit wasn't appearing because it was afraid of the bullet.

According to an account, this fellow was immediately pummeled by unseen hands and kicked to the ground, inspiring the men to leave—though not Jackson, who remained the night. What happened is not clear, but the next morning Jackson and his men were seen in nearby Springfield, en route to Nashville. Is it just a legend? Was he even in the area at the specific time cited? It has been reported that he owned adjacent land, knew the Bells, and once said, "I had rather face the entire British Army than to spend another night with the Bell Witch."

Danger. Much danger! One day, witchcraft would be allowed in military chapels.

Transgenders would be allowed to enlist.

O, Babylon: how far indeed have you fallen?

Did it not foretell it in Chapter 17 of Revelation?

"Then one of the seven angels who had the seven bowls came and spoke with me, saying, 'Come here, I will show you the judgment of the great harlot who sits on many waters, with whom the kings of the earth committed acts of immorality, and those who dwell on the earth were made drunk with the wine of her immorality.' And he carried me away in the Spirit into a wilderness; and I saw a woman sitting on a scarlet beast, full of blasphemous names, having seven heads and ten horns. The woman was clothed in purple and scarlet, and adorned with gold and precious stones and pearls, having in her hand a gold cup full of abominations and of the unclean things of her immorality, and on her forehead a name was written, a mystery, *'Babylon the Great, the Mother of Harlots and of the Abominations of the Earth.'* And I saw the woman drunk with the blood of the saints, and with the blood of the witnesses of Jesus. When I saw her, I wondered greatly. And the angel said to me, 'Why do you wonder? I will tell you the mystery of the woman and of the beast that carries her, which has the seven heads and the ten horns.'"

Might the beast one day rise from America—or was America preordained as the nation that would one day *fight* the "beast"?

In America, near "many waters," was New York, where, on the East River, flowing into the Atlantic—a thousand miles up the coast from St. Augustine—was the United Nations.

There was an old Hopi Indian prophecy (from more than a thousand years ago) that foresaw societal events preceding several "great shakings" of the United States. Leading up to the final shaking was a "house of glass" that would be built in the eastern part of what the Indians knew as "Turtle Island" (America). The house of glass, according to a man who studied the supposed prophecy, Lance Richardson, would be "where nations would come seeking peace but not to trust many of those nations, which would not be seeking peace but power." They claimed this auguration came from a "man out of Heaven" with a beard, a white flowing robe, and blue-green eyes" who, their legend had it, preached peace, instructed the Hopis how to cultivate corn, and spoke about the future. It's said that in the wake of that "visit" the tribe permanently became a peaceful one, burying its weapons.

They'd called him "Massow" or "Massuah" and some of his predictions already seemed to have materialized. One was that white men would come to North America and force Indians onto parcels of land (reservations). It was also prophesied, allegedly, that these arrivals would develop an amazing system whereby water would be available even in mountain villages (where people then had to haul water up from valleys) and a way whereby, with a mere touch of the wall, an abode would have light. The Hopis were also told, however, claimed Richardson, that they should not depend on such things, for one day the water would be unfit to drink and there no longer would be light. They were shown that white settlers would come in "carriages" pulled by animals (horses) and the day when these "carriages" would be able to move without animals and eventually would lift from the ground into the air (planes); that carriages would also move on rails (railroads); that there would be "bugs" (cars) on a "black ribbon across the continent" (highways). The first shaking, figured Richardson, was World War One, leading up to a second shaking and a "cobweb" that stretched across the world, allowing people to speak into it and be heard far away (telephones, radio, perhaps the World Wide Web). They were told that time would speed up, to the point where it was difficult for families to spend time with each other; females would wear skimpy clothing, or nothing at all; men would want to become women, and women become men; that the concept of family "would be destroyed" (Richardson wrote this before 2000); and that there would be a great commotion in nature—including great tornadoes, hurricanes, earthquakes, and an alteration of seasons: that during this period there would be darkness, destruction of life on the oceans, and upheaval; riots coast to coast; and a war against the "turtle" as the "bear" would join against America with the "country led by the red sign." They were shown that one of the carriages in the sky would drop a large "gourd" that turned the land below to inhabitable ashes (seemingly, Nagasaki and Hiroshima), and that such a "gourd" would later be dropped on the nation that had originally used it (America).

There would be a great famine, they supposedly heard, as part of the final "shaking" and that food should be stored for "three seasons" (some Indians had more than one growing season a year, making it unclear if it means three years or less).

Among the final signs leading up the shaking would be an unusual "alignment of planets."

Was this just occultism?

If so, the white men had their own brand of it.

In the same region of Upstate New York where Mormonism, feminism, and American Freemasonry were born, Spiritualism also germinated.

That involved seances to raise the dead and it would spread from Upstate New York to the rest of America and Europe, ensnaring everyone from Abraham Lincoln to Robert Browning, Victor Hugo, and Queen Victoria.

The whirlwind started innocently on a raw March night in 1848 as John Fox and his family extinguished the lamps in their small, box-shaped tenant house in Wayne County near Rochester, snuggling in for the night. Sleep was not to come. Suddenly, there was an eruption of strange sounds—rapping noises that started out fast, fizzled out, then recommenced.

Not given to superstition, John figured it was the wind, or maybe a neighbor hammering tacks. But wife Margaret, it seems, was less assured: her family had a history of sinister events, and she worried that the home was haunted. Margaret rustled out of bed to check on her two youngest, Kate, fourteen, and Margaret, twelve, and hurried back to bed as the sounds stubbornly went on.

To the family's distress, the noises continued through the following months, with two important facets. One was that the raps "responded" to questions by a code of one-rap-for-yes, two-for-no. The other was that the noises were heard only when either the two girls, or their older, married sister, Leah, was present.

Simple (but clever) chicanery?

Or was it poltergeists—known to draw energy from the young (especially pubescent girls): perhaps an entity that haunted the family line or something in the history of the Indian territory (this land so heavy with past such occultism)?

A committee including a congressman was set up to investigate and they exercised every conceivable precaution against fraud but were unable to explain the sounds. Though pressed to find just the opposite, they ruled that there was no earthly way such phenomena could be produced. A legendary newspaperman (and presumably hard-nosed skeptic), Horace Greeley, testified to the legitimacy of the phenomena (despite some who disputed it, as always there are such disputes), and by the time the girls were in their twenties, they had a following so large that it coalesced into the new psychic religion of "Spiritualism" (for an intelligence seemed to be behind it).

They called it Spiritualism but the Bible dubs—and condemns—it as "necromancy."

And it was dangerous.

As Church fathers knew—for cardinals and bishops themselves, especially in England, had themselves logged case studies—such happenings could occur due to demons or spirits of the deceased, with no sure way of telling one from the other.

The important point is that the outbreak spread across the new nation and the era became the Age of the Medium, its paranormality so numerous as to defy synopsis.

Fantastic—and often fraudulent—reports filtered in from all corners.

Mediums were soon not only communicating with the "dead" through the coded raps but also materializing spirits or going into trance and letting the "spirits" speak through them (what we now know as "channeling"). It was how the New Age took hold in America.

Pure danger!

But so impressive were accounts that Congress itself considered a bill to study it.

By December 1862, the psychic craze reached the White House. No one any longer knew where that original cornerstone—the Masonic one, at the President's House—had gone (it disappeared after the fire set by British), but now something new and related was afoot and all the rage.

At one White House séance, held in the Red Parlor, a medium fell into trance for the family of Abraham Lincoln (it was reported), producing a barrage of phenomena climaxed by a large piano levitating (levitation is well known to exorcists).

I knew about such matters first-hand. As a cub newspaper reporter during the mid-1970s, in Binghamton, New York, I had "investigated" a Protestant minister who was a medium. When in trance, a "spirit guide" spoke through him, but wouldn't let us record it (at one point two tape recorders clicked off by themselves simultaneously).

Was it a "gift" (as he believed)? Or an evil spirit?

Curious it was that the founder of Mormonism (Joseph Smith) experienced his alleged apparition of an angel called Moroni in the same "burned-over" region—just ten miles from where the Fox sisters would hear the rappings—and that the women's liberation movement had its beginnings a mere twenty miles from where the sisters lived, and the same year (1848).

In fact, Elizabeth Cady Stanton, the founder of suffrage, consulted "spirits" just as the Fox sisters did, and heard raps in her home.

No one can doubt the right women should have to equality (all men *and* women are created equal), but like so many movements, suffrage would one day be taken to an extreme—and be embraced by witches who sought (as they did too with rituals) to empower themselves. Although suffrage was good, radical forms of it shared in common with witchcraft—and perhaps this explains its connection to spiritualism—an occult need to empower women (and overpower men).

Noted one commentator, Mitch Horowitz: "You'd be hard pressed to come across a single significant figure in the Suffragist movement who didn't have some ties to Spiritualism, even the biggest names, like Susan B. Anthony. . . . It was more than an alliance—Spiritualism and early feminism were like two branches growing out of the same tree trunk. The first female presidential candidate in America, a woman named Victoria Woodhull, was a trance medium who ran for the presidency in 1872, as part of the Equal Rights Party, a consortium of suffragists and abolitionists. She was also a well known voting rights activist, and the first woman to address a joint committee of Congress on the question of voting rights. Into the late nineteenth century, this marriage between Spiritualism and suffrage was just a basic part of progressive and reformist politics."

So was the stage set for abortion, a blood sacrifice (at least for witches, who consider it a sacrament).

The occult was afoot, with potentially dramatic results.

Curiously, like rationalism, it detested Catholicism.

But at the same time as the occult took hold, there was an intervention of the Blessed Virgin with advice, grace, and warnings.

In France, she appeared during 1830 in the Miraculous Medal apparitions, warning that "the times are evil" and the "entire world will be overcome by evils of all kinds," while south of Grenoble, in the same country, more than seven thousand feet up a mountain, she appeared (two years before the Fox sisters, in 1846), warning that "*demons of the air together with the antichrist will perform great wonders on earth and in the atmosphere, and men will become more and more perverted.*" Civil governments, she said, would have "*one and the same plan, which will be to abolish and do away with every religious principle, to make way for materialism, atheism, spiritualism, and vice of all kinds.*" There would be "*so-called resurrected dead, who will be nothing but the devil in this form.*"

There would be a "*time of darkness.*"

Sinners would be introduced into religious orders.

The "*love of carnal pleasures*" would spread around the world.

Evil books would be "abundant."

A demon known as Asmodeus would find convents to be a "*grazing ground*" and as a consequence of it all, fire would fall in three places or "cities."

Chapter 16

When it came to fire, perhaps most relevant was what transpired four thousand miles from eastern France and nearly a thousand from western New York, near what was initially called Clarksville or Robinsonville and now is Champion, Wisconsin.

There, in early October, in 1859, a devout Belgian immigrant named Adele Brisé saw the Virgin bedecked in white, with yellow sash, between a hemlock and maple.

Shortly after, on October 9, Adele again saw Mary as the young Belgian woman was walking to Mass, and again as she returned from church.

In the official rendition, Mary had "a crown of stars around her head, and her long golden wavy hair fell loosely over her shoulders; such a heavenly light shone around her that Adele could hardly look at her sweet face. Overcome by this heavenly light and the beauty of her amiable visitor, Adele fell on her knees." Asked the young immigrant, "In God's name, who are you, and what do you want of me?"

This time the Blessed Mother—in an apparition that would become the only one ever fully approved on U.S.-Canadian soil—replied, *"I am the Queen of Heaven who prays for the conversion of sinners, and I wish you to do the same.*

You received Holy Communion this morning and that is well. But you must do more. Make a general Confession and offer Communion for the conversion of sinners. If they do not convert and do penance, my Son will be obliged to punish them."

At Adele's side were companions. "Adele, who is it?" said one of the women.

"Oh, why can't we see her as you do?" said another weeping.

"Kneel," said Adele, "the Lady says she is the Queen of Heaven."

Appearing in a way that reminds us of Lourdes, Mary turned, looked kindly at them and now said, *"Blessed are they that believe without seeing. What are you doing here in idleness, while your companions are working in the vineyard of my Son?"*

"What more can I do, dear Lady?" said Adele weeping when she heard these words.

"Gather the children in this wild country and teach them what they should know for salvation," came the response.

"But how shall I teach them who know so little myself?" insisted Adele.

"Teach them, their Catechism, how to sign themselves with the Sign of the Cross, and how to approach the sacraments; that is what I wish you to do," replied the radiant visitor. "Go and fear nothing, I will help you."

Just a year after the appearance, and her warning of "punishment," the U.S. (then thirty-seven states) found itself on a quick slope to what would be one of its greatest calamities: unwilling to give up slavery, South Carolina seceded from the Union, soon to be followed by a dozen others as the Civil War erupted, causing mayhem everywhere.

Brother shot brother; cousins fought cousins.

Americans killing each other!

Thousands—tens of thousands—dying.

Was it related to the Wisconsin warning?

In a proclamation drafted by Senator James Harlan of Iowa and appointing a national day of repentance and fasting—a president declaring a fast!—Abraham Lincoln proclaimed, on March 30, 1863:

"Whereas it is the duty of nations as well as of men to own their dependence upon the overruling power of God, to confess their sins and transgressions in humble sorrow, yet with assured hope that genuine repentance will lead to mercy and pardon, and to recognize the sublime truth, announced in the Holy Scriptures and proven by all history, that those nations only are blessed whose God is the Lord;

"And, insomuch as we know that by His Divine law nations, like individuals, are subjected to punishments and *chastisements* in this world [my italics], may we not justly fear that the awful calamity of civil war which now desolates the land may be but a punishment inflicted upon us for our presumptuous sins, to the needful end of our national reformation as a whole people? We have been the recipients of the choicest bounties of Heaven; we have been preserved these many years in peace and prosperity; we have grown in numbers, wealth, and power as no other nation has ever grown. But we have forgotten God. We have forgotten the gracious hand which preserved us in peace and multiplied and enriched and strengthened us, and we have vainly imagined, in the deceitfulness of our hearts, that all these blessings were produced by some superior wisdom and virtue of our own. Intoxicated with unbroken success, we have become too self-sufficient to feel the necessity of redeeming and preserving grace, too proud to pray to the God that made us. It behooves us, then, to humble ourselves before the offended Power, to confess our national sins, and to pray for clemency and forgiveness."

Nearly as if he had been there with Adele, and quoting Our Lady, Lincoln was calling for "confession" and declaring the Civil War no random event but a Divine chastisement!

This was dramatic, largely ignored stuff, not to be found readily in museums dioramas or libraries: one of the most revered presidents in U.S. history approving as official decree a document saying what Mary was saying, what seers have warned of since—that there was this thing called chastisement, and that America was tempting the Justice of the Almighty—and not only was formalizing his belief in that but also declaring that the nation had "forgotten God" and was attributing its success to itself, instead of the Almighty. It was an early fruit of the "enlightenment": as in the French Revolution, many—at least 750,000 and perhaps closer to a million Americans—died in what was likewise an uprising.

This was in 1863. And to draw a sense of the tragedy, one need only visit the battlegrounds of Gettysburg, where massive rolling fields memorialize the war dead and where ghost tours (a big business in town) tout and taunt the spirits alleged to haunt the vicinity—the tragedy.

It was strange, how the occult seemed to go hand in hand with tragedy.

Even Lincoln and wife Mary Todd, grieving over a son who died in 1862, sought the reassurances of a spiritualist named Charles J. Colchester.

As *Smithsonian Magazine* recounted:

"Lincoln was particularly intrigued with Colchester's eerie ability to summon noises in different parts of a room," said *Smithsonian*. "Like any rational person, the president wanted to understand what was happening, so he asked Colchester to submit to an examination by Joseph Henry, the Secretary of the Smithsonian Institution. The medium agreed, and a chagrined Henry reported back to the president that he had no immediate explanation for the phenomenon."

But because a happening is paranormal hardly means it is good. And brushing against it can draw misfortune.

Another prominent person intrigued by spiritualism was John Wilkes Booth—who, ironically (if you believe in coincidence), was also a friend of Colchester's.

According to *Smithsonian*: "The pair spent a considerable amount of time together, said George W. Bunker, the National Hotel's room clerk, and they often went out in company. Bunker observed that Colchester was not merely Booth's friend. It was more than that. Colchester was Booth's 'associate.'"

Colchester had often warned Lincoln that the president might be in danger.

Did he get this supernaturally—or had he heard Booth's assassination plot?

We know only that right after the assassination, the medium disappeared.

Chapter 17

"Coincidence" was a funny thing. There were certainly coincidences when it came to presidents, ironies, for example, between the assassinations of Lincoln and (a century later) Kennedy.

Abraham Lincoln was elected to Congress in 1846 and John F. Kennedy was elected to Congress in 1946. Lincoln was elected President in 1860 and Kennedy in 1960. The names Lincoln and Kennedy each contain seven letters. Both wives lost children while living in the White House. Both presidents were assassinated on a Friday. Both were shot in the head. Kennedy's secretary was named Lincoln (Evelyn). Both were slain by southerners. Both were succeeded by Southerners. Both successors were named Johnson. Andrew Johnson, who took Lincoln's place, was born in 1808. Lyndon Johnson, who succeeded Kennedy, was born in 1908. Lincoln was killed at Ford Theatre while Kennedy was killed in a Ford Lincoln.

Nor did happenstance halt there. Three of the five founding presidents had died on a July 4: Jefferson and John Adams on the same Fourth in 1826— the fiftieth anniversary of the Declaration—and James Monroe in 1831. Noted Daniel Webster, in his eulogy for Adams and Jefferson, "It cannot but seem striking and extraordinary, that these two should live to see the fiftieth year from the date of that act, that they should complete that year, and that then, on the day which had fast linked forever their own fame with their country's glory, the heavens should open to receive them both at once. As their lives themselves were the gifts of Providence, who is not willing to recognize in their happy termination, as well as in their long continuance, proofs that our country and its benefactors are objects of His care?"

One thing that was not happenstance was that warning from the Virgin Mary near Green Bay.

There were the words: *"If they do not convert and do penance, my Son will be obliged to punish them."*

They still hung in the air.

For, incredibly, twelve years to the week of the Blessed Mother's appearance (some say it may have been to the day, between October 8 and 10 in 1871), the very region of the upper Midwest, this precise part of Wisconsin, along with parts of upper Michigan, encountered the *greatest wildfire* in America's recorded history, consuming at least 1.2 million acres (an area larger than the state of Rhode Island); killing more than a thousand; forming fire tornadoes that plucked trees from the earth (hurling them like flaming spears); and moving at speeds later estimated to have been about a hundred miles an hour, with the temperature of a crematorium. It had been preceded by what a local priest, Father Peter Pernin, in *Firestorm At Peshtigo,* said was "a vague fear of some impending though unknown evil haunting the minds of many, nor was I myself entirely free from this unusual feeling." There had been little wildfires for weeks as exceptionally dry weather and strong winds nurtured the sporadic flames—ignited, perhaps, by the lumberjacks, rail workers, or hunters with their campfires. "In response to the danger, itinerant preachers suddenly began stalking the countryside, appearing in settlements waving their Bibles until they became as familiar as the smoke," wrote Father Pernin of the conditions just before hurricane winds. The preachers were suggesting, noted a secular history, that the work of all around "was about to explode before their eyes unless they all made an effort to ask forgiveness." As a newspaperman named Benjamin Tilton of the Green Bay *Advocate* further recounted, "Whether we were all unrighteous, or lacking in faith, or doomed to chastisement for our sins or for a solemn warning to the world, we leave to others to decide." The epicenter: Robinsonville (Champion) and the Peshtigo River.

Lust. Serving the loggers had been houses of prostitution.

Greed. In Wisconsin, lumber barons were stripping the landscape with no regard for nature.

Violence. In their caulked boots, loggers often stomped on rivals or passersby (apparently for fun, with an audience watching).

"Half wild, half-civilized, Peshtigo was synonymous with progress," noted an authoritative account of the fire.

The Faith—as Mary had warned—was lost.

A fire here. A fire the next day elsewhere. Another fire. A repeat. In increments, the scourge had increased.

Larger and larger in size, starting in September. One preacher in Peshtigo warned a lumber camp that "God is very angry with some of His children in Peshtigo. He is going to send doom of some sorts."

This was just days before the conflagration.

This was something altogether different, not simple wildfire. An inferno seemed to fall from the sky. There were massive cyclonic flames. These formed a ceiling over the Peshtigo River, while elsewhere, as the priest reported, "people simply became piles of ashes or calcinated bones, identifiable only if a buckle, a ring, a shawl pin, or some other familiar object survived the incredible heat. The survivors would never forget the sound. The sound 'of judgment,' some said. The sound of an angel heralding the end of the world, blasting gusts of fire from his horn. 'Like a thousand locomotives rushing at full speed,' some wrote. Like the devil had opened his mouth with a 'deafening, persistent roar that never stopped but kept growing louder,' or 'a pounding waterfall,' or a 'hurricane.'" Perhaps it was campfires. Perhaps it was from marsh gases. Perhaps something else.

So hot was the conflagration and so widespread—so encompassing and inescapable—farm folk who climbed into wells or wrapped themselves in wet blankets on hillside pastures were incinerated anyway. Sand turned to glass. Bizarre black clouds spat lightning, recalled Father Pernin. The flames were as like "a thousand screaming valkyries," in the words of a second chronicler. There were mysteries within the mystery. Was it just campfires, or something more perplexing? "The heat has been compared to that engendered by a flame concentrated on an object by a blowpipe; but even that would not account for some of the phenomena," said yet another spectator. "For instance, we have in our possession a copper cent taken from the pocket of a dead man in the Peshtigo Sugar Bush, which will illustrate our point. This cent has been partially fused, but still retains its round form, and the inscription upon it is legible. Others, in the same pocket, were partially melted, and yet the clothing and the body of the man were not even singed. We do not know in what way to account for this, unless, as is asserted by some, the tornado and fire were accompanied by electrical phenomena."

Electrical phenomena? Even the roots of trees burned and witnesses claimed that flames came not horizontally, through the trees, but from above them. Dark, round objects, perhaps sap, streaked down like napalm. Wildlife, shrubs, and trees: gone. Countless fish floated on the river. Noted a website of that October 8 holocaust: "Evening church services ended at 8:30. Around 9:00, a dead silence fell over the town, followed by a roar which could soon be heard over everything. The crimson horizon to the south turned bright as day. The winds became hurricane force. White ash fell in blizzard proportions. Showers of hot coals rained down, starting fires in the town and the forest beyond. Peshtigo wasn't destroyed. It was incinerated by a fire of biblical proportions. A perfect storm of wind, drought, terrain, and combustion stirred up a witch's brew for weeks that finally exploded into a cataclysmic firestorm very much like those that destroyed Dresden and Tokyo in World War Two. Survivors remarked that, 'this must be what hell looks like.' When it was done, there was nothing but ashes."

Nor did it stop there: on the same day (some said at the same *hour*), but more than 260 miles to the south, erupted a tremendous fire in Chicago: the most famous *urban* fire in American history (as Peshtigo was the most famous wild one), as if part of the same event. Three places: Wisconsin, Michigan, and Chicago.

Coincidence?

We know this: once begun, the Chicago blaze, like Peshtigo, was whipped into a frenzy by "fire devils" that one account described as "whirling pockets of gas and air that rolled through the city for two days, knocking down buildings and sending survivors scurrying for safety in the waters of Lake Michigan." A city of saloons, brothels, mediums, and unsavory businessmen, nearly leveled.

As one publication recalled, "Residents noticed that a freakish wind whipped the flames into great walls of fire more than a hundred feet high, a meteorological phenomenon call 'convection swirls'—masses of overheated air rising from the flames and spinning violently upon contact with cooler surrounding air." And as yet another remarked, "The wind, blowing like a hurricane, howling like a myriad of evil spirits, drove the flames before it with a force and fierceness which could never be described or imagined."

Residents fled in terror down the streets.

"The great, dazzling, mounting light, the crash and roar of the conflagration, and the desperate flight of the crowd combined to make a scene which no intelligent idea can be conveyed in words," wrote a journalist named J. E. Chamberlain.

Hell indeed. A glimpse of a fiery netherworld. One third of Chicago was left homeless, likened to what Moscow suffered after Napoleon's siege. A church dedicated to St. Michael was one of just six structures to survive that simultaneous fire, which to this day is unexplained.

Enter now another set of curious facts.

Those pertain to a comet called "Biela." Back in 1772, astronomers discovered the object as it approached earth from the reaches of our solar system (near Jupiter). It circled the sun every six or seven years, and it was known there were times it missed earth by a narrow margin, with earth dissecting the comet's orbit a month after it passed. In other words, had the comet appeared a month later, or earth traversed its path a month earlier, they could have collided. Indeed, when it passed in 1832, some astronomers predicted impact.

That didn't occur, but upon the comet's return in 1845–1846—the period of LaSalette—something different had been noted. It was at this time an astronomer named Matthew Fontaine Maury observed that there were now *two* luminous objects. Biela had broken apart and a second chunk was separated from the larger one by a distance comparable to two-thirds the span between earth and moon. Both had tails, and soon the main chunk developed a second, but more relevant was the fact that between the comets was an arc of luminous matter, what some called a "gaseous prolongation." It connected the two chunks like a glowing bridge of debris. Orbiting in 1852, "both comets returned at the predicted time, though they were over two million kilometers apart," wrote experts at NASA. "Once again the two comets took turns as the brighter of the pair. On at least one occasion a bright jet was seen between the two heads."

"Each year the earth passes through the remains of Biela, but with varying consequences," noted a science website. "And the effect today is trivial by comparison with the November 1872 occurrence."

Was it even more intense the year before—in 1871, the year of the two greatest fires in U.S. history?

To the point: had earth passed through the gaseous prolongation, a foregoing of debris, with the upper Midwest directly impacted?

There were those bizarre clouds, those "napalm" balls, those sheets of flame. There was the spectator in Wisconsin who noted that "the fire did not come upon them gradually from burning trees and other objects to the windward, but the first notice of it was a whirlwind of flame in great clouds from above the tops of trees, which fell upon and entirely enveloped everything." Curious also was that at LaSalette, in one part of Melanie's alleged "secret" (it did not have official sanction) was that mention of *"the fire of Heaven"* that would *"consume three cities"* and that *"water and fire will give the earth's globe convulsions."* Did this pertain to Europe, which was in the throes of rebellions and wars in the 1800s; to a future global event; or might "three cities" have signified three *regions* fitting what occurred in 1871 as fire destroyed massive parts of eastern Wisconsin, western Michigan, and Chicago (the latter, of course, an actual city)?

Whether or not connected, a meteorite was located in one part of Michigan that had burned.

The clues are tantalizing, hidden in obscure details.

There are always warnings, it seems—in the weather, in society, in revelations—and such was the case, whatever the physical cause (or *causes*) in the disasters—the chastisement—of 1871. Chastisements involve the confluence of conditions and events. The Lord uses nature. He also can protect in any circumstance (Father Pernin not only survived, but so did a *wooden* tabernacle he had).

One thing we know for sure is that the Peshtigo territory had been reduced to a sea of ash, all but total devastation, most everything just gone, but for a spot of green—what one chronicler called "an oasis of emerald"—in the midst of the ash.

This was at Champion, a twelve-acre area where Adele Brisé and friends had erected a small chapel commemorating her apparitions—a shrine where they had taken refuge during the fire, which roared toward the site, licking and scorching its fence, but never entering the shrine itself.

Chapter 18

Peshtigo.

Chicago.

Western Michigan.

Three "cities."

Were they harbingers?

In Europe, a tremendous display of the aurora borealis occurred just before France was invaded by Germany.

And once more, Mary:

She appeared to two boys assisting their father in a barn at a farm in a small hamlet called Pontmain.

One of the sons, taking a break to gaze up at the stars out the front door, was astonished to note that in a patch of the sky, above a neighbor's house, the stars were oddly missing.

Suddenly in their place was a beautiful, smiling woman, there mid-air in a blue gown covered with gold stars and a black veil under a crown. As a small crowd that gathered prayed, a luminous banner or scroll unfolded beneath her feet, with gold lettering that materialized one at a time. *"God will soon hear your prayers,"* it said. *"My Son is waiting for you."*

As they implored her help for France, she smiled with love and pointed to a red cross near her heart.

A star broke loose and seemed to extinguish four candles that surrounded the Blessed Mother.

And after the parish priest recited the *Ave Maria Stella*, a Crucifix likewise vanished and two small crosses appeared on her shoulders and a large white "veil" floated up, covering the apparition, which then disappeared entirely.

Three days later the Germans, though outnumbering local soldiers, began to retreat and within eleven days a peace treaty was signed.

So potent was it all that Pontmain was approved by the Church within four years.

Displaying, in a vivid way, the conflict between good and evil, a demon appeared six years later at Pellevoisin in another part of France to a woman who was dying from pulmonary tuberculosis as well as an abdominal tumor but almost immediately Mary also appeared and cast the demon away. *"Fear nothing, you are my daughter,"* she told the woman, Estelle Faguette.

The next night the same happened, this time Mary telling Estelle not to fear because her Son was showing mercy and would heal her four days later. In a short review of her life, Our Blessed Mother allegedly showed Estelle the "mistakes" she had made, some of which, in the gravity with which Mary viewed them, stunned the woman, who had thought them minor infractions. "I remained silent about what she said," recalled Estelle. "I know it was deserved. I wanted to shout for forgiveness, but was unable to do so as I was overwhelmed with sorrow. The Virgin looked at me with an expression of goodness and then she disappeared without a word."

Still rattled by the mistakes she had been shown, Estelle heard consoling words from Mary, who said, *"That is all past. By your self-denial you have put right the wrongs."* And now Estelle was shown some of the good she had done and how her intense prayers had touched Mary's *"motherly heart."*

There was mercy—and healing, Estelle was told—because of her sacrifices and patience.

It was *impatient*, said Mary, to want to know everything *before learning* and to understand everything *before knowing.*

But was this not, soon, back in the U.S., a great failing of modern society?

Indeed, Americans were embarking on the greatest technological quest in history, but without devotion, patience, or sacrifice.

Soon, society would experience fantastic transformation.

An ersatz world, a sterile and less personal world, was set to emerge as Thomas Edison dabbled with electricity (calling to mind how the Hopis claimed to have been shown that the white men would bring light into their homes by simply touching a wall). Soon the power of nature would not just be subdued but altered completely—and in some instances, obliterated.

Materialism ruled the day.

Was there a bit of occultism also?

One of those who influenced Edison, at least to some degree, was Madame Blavatsky, who traveled the world studying with ancient Hindu masters and putting on public displays, from Europe to the U.S., of spiritualism (rapping noises followed her everywhere, it was said). She founded what was called Theosophy and published a magazine boldly titled *Lucifer* (apparently considering him an agent of wisdom). Born the year after that warning at Rue du Bac, Blavatsky's society would one day capture the attention—again, to whatever extent—of celebrities like William Butler Yeats, Lewis Carroll, Sir Arthur Conan Doyle, James Joyce,

Thornton Wilder, Kurt Vonnegut, Carl Jung, Mohandas K. Gandhi, Adolph Hitler, and later feminist Gloria Steinem and actress Shirley MacLaine, most of them unaware of the true implications (and looking upon Theosophy more as an alternative religion, melded with philosophy). Accused of black magic, Blavatsky was in essence a trance medium whose apparitions were of the goddess Isis (another coincidence: ISIS) and included in her mystical brooch was a swastika—this years before Nazism (she died in 1891)—and a hexagram. Blavatsky's seminal work, which one day would inspire even an international group working at the United Nations, in New York, was *The Secret Doctrine*, a book of "ageless wisdom."

Both Edison and Nikola Tesla (the genius who once worked for Edison, and is more responsible for our current system of electricity than was Edison, inventing alternating current), had keen paranormal interests and may even have been trying to invent a way of contacting unseen sources (spirits of the dead and "extraterrestrials"). An assistant named Dr. Miller Hutchinson wrote that "Edison and I are convinced that in the fields of psychic research will yet be discovered facts that will prove of greater significance to the thinking of the human race than all the inventions we have ever made in the field of electricity"—while Tesla thought electromagnetism might come from an overarching spiritual force.

Both Tesla, who invented the fluorescent light and established principles of wireless telegraphy, as well as radio, and Guglielmo Marconi, who actually produced the first radio, were said to have picked up strange, inexplicable voices on their electromagnetic frequencies (ones not given to transmission of normal human sounds), while Edison's resumé would include everything from that first incandescent bulb (in the 1870s) to the phonograph. These inventions, in their turn, led to mass production and large corporations that soon reconfigured Creation (leading even to artificial fertilizer and food on franchised assembly lines).

The power of Niagara would be transformed into alternate current that coursed with unfathomable dispatch over wires—causing a diversion of water at a massive hydroelectric plant near (coincidentally) Devil's Hole. Electricity would beget the motor which would beget endless inventions. The list of inventions based on internal combustion or steam engines and electricity during this and the first part of the next century was relentless: steamboat, locomotive, battery, the telegraph, canning, telephone, phonograph, and—of major consequence—the first plastic, along with penicillin, television, the electron microscope, rockets, and the atom bomb. The internal combustion engine begat automobiles ("carriages without animals") that soon dominated the landscape and began to traverse on "ribbons" strewn across America.

The world was not changing. It was being reinvented.

An ersatz world, moving swiftly. Turmoil.

There was also abrupt change in politics.

President Garfield was assassinated in this era, and by the beginning of the 1890s, so was President McKinley (both on Friday, McKinley the day after riding past Devil's Hole, on a scenic gorge trolley).

In society then, as now, San Francisco was a bellwether, and those with an affinity for the spiritual warned that it was becoming another Sodom, what with its brothels, opium dens, gambling, slavery, and theft, so pronounced that there were those who—as in Wisconsin—openly fretted about God's Justice. And that seemed to come in short order, with the great earthquake of 1906, which destroyed a third of the city, sending fire and smoke billowing from the windows of august places like a landmark Episcopalian church (Grace Cathedral) where, in later decades, there would be promotion of yoga. Much of it had started in the 1800s on the Barbary Coast, where greedy miners dominated the populace and where a disproportionate number of men led to certain of them assuming on the role of women and giving birth to the homosexual/transvestite culture that one day would make San Francisco the "gay capital" of the world.

Drifters and conmen were common—dodging in and out of the profligate opium and gambling dens connected by secret passages.

While triggered by tremors, most of the devastation, in 1906, was—again—by way of *fire*. Building after building—28,000—burned. Neighborhoods had to be dynamited to create a firewall.

The entire city was nearly reduced to ash.

"When Thy judgments are in the earth, the inhabitants of the world learn righteousness," said Scripture (*Isaiah* 26:9).

"Then the earth shook and trembled, the foundations also of the mountains moved, and were shaken because He was wroth. There went up a smoke in His wrath, and fire out of His mouth devoured. The Lord thundered from Heaven, and the Most High uttered His voice. Then the channels of the sea appeared, the foundations of the world were laid bare, by the rebuke of the Lord, at the blast of the breath of His anger" (*Psalm* 18).

Wrote one evangelist: "The message of warning should be sounded in the large, wicked cities, such as San Francisco. San Francisco and Oakland are becoming as Sodom and Gomorrah, and the Lord will visit them. Not far hence they will suffer under His judgments."

That was penned on April 20, 1903, three years before destruction.

One day, San Francisco would also be notorious for its palm readers, psychics, and New Age shops, as well as its daunting network of witches, just upstate from what would become the center of high-tech (Silicon Valley).

Electricity!

A funny thing it was: something none of us wanted to live without (think air conditioning) though also how Satan fell from Heaven (lightning).

Everything had its good side and its bad side and the problem was when society made progress but did so of its own volition, its own "ingenuity," without the proper guidance of God.

Here was a reputed word of knowledge or prophecy: *"Know this about the world: I would not appear on television, nor ride a car, nor travel in an airplane. Would I come in such a manner? Would I live in such a world? You think of the changes in very simple ways, without realizing the fundamental mistakes of mankind. The very artifice of your societies is false and against the accordance of God's Will. This artifice shall not last. Your very conceptions of happiness and comforts are a great evil and falsity. They will not stand. My greatest nemesis is science, even more so than the media. The science that alters life, the science which creates a counterfeit heaven, the science that toils with the womb and genes, the science that has filled the air with the power of the enemy, the science which creates chemical witchcraft and fouls the earth, the science which seeks to create life but cannot in actuality even sustain it, the science which has denied God. This will fall, and all of its creations with it."*

An angel of light indeed! Touch the wall. Turn on the switch. Rev up the motor. Hit the "enter" button and send a message around the world.

Magic.

How much was good? How much blessed? How much human hubris?

This was a challenge of discernment.

There were those who insisted earthly inventions had their origin in heavenly realms—that spirits were up or out there designing ways to abet humans, and then transferring this knowledge into the inventor's intuition—and, in fact, there *were* those who received their inspiration, good or not, with hardly a forethought, out of the blue, sometimes in dreams. (James Watson had "seen" the molecular shape of DNA—foundation for genetics—in a dream that, curiously, also involved a snake). What about chemicals? What about cars?

There was this oil, and here too were questions: Was petroleum of benefit to mankind? Or a transgression of the natural order?

A devout and illiterate peasant from Serbia named Mitar Tarabich, who died in 1899, had experienced prophetic visions that were recorded by a local Orthodox priest, Zaharije Zaharich (1836-1918)—decades after gas and oil, which Indians had used to grease their bodies, was quietly first drilled, natural gas was, in Upstate New York, near Lily Dale. "People will drill wells deep in the ground and dig out gold, which will give them light, speed, and power, and the earth will shed tears of sorrow, because there will be much more gold and light on its surface than in its interior," wrote Father Zaharich, quoting his alleged seer. The earth will suffer because of these open wounds.

"Instead of working in the fields, people will dig everywhere, in right and wrong places, but the real power will be all around them, not being able to tell them, 'Come on, take me, don't you see that I am here, all around you.'

"Only after many a summer, people will remember this real power, and then they will realize how unintelligent it was to dig all those holes. This power will also be present in people but it will take a long time before they discover it and use it. Thus man will live for a long, long time, not being able to know himself. There will be many learned men who will think through their books that they know and can do everything. They will be the great obstacle for this [self-knowledge], but once men get this knowledge, then people will see what kind of delusion it was when they listened to their learned men. When that happens, people will be so sorry that they didn't discover it before, because this knowledge is so simple."

Put another way: Was progress always a benefit? Or were there sometimes, and even often, the fingerprints of Lucifer (prince of the power of the air, in this era whereby the atmosphere now consisted of radio waves)? That word of knowledge had said: *"The very artifice of your societies is false and against the accordance of God's Will."* One might look at it a simple way and declare that whatever glorified God and His Creation was good and whatever tried to replace what He'd made was not good but rather an attempt at self-aggrandizement, reminiscent of how Satan was cast out of Heaven because he aspired to the Throne of the Almighty.

There were certainly major scientists—and inventors—who believed in the Lord: Max Planck, Rene Descartes, Albert Einstein, Louis Pasture, Arthur Compton, Marconi.

Some dreams led to inventions that seemed good, some more questionable, some outright nefarious.

The sewing machine came to Elias Howe in a dream. A nighttime vision was also how Descartes came upon the "scientific method." The first proven human carcinogen, benzene, arrived to Friedrich August Kekulé in a dream (of snakes swallowing their tails). There was also Sigmund Freud, who explained the thought/dream process in a way that framed the universe—Creation—in a mechanical, humanistic way. An undercurrent of occultism here too? In public, Freud spoke of everything in a "rationalistic" manner (planting logic in the place of faith), while privately demonstrating a fascination with voodoo artifacts. As a researcher named Dr. Pravin Thevathasan once noted: "Freud is now best known for his psychoanalytical method. It has been recognized that there are similarities between psychoanalysis and the occult doctrines of the Kabbalah. They both share an emphasis on male and female elements, in a fixation with numbers and in the exploration of a variety of symbols. Some fundamental themes can be found in the Zohar or Book of Splendor such as bisexuality, malevolent childhood impulses, and dream interpretation. Freud was also deeply interested in witchcraft and other occult phenomena. On Saturday evenings, he would frequently play tarot—a card game associated with the Kabbalah. However, he appeared to have a conscious hatred of religion—both Orthodox Judaism and Christianity. In 1937, when he was urged to flee Nazism, he responded that his real enemy was the Roman Catholic Church. Interestingly enough, his childhood hero was Hannibal, the Carthaginian besieger of Rome."

How many knew that the very case upon which he formed his theory of psychoanalysis involved a woman who later insisted she wasn't psychologically afflicted but rather possessed (and ended up convincing Freud's partner, who became frightened at what he witnessed)?

And so we see that as mankind headed into the twentieth century, evil was on the move, in large and small ways—as foreseen in the famous vision Pope Leo XIII reportedly had around 1884, a vision that has come down through the decades in various versions: one saying the Holy Father had it while at Mass (seeing it over the head of a concelebrating Cardinal), another *after* Mass; in one version, so shaken he fainted and needed assistance, even brief medical attention, in other versions simply staring for a moment in amazement and dread and later describing it (to his secretary, Monsignor Rinaldo Angeli): a vision of "demonic spirits who were gathering on the Eternal City."

Other accounts had the Pope hearing the voice of Satan ask God for more power with which to test the Church and being granted fifty or sixty years to do so (not a "century," as often quoted). So affected was Pope Leo, say reliable accounts, that he not only polished up the St. Michael prayer but had it promulgated to parishes for solemn recital kneeling down at the end of every non-chanting Mass and himself often reciting it.

"In fact," wrote Cardinal Nasalli, "another prelate familiar with the Pontiff used to tell us that even on his walks through the Vatican Gardens, he would take out a small book—worn from much use—from his pocket and repeated his exorcism with fervent piety and deep devotion."

The prayer, it has been shown conclusively, dealt mainly with that threat of Freemasonry, and while Masonry would soon wane in Europe as well as America, it had spawned movements and sects such as the Rosicrucians and took different and often camouflaged forms, reaching into many walks of life. It was a *spirit*, was Masonry, more than a secret sect. The true architectures of darkness, in science or superstition, in churches or covens, in universities and laboratories, came with the grand orchestration of Satan—not men.

But in the eighteenth century, Freemasonry had escalated, and in addition to promotion of the Prayer to the Archangel Michael, Pope Leo had written an entire encyclical on the danger of secret groups.

So many were these! The devil was at every turn. He is a superintelligence. Among his agents was Aleister Crowley, who considered Blavatsky to be his predecessor, noted with pride that he was born the very year Theosophy was founded, and in 1900 announced, with a grandiose poem, that the twentieth century was Satan's: the end of Jesus' "eon" (as he phrased it). One of history's darkest occultists, a man whose own mother called him "the Beast," Crowley would one day be indicated as the inspiration for the first Church of Satan in America (in San Francisco). His devotees included John Whiteside Parsons, a famous rocket scientist and close friend of L. Ron Hubbard's.

If most scientists held no such beliefs (many of them skeptical of anything spiritual), they too practiced idolatry in the way they worshipped at the altar of technology.

Electricity replaced the Holy Spirit.

And anything was wrong if it was invented without God.

What would Pius X call modernism?

The "synthesis of all heresies."

It would bear bad fruit.

It would cause harm.

Soon, to see this, one would only have to visit Nagasaki.

It promoted hedonism.

Crowley's credo—"Do what thou wilt shall be the whole of the law"—became the law of the land.

"Lust ye men! Enjoy all things of sense and rapture."

That was the notion. That was the chant, the anthem. And chant they did: while most of those affected by the occult were influenced subtly and indirectly, without knowing it, there were those who formed the modern world and practiced overt "magick" (as they spelled it).

Chapter 19

It was true, what was warned about during apparitions, what Pope Leo had "heard" in a locution: Satan was rising on all sides, like the surge of a cyclone. *"Now is the time the abyss is opening,"* said Our Lady of LaSalette. A *"time of darkness"* would cause the Church *"a frightful crisis,"* she'd said in 1846, as she also warned at Rue du Bac, to Saint Catherine Labouré (*"The times are evil."*)

Secret doctrines? Exotic wisdom? "Ageless"—like Satan was ageless?

Among others, Blavatsky had imparted her "wisdom" to devotees like Margaret Sanger, who was to champion the most dangerous and dark trend of the coming era, the "right" (always, there is this deception of a new "right") to abortion.

I won't delve too deeply into her personal life but Sanger was a famous adulteress who treated her first husband with cruelty and neglected her children. Sexual promiscuity was her real cause and as a writer named Mabel Dodge described her, "it was as if she had been more or less arbitrarily chosen by the 'powers that be' to voice a new gospel of not only sex knowledge in regard to contraceptions, but sex knowledge about copulation and its intrinsic importance. She was the first person I ever knew who was openly an ardent propagandist for the joys of the flesh."

Her own husband complained that Sanger's movement was "not noble but an excuse for a Saturnalia of sex." (A "Saturnalia" is a pagan sex festival.)

We see then how paganism, a form of demon worship, was infecting not just politics, philosophy, and science back at the turn of the twentieth century, but personal morality. The evil seed she helped to plant would grow into a towering redwood that still grows. Sanger was a Rosicrucian and editor of a newspaper called *Woman Rebel*, the motto of which was "No gods, No masters." Quite the women's libber, she urged women to "look the whole world in the face with a go-to-hell" attitude. She was also an unabashed racist who thought the birth rates of blacks, poor, disabled, and other "inferior" people should be limited—a cause that Planned Parenthood has maintained, for black babies are now a majority of those aborted. She advocated prevention of the "feeble-minded" from propagating, saying, "[We should] apply a stern and rigid policy of sterilization and segregation to that grade of population whose progeny is tainted, or whose inheritance is such that objectionable traits may be transmitted to offspring."

Unknowingly controlled by what Crowley called the "secret chiefs," by what Blavatsky taught as ancient wisdom, she was trying, in essence, to involve an entire society in the occult ritual of Saturnalia. A massive sex rite! The sexual revolution was on its way (made possible by contraception) and its fruit, abortion, was tantamount to another ritual of occultism: blood sacrifice.

For centuries witches had promoted just what Sanger, whose cause was so linked to that "suffrage" effort in Seneca

Falls, was promoting: free extramarital sex and the sacrifice of innocents.

Now this too would be done, during the 1900s, on a ghastly scale—by the staunchly "feminist" organization she started, Planned Parenthood (America's largest abortion-provider, and also a supplier of baby parts, reminiscent of Nazism). Was there anything "feminine" about killing the unborn? How many women would have gone through with an abortion if they had seen an ultrasound of what was in their wombs—what was struggling and yearning to live there? How many would have paid for the termination of a child if they knew the body parts would be sold like automotive ones but to medical researchers—hearts, brains, the pancreas ("What's the pancreas forecast like today?" a procurement agent would one day joke, in inquiring at a clinic.)

The occult spirit engendered by Spiritualism and nurtured by the secret cults was now integrating itself in society's mainstream under the disguise of liberated sex and feminism. Sanger, the Marx of sexuality, described herself (in *My Fight For Birth Control*) as part of a "secret society" of "agnostics and atheists"—lying in wait for just what Pope Leo was shown: the "coming revolution." As an exorcist wrote, "the age of enlightenment caused a laxity in the use of the ecclesiastical powers of exorcism" while another noted the history of mankind demonstrates that Satan is in constant warfare fighting for his kingdom, ever urging the wicked against the good, and using the powers of darkness against those of light."

When he was around, there was always a hiss. There was depression. There was obsession. There was oppression. There was regression. When taken to the extreme—when there was loss of overt consciousness—there was possession. Hear the hiss? There was in Germany the "SS."

"Paranoia" or obsession? "Schizophrenia" or what the Bible calls "double-mindedness"?

"Multiple personality," or "legion" (*Luke* 8:30)?

The first signs of the enemy were often confusion, antagonism (coming in a flash), and anxiety. That was the brave new world: disoriented. Where was the compass Columbus had used! Said the last exorcist I quoted, "Satan is still prince of this world and he will maintain his position until the world is converted by fire, that is, by a burning zeal of love through the sacrifice of self. The day will come when Christ's complete victory will be made known to the entire world, and when the prince of this world will be cast into exterior darkness together with his clients. Then the world will be judged" (*John* 12, 13).

Or *would* there (as in Peshtigo) be actual fire?

"Lo, the day is coming, blazing like an oven, when all the proud and all evildoers will be stubble, and the day that is coming will set them on fire, leaving them neither root nor branch, says the Lord of hosts. But for you who fear my name, there will arise the sun of justice with its healing rays" (*Malachi* 3:19-20).

Below the surface, under society's radar, beyond the template of modern belief, Satan was now working unencumbered, wreaking havoc both subtly and with first Nazism and then Communism in a way that stole the breath. Karl Marx wrote poems about "hellish vapors" that filled his brain, and did they! When it came to smoke, every crack was a grand opening. The vast majority of those who engineered society had no notion of the occult that limned popular movements, nor the negative sway that could reside in entertainment, in celluloid, in the new motion pictures—movies—that had been spawned from the inventiveness of men such as Edison. (It was still in the late 1800s that

Edison, working feverishly also on better phonographs, built a film studio known to employees as the "Black Maria.") Curious it was how the name "Hollywood" had its origins in "holly" or "holy" wood, sacred to ancient wizards, used even in magic wands, its beginnings traced by some to pagan rituals in Nordic times—to Druids—who considered holly as their most hallowed symbol because it was important to the Norse goddess of the underworld (*Holle* or *Hel*). In Los Angeles was Mickey with his wand at a "magic" kingdom.

Magic got you a long way on earth (celebrity; the "magic" of the silver screen), but a price came with it.

Did this mean *Mickey* was evil, and that movies got you condemned, and that we should toss away all the modern world gave us?

Of course not. Who wanted to live without light bulbs, penicillin, clean water? It was the way we had formulated inventions. It was the way we created new idols in Hollywood (we even called them "idols"). It was to note the wrong user of ingenuity when it is not totally in accordance with God.

How many would pay for it! How many "famous" died in a way that was ignoble, even hair-raising?

This was often because they simply didn't know the devil was there.

The Bible said clearly: "Fools die for lack of understanding" (*Proverbs* 10:21).

"Be brave and fight the ancient serpent and you will gain the eternal kingdom," the exorcist intones, in Latin [my italics].

And so it was: one could not allow the enemy any fissure, the smallest crack, through which to slither, or pour smoke—turning the atmosphere, the life breath, fetid, fuliginous, and venomous. The cracks came from laziness, unforgiveness, jealousy, hatefulness, promiscuity (for sure), atheism (also certain), glances of lust, habits of gluttony. In many ways, atheism *was* hatred. Any imperfection could widen an aperture. The "cardinal sins" were of particular relevance (along, of course, with the Commandments—and also the Beatitudes).

How many knew the Sermon on the Mount as well as they needed to?

Reading the Bible was another way—with Holy Water, blessed salts, other sacramentals, especially a Crucifix—to distance oneself from the omnipresent but not omnipotent demons. Hold high the Cross! Those early explorers were knowingly or unknowingly—certainly in many cases knowingly—conducting exorcism. They were planting a flag of battle. Didn't they set the standard—daring into pagan territory and fearing not to raise that symbol of victory, the monument of Calvary?

Any self-respecting exorcist had this in his tool kit: a Crucifix. For how the Power of Christ rained down when He was approached with prayers that came not just through rote, nor just by reading them, but from the heart, in front of a Cross.

This pierced the clouds.

This sent warring angels.

Crowley?

He would have scurried away at the site of a little old lady holding the beads of a rosary.

The more they were in darkness, the more cowardly. When there is dark, it is for Christians to simply light the candle; send up thanks; send up glory, with the dance of the flame.

The Flame of His Heart.

Or else: one day the flame would be sent upon us, roaring from above the forest, replacing the melody of a woodnote.

It was the verb Leo XIII used when he described evil as "prowling" as in the Scripture that speaks of "a roaring lion" who prowls about the world (1 Peter 5:8) seeking destruction.

How many knew that in etymology, the name "Osama" (as in Bin Laden), meant "lion"?

Chapter 20

Big loud roars—roaring locomotives now, across America, in the 1900s, roaring oil gushers in Texas, the roaring of factories in mass production: a roaring economy in the Roaring Twenties.

Yet nothing would make humans more vulnerable to future breakdown than mass production, such that at the dinner table it would become normal to have vegetables, meat, fish, or fruit that had come from a thousand or even *thousands* of miles away.

This led to the next query: What would occur if that oil suddenly halted, due to a massive outage of electricity?

Was this why the Hopis were (allegedly) warned about relying totally on the way white men would teach them to light up their homes by touching the wall, and why they were, in that legend, of a prophecy from long before to not rely completely on the new ways they would be taught of getting water (which involve electrical pumps)?

If the end of the eighteenth century and the first part of the nineteenth could be defined by anything, it was mass production, which soon would create a fast-food industry and what another Pontiff would rail against one day as the "throwaway culture": use a plastic bottle once, or a plastic bag, and send off to the landfill, where it would take decades to dissolve, if ever it did, or allow it to be swept as litter into a swale to a creek to a river to the ocean where now micro-particles of plastic were as numerous as phyto-plankton (the tiny organisms on which small fish—the beginning of the ocean food chain—fed). If there was residue or waste that hurt His Creation, it wasn't in God's Plan. Period. The Lord made everything dissolve back into nature—made it so that when something was used by the nature He created, what *it* left (for example, manure) nourished something else, feeding a cycle, an endless, brilliant, incredible feedback system—instead of harming it. No scientist could possibly design anything a millionth as intricate. And if scientists worked with God, the result would have been products that left useful, non-toxic waste, residues that were gladly received back into Creation, and energy that was renewable. The earth was not created to be left in darkness, but also not to be depleted. With God, there would be plastic-like materials but ones that readily dissipated into natural components—energy configurations that utilized the sunlight and magnetism abounding all around us. It was when something was too "convenient, and more to the point, conducive to making big money, for an elite few—that it strayed from His Plan and hurt the surroundings and people and fauna in it. With God, inventions vastly more impressive than anything that came out of the Edison Illuminating Company would have been and could be concocted. It didn't mean an end to cars and air conditioning. It meant an end to powering air conditioning in an artificial way. This was not a political issue. It was not liberal or conservative, Democrat or Republican. It was an issue of rationality blending with the spiritual. The mystic Maria Esperanza gave me messages she'd received (decades before) that said exactly this: with God, ingenuity would exceed the imagination while solving problems and disrupting nothing. Instead, our scientists were going their own way without even believing in Him. For years, Esperanza had warned that such misuse of technology—Godless technology, especially human cloning—would be a disaster. In a world where science was in tune with spirituality, Esperanza said there would be "great events" and a "conquest" of what she called the "spatial era." *"You must know that if you obey, the fullness of a wonderful light shall reflect upon you,"* she quoted Jesus as saying. *"Great luminaries will work lively splendors that you may see next to you, guiding your footsteps because of your love for Me. Great events are near and the next one will shake the world of science. Electronic computers will [cause] the utmost revolution people could imagine,"* Maria quoted a message from Mary, on March 18, 1981, as stating. If we prayed, and consulted Heaven, said the Church-sanctioned seer, society would even find a way to eliminate harmful radioactivity. "Its reactions will grind to a halt, and then the time will come in which it will be used for pacific purposes, for man's well-being and for the probable happiness of better days," she recorded in a diary. "This will come about with the sun and with the drive of magnetic forces of earthly energies: volcanic forces, wind, water, certain kinds of seaweed because phosphorus will be better assimilated. In short, no element will be wasted; everything will be used."

Such developments would come only at the end of the current era, she claimed, warning that the world would undergo purification (due to sinfulness, especially our lack of humility, charity, and love, and a lack of devotion to the Eucharist). *"Men cannot think, cannot imagine for a moment, the great struggle among nations that will take place, brother against brother,"* she quoted Jesus as saying. After that cleansing, however—if mankind reverted back to the Lord, and lived a simpler, more harmonious life (as He did, in concert with nature), would come what she described as devices more revolutionary than even computers. There would be "amazing devices" with the capacity to diagnose and heal human sickness—if science and religion join forces in God's Plan.

One example: a technology that would create new means of illumination, turning dark into day. She foresaw that as tapping into a "stellar curvature."

She also saw forces of light and music combined together in ways that currently were unimaginable.

In equally surprising language (most of her images were simply means of devotion), the great mystic, whose cause has been initiated—in a diocese near where Edison lived—foresaw "the registration of equations to their final expression" and computer devices that would replace many of the functions of a doctor. She described such inventions as coming from "secret forces" hidden in rhythms of nature and what she labeled the "sacred canticles."

But that wasn't what was seemed set back at the beginning of the nineteenth century. Instead, there were the Roaring Twenties. A roaring culture, for sure. That silver screen. Valentino. Chaplin. Instant unprecedented wealth. Celebrities. Theatre palaces. Even back then, provocative stars. A roaring economy. Flying freight planes!

But after all this prosperity, fun, and wanderlust, there was the Wall Street crash; there was a monstrous global plague of influenza (killing two of the Fatima seers). There were the *secrets* of Fatima. It was also a time of ferocious *hurucans*: In 1926 Miami Beach, locus of amusements, nearly vanished from one direct hit from the Atlantic (some believed Miami was in such a location that one day it would vanish in a much greater disaster—that its very location was not feasible. FM radio! Technicolor! What had LaSalette said? *"People will think of nothing but amusement."* Was the clock, reset after that hurricane, ticking again?)

Chapter 21

In apparitions to four girls in Heede, Germany, Our Blessed Mother, holding the Infant in one arm, a globe, with Cross, in the other, summed up the state of the world in 1937 when she said, "*Girls, pray the Rosary in reparation for the sins of the world.*" That was just before the rise of Hitler and a fantastically dark period during which not just millions of Jews but also millions of Ukrainians and others trapped in the Soviet Union would be executed under Communism.

In the U.S. were strong hurricanes and, after that roar of the Twenties, the Great Depression. It was claimed that years after the first apparitions (which the diocese authenticated), Jesus came with an "angel of justice." Keep in mind: this was now after World War Two and the Holocaust. Apparently, the sinfulness of mankind continued. And would—for the rest of the century. Danger had begun to build up again. Said one alleged message (in 1945): *"Humanity has not heard My Mother. The times are serious. The angels of justice are spread throughout the world. For those who do not have Grace it will be scary. What will happen will be terrible. Humanity is worse than before the Flood. The world lies in an obscure darkness. I want to save everyone. This generation deserves to be destroyed, but looking at what is right [with the world], I will leave, that My Mercy eventually triumphs."*

At LaSalette, had Our Lady not warned of the same, lamenting a world in which *"people will think of nothing but amusement"*?

And so now let us take a look at those amusements, and especially the origin of a great entertainment called rock and roll, for here again we have to diverge into the possibility (let's just call it a chance) of an occult influence and even underpinning.

Few realize that much of modern rock and roll found its wellspring in a blues singer named Robert Johnson.

Johnson, from Hazlehurst, Mississippi, had been known as a very average musician roaming from gig to gig with his uninspired guitar. Famously, Johnson went to a crossroads near Dockery Plantation in his home state at midnight one night, according to legend, where he was met by a "man" who took his guitar, tuned it, and in exchange for his soul, granted him the gift of blues—a classic Faustian pact. (In superstition, intersections are special places.) After, friends and colleagues were stunned at his newfound genius for both style and lyrics: songs like "Me and The Devil Blues," "Hell-hound On My Trail," and "Up Jumped the Devil," not just blues but jazz and country music also. Said *Rolling Stone* magazine, "[Johnson] often claimed that he learned to play guitar from the Devil himself, and many of his recordings evince a haunting, otherworldly inspiration." Bob Dylan wrote that "when Johnson started singing, he seemed like a guy who could have sprung from the head of Zeus in full armor. I immediately differentiated between him and anyone else I had ever heard. The songs weren't customary blues songs. They were so utterly fluid. At first they went by quick, too quick to even get." Whatever the veracity of this story, future rock stars—Mick Jagger, Robert Plant (of Led Zeppelin), John Fogerty (of Creedence Clearwater Revival), and Eric Clapton were known by their own admission to have visited the legendary spot, with success following. There was the tincture of voodoo. Some said it reflected back to the music of an African cult that followed a god named Legba. When asked by Ed Bradley of CBS why he kept touring at an old age, Dylan would one day explain that "it goes back to the destiny thing, I made a bargain with it a long time ago, and I'm holding up my end." When Bradley asked what the bargain was, the famous songwriter replied, "To get where I am now." And who was the bargain with? "With the chief commander." On this earth? "On this earth and in the world we can't see." Added Dylan (in another interview), "I also went to the 'crossroads' to make a big deal like [*whistles*] one night and then went back to Minneapolis, and like, *hey* . . . " Success. As guitarist Keith Richards of the Rolling Stones listened to Johnson's music, he wondered, "Who is the other guy playing with him? I was hearing two guitars, and it took a long time to actually realize he was doing it all by himself."

In one of the few photos of him, Johnson is strumming his guitar cross-legged on a stool and there is a large smoke-like effect in the picture, a light bleed or tobacco cloud, that bears a strong resemblance to a demon.

(A womanizer, Johnson died at twenty-seven, killed by a jealous husband—whether by poison or knife, no one is certain.)

Those who followed would incur their own stardom and misfortunes in subsequent decades (often at age twenty-seven).

No doubt, God could move in music. But so could the forces of dark. The fruit of the darkness was disarray, division, lust, addiction. When something came from the devil, it led to a dissembling. It caused destruction. Noted a non-Christian writer, "Spurred by the holy drums [in central Africa], deep in the meditation of a dance, one is literally entered by a god . . . and it can happen to anyone. In Abomey, Africa, these deities that speak through humans are called vodun. The word means 'mysteries.' From their vodun comes our voodoo, and it is to voodoo that we must look for the roots of our musicElvis Presley was the first [product of African music in America which the official culture could not ignore . . . The voodoo rite of possession by the god became the standard of American performance in rock and roll. Elvis Presley, Little Richard, Jerry Lee Lewis, James Brown, Janis Joplin, Tina Turner, Jim Morrison, Johnny Rotten, Prince—they let themselves be possessed not by any god they could name but by a supernatural spirit they felt in the music. Western performers transmitted their possession through their voices and their dance to their audience, even through their records."

It was a music that wouldn't stop. It latched on and burrowed in. Did anything go as quickly to the soul?

Was it true that before he fell, Lucifer had been in charge of heavenly choirs?

Demons were being invoked, unknowingly, in many places: soon, everywhere.

The Forties had turned into the Fifties with much shifting in the culture and it was a tectonic shift. No small temblor, this! The change was everywhere. There was no end to examples that linked modern music and many movies and soon TV then the internet with forces of darkness. All bad? No. But enough. Strange phenomena, also. In 1947 the term "flying saucer" was coined by a pilot named Kenneth Arnold who spotted a number of inexplicable aerial objects in Washington State near Mount Rainier moving at impossible speeds. In subsequent weeks, there would be dozens of similar reports across the U.S., including the famous incident near Roswell, New Mexico, whereby, it was claimed (in the folklore of ufology), that a "saucer" with humanoids aboard had crashed. Fascinating it was how often other spiritual phenomena were attendant to such experiences, and how widespread these supposed experiences were among musicians like Elvis, who told friends that when he was born (around 3:30 a.m., on January 8, 1935, in Tupelo, along with a twin brother who was still-born), an inexplicable blue light was seen around the Presley home. Some claimed bottles shook as if by a raucous storm, though the wind outside actually had come to a strange standstill. It was also claimed that when he was eight, two apparitional strangers touched the future super-star and he "sort of" felt a floating "light inside me." It was said the two men had played music for Elvis and showed the youngster a vision in which he was dressed in white under stage lights—an outlay of his future. Often Elvis heard voices. Was this myth, or like a scene out of *Poltergeist*?

This we know: Elvis Presley was serious about "extraterrestrials" and had a fascination that bordered on obsession (often staring at the stars, saying that he was from another planet, and asserting the "space" beings were here to "prepare us for transition into the New Age."

New Age indeed: remember that Elvis followed the works of people such as Madame Blavatsky.

During the Fifties the singer also asserted (to a friend named Wanda June Hill) that he and a bodyguard spotted a large "cigar-shaped, oblong, and rounded" object in the sky and heard what sounded like an electrical buzz as the hair stood up on the napes of their necks (spiritual phenomena is often accompanied by electrical disruption, as well as the goose bumps). Peculiar as it is, he never backed down from these accounts and a friend claimed he and Elvis also saw a

"UFO" above Elvis's mansion in Bel Air, California (in 1966).

Drugs? This much can be ascertained: Presley seemed haunted by *something*. And music affected our culture. In the late Sixties the singer reported another sighting while driving through New Mexico on Route 66 with two other men, Jerry Schiling and Larry Geller. New Mexico, where those Franciscans had tried to drive away the demonology of Indians—who knew such luminosities in the sky as "spirit lights" (they are common over Indian mounds).

None of it is to imply that Elvis himself was evil. This was a singer who is not only in the country and rock "halls of fame," but also the *Gospel* Music Hall of Fame, known for his incredible rendition of "How Great Thou Art" and "Ave Maria."

But certainly he was deceived, as so many of us have been, at least as far as his interest in the occult (which so upset his manager, Colonel Parker, he burned Elvis' books, and was nearly fired for it). Some claimed Presley could miraculously heal people or cause objects such as an ashtray to move or levitate—like those table-rappers a century before. One of Elvis's favorite symbols was that of a phoenix—the mythological bird of resurrection—that was identical to that reported by a woman in Massachusetts who claimed to have been "abducted" by "aliens" wearing just such a symbol on their uniforms. After he died, a security guard at Graceland said he often saw orange-lit saucers hovering over Elvis's tomb between two and four in the morning (the median of which is three, again, the famous "witching" hour).

Were incorporeal spirits at work, displaying themselves in luminosities and then miching in the shadows? How much to believe? How much was drugs? How much was simple yarn? If any of it was true, and demons were behind it, were they imbuing celebrities with talents and charisma?

The list of other "superstars" who have spotted or closely encountered what they believe were extraterrestrials was long. John Lennon (who had a personal Tarot-card reader) claimed he and a mistress named May Pang saw one up close from the balcony of an East Side Manhattan apartment (the very name "Beatles" was given to him as a youngster, John said, by a man he saw in a vision who was "on a pie of flame" and in fact Paul McCartney later called a solo album "Flaming Pie" (shades of Ezekiel). The occult? Aleister Crowley is among those on the cover of *Sergeant Pepper.* UFOs? Mick Jagger said he saw a giant spacecraft larger than a football field at Glastonbury Tor in England (circa 1968), a year after he'd donned a robe and wizard's hat—planets in the backdrop—on the cover of an album called *Their Satanic Majesties Request*, while his close friend and bandmate Keith Richards saw *his* flying saucer in Sussex the same year. ("We receive our songs by inspiration, like at a séance," commented Richards.) To the point was also singer Michael Jackson—a UFO aficionado and close friend of famed psychic Uri Geller—who often spoke about his talents in terms of "magic from somewhere." Meanwhile, the iconic Led Zeppelin song "Stairway To Heaven," one of the most popular songs in history, came so fast and furiously to the two men writing it that they could hardly get it all down (at the time, they were staying at a cottage on Loch Ness that once had been owned by Crowley).

The dots did not seem hard to connect. Jim Morrison of The Doors claimed that as a boy the spirit of an Indian entered him ("his eyes roll back ever so slightly in his head and he was gone," noted a friend of that singer's guttural utterances), and before he died, Jimi Hendrix sought help, believing he was possessed by a spirit (one of the songs he recorded was "The UFO," connected perhaps to his *own* claim to have seen one in 1970.

Was something infiltrating—invading—from the world of spirits, as opposed to "outer space"? No wonder the big TV series had been "The Twilight Zone." And was now "Star Trek." Strange lights were seen in the skies above Woodstock, while on the other side of America, Jerry Garcia of The Grateful Dead said he had been abducted for two days by large insect-like beings similar to another account from John Lennon in which the Beatle had said "insectoid" beings once came to his apartment in a blazing light outside his door, again reminding us of a Spielberg movie, this time *Close Encounters.* (During the filming of that movie, the director reported poltergeist activity.) Songwriter Cat Stevens claimed he had been "sucked up" by a saucer that later dropped him on his bed; singer Phoebe Snow said she talked to "aliens" via a Ouija board. A writer for a satanic heavy-metal band called Blue Oyster Cult was another who was "abducted" by a cigar-shaped "mother ship," while David Bowie—to carry forth this incredible litany—starred in a movie called *The Man Who Fell To Earth,* made himself up to look like an extraterrestrial during concerts, and once said, "Rock has always been the devil's music." Even those who looked like clean-cut no-nonsense All-Americans, such as Brian Wilson (of the Beach Boys), had a link to the bizarre; he heard "voices" that directed his music (when they stopped, so did his hits), while more blatantly suspect musicians such as Ozzie Osbourne wrote an ode called simply but unambiguously "Mr. Crowley." Why did no one question it, when the fruit so often was bad? A "UFO" was seen above a violent outbreak at Altamont Speedway in California (during which Hell's Angels serving, as the Rolling Stone's security, knifed a man to death).

Chapter 22

Ironic it was, how aliens described now as "grays" but similar to those insects left with the smell of sulfur!

Let's briefly recap.

At the Miraculous Medal, the Blessed Mother said there would be "*evils of all kinds.*"

At LaSalette, she said that "*fire and water*" would give "*the earth's globe convulsions.*"

She said the spirit of "Asmodeus" would infiltrate convents (Asmodeus is a major demon), and sure enough, nuns in the West would soon find themselves swooned by the New Age.

She said there would be priests who would become "*cesspools of impurity,*" and in the 1950s and 1960s clerics came up through the ranks who began an incredible period for abuse of youngsters (especially altar boys).

No one liked to recite this litany. But it was the truth—not ornamentation, not cosmetics—that set us free.

There would be the "*demons of the air,*" it had been warned—deception. UFOs?

So we see how she is always there. The Virgin was in Hungary. She was in Michigan. She had appeared in San

Francisco (long before the quake). She appeared again in Belgium. She came with a sun miracle at Casanova, Italy. In one of the most dramatic cases, she appeared near Rome on April 12, 1947, to a virulent Seventh-Day Adventist named Bruno Cornacchiola who had made a vocation of speaking against Catholicism and who even had plans to assassinate the Pope (on her birthday of September 8)! At Tre Fontane, site of Saint Paul's martyrdom, though by the 1940s a park-like area known to occasionally harbor the bodies of slain unborn infants and other forms of sinfulness, was a shrine with a statue of the Virgin on which this angry, militant Protestant penciled in, "You are neither virgin nor mother." He was carrying the pencil because, though simply a rail worker, he intended on writing a speech arguing against the Catholic notion of the Immaculate Conception, to be delivered in the town square. He was interrupted from this, however, when one of his children asked if he could help find a ball they'd lost. While searching, Cornacchiola spotted upon his youngest son kneeling oddly at the entrance of a small dark cave, engrossed, his hands positioned in prayer. "Beautiful lady!" the young boy kept repeating. "Beautiful lady!" as his eyes fixed on a single point in the cave. Suddenly, to Bruno's astonishment, his other two children also fell to their knees, repeating the same exclamation. When Bruno tried to nudge them, it was as if they were glued to the ground. And suddenly he was overcome himself with an intense light that filled the area and felt weightless, as if leaving his body. In the brightest part of the cave was now a woman of ineffable beauty. She identified herself as the "Daughter of the Father, the Mother of the Son, and Spouse of the Holy Spirit." She also called herself the "Virgin of Revelation." Bruno had recently agreed to a challenge from his wife, a devout Catholic, to recite the nine First Fridays of the Sacred Heart (his wife had promised, if he did so, and did not convert, she would give in to his religion), and this, said Mary—those prayers, recited as sort of a bet—had saved him. A special place in Heaven was reserved, she also explained, for those who recited the Rosary for the conversion of unbelievers. Bruno not only converted back to Church (he had been born Catholic) and never again considered violence against the Holy Father (Pope Pius XII, who a few short years later would proclaim the dogma of the Immaculate Conception), but became "Brother Maria Paolo."

These aren't ancient myths. One can only relate a fraction of the examples. They lead up to our own time. Apparitions were claimed from Austria to Canada to Bellmullet, Australia.

From April 25 to June 25, 1946, the Blessed Mother appeared at the German town of Marienfried, a name which meant "the peace of Mary."

There, another secret was given to a visionary and she again urged recitation of the Rosary to ward off sin and Satan, stating that "*the world will have to drain the cup of wrath to the dregs because of the countless sins through which His Heart is offended. The Star of the infernal regions will rage more violently than ever and will cause frightful destruction, because he knows that his time is short and because he sees that already many have gathered around my sign. Over these he has no power, although he will kill the bodies of many, but through these sacrifices bought for me, my power to lead the remaining host to victory will increase. Some have already allowed my sign to be impressed on them and their number will keep growing* (5/25/46). *The Father pronounces a dreadful woe upon all who refuse to obey His Will*" (6/25/46).

Some bishops liked this apparition. Others didn't. Most I have mentioned are "approved."

What did the Blessed Mother mean when she said time was "short," or when, in prophecy—in alleged prophecy—we saw the term "soon"?

Heaven's time was different than ours; no one knew how many eons ago the planet had been configured; Catholicism alone spanned twenty centuries. But from Miraculous Medal to our current time, the word "soon" obviously merited notice—meant that it was within the modern era that a great new danger lurked. It wasn't predicated on politicians. It was predicated on people. A year after Tre Fontane, a seer in Lipa, Philippines, claimed to have been given a secret that pertained to China. "*Be humble and simple because humility and simplicity are the two virtues I love most,*" Mary supposedly had said (9/26/48, though we can no longer take these words as Mary's, for the Vatican has ruled against them, despite the local archbishop's approval).

Oh, the confusion! The same had occurred around apparitions in Amsterdam, Holland, to a woman named Ida Peerdeman, with initial rejection all the way up to Rome again (or at least discouragement) but formal and Rome-accepted approbation much later (on May 31, 2002, after forty-five years of controversy and investigation).

Here Mary mentioned the United States by name when she said (12/31/49), "*America, remember your faith. Do not sow ideas and confusion among your people and abroad. The Lady of All Nations exhorts America to remain what it has been.*"

There would be periods of tranquility, she said, but they would not last. "Child," Mary intoned, "*there will be a fierce struggle. We have not seen the end of this struggle yet. Economic disasters will come.*"

They still seemed, if the message was valid, to be in the future. "For as in those days before the flood they were eating and drinking, marrying and giving in marriage, until the day that Noah entered the ark, and they did not understand until the flood came and took them all away (*Matthew* 24:38-39).

We take that and jump back to Italy, where Mary allegedly appeared at Montichari to a woman named Pierina Gilli. When I visited the site in 1991, I witnessed what I believe was the miracle of the sun—pulsing—but was taken aback when upon entering the large church at the center of the apparitions I read an official *noticia* from the bishop dissuading the faithful from placing credence in the manifestation. Here there was confusion again, for a previous bishop had accepted the apparitions and ordered a statue of Mary carved in accordance with Pierina's depiction, a likeness now known as Rosa Mystica. "*Our Lord, my Divine Son, is tired of the many offenses, the severe offenses, the sins against holy purity,*" she had quoted Mary as saying. "*He wants to send another flood of punishments. I have interceded that He may be merciful once more.*"

This was in 1947. Around the same time, Sister Lucia dos Santos, the sole living Fatima visionary, now cloistered as a Carmelite, saw that the devil was in what she said was "the mood for a final battle" and that the world was being engulfed by a "diabolical disorientation." Evil would seem good and good as evil. There would be false lights. One day, following certain passages from the Bible—for example, biblical teachings on homosexuality—would be considered "hate" speech. My goodness!

This time we risked a *global* holocaust. In Ukraine, at Seredne, in the 1950s, a seer saw fire falling, as did many others, as had Sister Lucia, if not for Mary. Wrote Archbishop Fulton Sheen in 1948, "[Satan] will set up a counterchurch which will be the ape of the [Catholic] Church . . . It will have all the notes and characteristics of hurch, but in reverse and emptied of its Divine t . . . We are living in the days of the Apocalypse, the ys of our era. The two great forces—the Mystical Body st and the Mystical Body of the antichrist—are begin- draw battle lines for the catastrophic contest. The ophet will have a religion without a cross. A religion without a world to come. A religion to destroy religions. There will be a counterfeit Church. Christ's Church—the Catholic Church—will be one; and the false Prophet will create the other," wrote the famous archbishop (*Communism and the Conscience of the West*).

The False Church would be worldly, ecumenical, and global, said the archbishop. It would be a "loose federation of churches and religions," forming some type of global association. "A world parliament of Churches," was the phrase he used, and once emptied of all Divine content, it would be "the mystical body of the antichrist."

"The Mystical Body on earth today will have its Judas Iscariot, and he will be the false prophet," warned Sheen. "Satan will recruit him from our Bishops. The antichrist will not be so called; otherwise he would have no followers. He will not wear red tights, nor vomit sulfur, nor carry a trident nor wave an arrowed tail as Mephistopheles in Faust. This masquerade has helped the Devil convince men that he does not exist. When no man recognizes him, the more power he exercises. God has defined Himself as '*I am Who am,*' and the Devil as 'I am who am not . . .'

"Nowhere in Sacred Scripture," continued Sheen, "do we find warrant for the popular myth of the Devil as a buffoon who is dressed like the first 'red.' Rather is he described as an angel fallen from Heaven, as 'the Prince of this world,' whose business it is to tell us that there is no other world. His logic is simple: if there is no Heaven there is no hell; if there is no hell, then there is no sin; if there is no sin, then there is no judge, and if there is no judgment then evil is good and good is evil. But above all these descriptions, Our Lord tells us that he will be so much like Himself that he would deceive even the elect—and certainly no devil ever seen in picture books could deceive even the elect. How will he come in this new age to win followers to his religion?

"The pre-Communist Russian belief is that he will come disguised as the Great Humanitarian; he will talk peace, prosperity and plenty not as means to lead us to God, but as ends in themselves . . .

". . . The third temptation in which Satan asked Christ to adore him and all the kingdoms of the world would be His, will become the temptation to have a new religion without a cross, a liturgy without a world to come, a religion to destroy a religion, or a politics which is a religion—one that renders unto Caesar even the things that are God's.

"In the midst of all his seeming love for humanity and his glib talk of freedom and equality, he will have one great secret which he will tell to no one: he will not believe in God. Because his religion will be brotherhood without the fatherhood of God, he will deceive even the elect. He will set up a counterchurch which will be the ape of the Church, because he, the Devil, is the ape of God. It will have all the notes and characteristics of the Church, but in reverse and emptied of its Divine content. It will be a mystical body of the antichrist that will in all externals resemble the mystical body of Christ."

Chapter 23

It would focus, was my bet, on materialism.

Only Heaven—and for now it was doing so through Mary—could intervene.

On November 1, when the dogma of her Immaculate Conception was defined, the sun moved so oddly and brightly that afterward Pius made inquiries to the Vatican Observatory.

The more Mary was invoked, the more she was officially recognized, the more she could intervene. Between 1947 and 1954 four times as many apparitions were reported as in preceding or subsequent years and what Mary seemed to be saying was that a danger lurked that would make World War II but a prologue. At the onset of the next decade a mystic named Elena Aiello in Consenga, Italy, was shown a vision of the netherworld while Our Lady said, "*Satan reigns and triumphs on earth! See how the souls are falling into hell. See how high the flames are, and the souls who fall into them like flakes of snow look like transparent embers! How many sparks!*"

How many, indeed.

On Good Friday in 1951, Elena claimed to have heard Mary tell her that "*all nations will be punished, because sin has spread all over the world! Tremendous will be the punishments, because man has arrived at an insupportable contest with his God and Father, and has exasperated His Infinite Goodness!*"

How, wondered the messages, "*can the world be saved, from the disaster that is about to crash down upon the misleading nations, if man does not repent of his errors and failings?*"

The "*wrath of God*" was "*near.*" "*Soon the world will be afflicted with great calamities, bloody revolutions, frightful hurricanes, and the overflowing of streams and the seas.*"

"*Once there was the chastisement by water, but if there is not a returning to God, there will come the chastisement by fire, which will cover the streets with blood.*"

"*Clouds with lightning flashes of fire in the sky and a tempest of fire shall fall upon the world,*" said Mary—according to the mystic—in 1954, and "*this terrible scourge, never before seen in the history of humanity, will last seventy hours; godless people will be crushed and wiped out . . . Mankind is obscured by a thick fog, as a result of the many grievous sins, which are well-nigh covering the whole earth.*

"*If men do not amend their ways, a terrifying scourge of fire will come down from heaven upon all the nations of the world, and men will be punished according to the debts contracted with Divine Justice. There will be frightful moments for all, because heaven will be joined with the earth, and all the ungodly people will be destroyed. Some nations will be purified, while others will disappear entirely.*

"*The world will be once more afflicted with great calamity, with bloody revolutions, with great earthquakes, with famines, with epidemics, with fearful hurricanes, with floods from rivers and seas. If men do not return to God, purifying fire will fall from the heavens, like snowstorms, on all people, and a great part of humanity will be destroyed."*

Chapter 24

Did this not redound back to Peshtigo, back to Adele, back to Chicago?

Woe.

Might a single leader, rising to the scene, to the challenge, halt this slide? It was possible. But he would have to be moral.

What a juxtaposition was Mary—were these experiences—with the rising culture. She never left us. There had been *hundreds* of apparitions and manifestations (not the nine or sixteen often cited by writers) that met with the embrace of bishops, who in early times, before scientism, simply visited a site of phenomena, thereby discerning, thereby personally judging. If his view was positive, a shrine was built. A statue was placed. Often, a church rose. It was largely the way Catholicism was established in Europe. In the U.S., not one, aside from Adele's, was approved, but there were ones of great interest reported by a nun named Sister Mildred Mary Neuzil, starting in 1956 in Illinois and Ohio. It was on the eve of the North American Martyrs feast that they began, the Virgin appearing with a white veil reaching almost to her waist and a mantle and robe of pure white with no decoration. An oblong brooch or clasp held the ends of the mantle, all gold, as was the tall brilliant crown she wore. Her hair and eyes: medium brown, said Sister Mildred, her feet bare but not always visible—sometimes covered by clouds. Often she smiled and revealed a heart encircled by roses that sent forth flames of fire. At times light twinkled from Mary's hair, wrote the nun, radiating from within her. "*I am Our Lady of America,*" she allegedly said. "*I desire that my children honor me, especially by the purity of their lives.*"

It was purity of family, said Mary, that would prevent "*a terrible purification.*"

In this cause—personal morality, and sanctification of the family—America was to lead the world.

That the U.S. should be assigned a spiritual (not economic, not just political) role in the world was a bracing thought. Already, by the 1950s, in this time of incipient rock music, and nascent libertine ways, it and the world were steering in an opposite direction—the direction of sensuality and technological comfort as a "good" and those amusements as a "spirituality." "*My Father is angry,*" Sister Mildred quoted Jesus as saying. "*If My children will not listen to My Heart, which is a voice of mercy and instruction, punishment will come swiftly and none shall be able to stay it. The pleadings of My Heart have held back the Divine justice about to descend on an ungrateful and sinful generation.*

"*Woe to parents who set a bad example to their children,*" continued the messages. "*Terrible will be their judgment. I will demand a strict account of every soul entrusted to their care. Woe to parents who teach their children how to gain materially in this world and neglect to prepare them for the next! Woe to children who disobey and show disrespect towards their parents.*"

In addition to purity—and sanctification of children—what was most lacking in the world, the nun quoted Jesus as saying, was faith.

"There are so few souls that believe in Me and My love. They profess their belief and their love, but they do not live this belief. Their hearts are cold, for without faith there can be no love."

Born in Brooklyn, Sister Mildred had professed as a religious in 1933 and began to encounter mystical experiences in 1938. Only ten years later, in 1948, had she brought them to the attention of her confessor as they grew increasingly pressing and vivid—with the special, urgent, alleged warnings for the United States. In May of 1958 Sister Mildred entered a cloister. She died on January 10, 2000, at the age of 83.

"Tell the bishops of the United States, my loyal sons, of my desires and how I wish them to be carried out," Mary further conveyed, allegedly, to Sister Mildred, who left leaving a small booklet of messages and detailed correspondences with the archbishop. What the Virgin desired was the moral leadership of a nation that had been consecrated to her and was now straying—badly. This was back in the 1950s! *"I wish it to be the country dedicated to my purity,"* said Mary in a dramatic revelation of America's role in a spiritual territory that has long been dominated by foreign apparitions. *"I desire, through my children of America, to further the cause of faith and purity among peoples and nations. I come to you, O children of America, as a last resort. I plead with you to listen to my voice. Cleanse your souls in the precious Blood of my Son. Live in His heart, and take me in that I may teach you to live in great purity of heart which is so pleasing to God. Be my army of chaste soldiers, ready to fight to the death to preserve the purity of your souls. I am the Immaculate one, patroness of your land. Be my faithful children as I have been your faithful mother."*

There was drama in every aspect of the apparitions. At times the Virgin stood on a globe, her right foot on a crescent or quarter moon—as depicted at Guadalupe. On at least one occasion Sister Mildred described a white rose on each of the Virgin's feet (as at Lourdes) and above her head was a scroll on which was written in gold letters, *"All the glory of the king's daughter is within."* While supported by her confessor, who became archbishop of Cincinnati and whose imprimatur graced the booklet of messages, there never was full recognition in the way of a formal pastoral letter.

Nothing is accomplished in life without pain, the Virgin purportedly told Sister Neuzil. When she was portrayed with a sword in her heart, said Mary, it was because of the "*grief plunged therein by my children who refuse to let me teach them the true way.*" She expressed special sorrow over priests who rejected her appearances, while promising grace to those who showed their respect.

Her wonders, she said, would be more spiritual than physical.

"When a picture or statue of myself as Our Lady of America is placed in the home and honored there, then will my Son bless His people with peace," said the Virgin—who specifically requested such a statue also be placed in the National Shrine of the Immaculate Conception in Washington after a solemn procession (a request that was never met). *"I desire to make the whole of America my shrine by making every heart accessible to the love of my Son."*

The Virgin emphasized the importance of the mission and according to Sister Mildred asked that it be expressed to Church authorities—who would be charged with establishing a new devotion in America. *"My Son's patience will not last forever," the nun quoted Mary as saying. "Help me hold back His anger, which is about to descend on sinful and ungrateful men. Suffering and anguish, such as never before experienced, is about to overtake mankind."*

Unless there was penance, said Mary, God would visit men *"with punishments hitherto unknown to them."*

"My dear children," said Mary. *"Either you will do as I desire and reform your lives, or God Himself will need to cleanse you in the fires of untold punishment. You must be prepared to receive His great gift of peace. If you will not prepare yourselves, God will Himself be forced to do so in His justice and mercy."* There was that idea of fire again.

"Oh, the pride of souls!" Sister Mildred quoted Mary as lamenting. *"How they resist my grace. O my priests, my religious, what would I not do for you if you would only let me! I come daily laden with graces, which you daily refuse. How long will I bear with you, O my chosen ones? How long will you spurn my approaches?"*

There was a bright future if America would take up penance, if it would take up Christ, if it would unite with Mary as its mother. If not, *"the punishment will be long and for many forever."*

"If my desires are not fulfilled much suffering will come to this land," the Virgin allegedly said. *"My faithful one, if my warnings are taken seriously and enough of my children strive constantly and faithfully to renew and reform themselves in their inward and outward lives, then there will be no nuclear war. What happens to the world depends upon those who live in it. There must be much more good than evil prevailing in order to prevent the holocaust that is so near approaching. Yet I tell you, my daughter, even should such a destruction happen because there were not enough souls who took my warning seriously, there will remain a remnant—untouched by the chaos who, having been faithful in following me and spreading my warnings, will gradually inhabit the earth again with their dedicated and holy lives."*

Mary said her Immaculate Heart was *"the channel through which the graces of the Sacred Heart are given to men"* and warned that *"the false peace of this world lures them and in the end will destroy them."*

In the revelations, the Virgin allegedly referred to herself as a "co-redemptrix of the human race"—as did St. Joseph, her earthly spouse, who was also said to have appeared to Sister Mildred.

Yet the nun's emphasis in her last years, say those who knew her, was on how these events could be prevented. She was a cheerful soul with a sense of humor despite physical torments. "She said that if the world would listen and do what God asked, everything would be fine," one of her close friends told me. "But if they didn't, something eventually was going to happen. With all the abortion and that, God isn't going to take that. She was concerned about the whole world and America leading the world. The impurity of the youth—she was very concerned about that."

"It is the United States that is to lead the world to peace, the peace of Christ, the peace that He brought with Him from heaven," Sister Millie (as some knew her) quoted the Virgin as saying. *"Dear children, unless the United States accepts and carries out faithfully the mandate given to it by Heaven to lead the world to peace, there will come upon it and all nations a great havoc of war and incredible suffering."*

"It is the darkest hour," said another message. "But if men will come to me, my Immaculate heart will make it bright again with the Mercy which my Son will rain down through my hands. Help me save those who will not save themselves. Help me bring once again the sunshine of God's peace upon the world." Asking that a prayer to the Immaculate Conception (patroness of the U.S.) be recited once a day, the nun said it was "evident that the forces of evil are enveloping the world. Their hatred, however, is now partic-

ularly focused on the United States because of the Divine Mandate given to it to lead the world to peace. Weep, then, dear children, weep with your mother over the sins of men. Intercede with me before the throne of mercy, for sin is overwhelming the world and punishment is not far away."

Chapter 25

A potent poison was harming souls in the same way potent chlorinated or oil-based compounds (of the ilk exposed in *Silent Spring*) tainted the planet.

Soon, birds would no longer lay viable eggs (thus the "silence") and the eagle—very symbol of the young, bustling nation—headed toward extinction.

A new, synthetic biosphere was in the offing, along with new, synthetic sounds (the electric guitar was supplanting the old wooden ones).

There was Dick Clark on TV (now so tame in comparison) while in politics a suave congressman named John Kennedy was on the rise.

There were tests in the far-off Pacific of potent atomic weapons. (In the cloud of one would be seen a remarkable likeness to Jesus on the Cross and Mary kneeling in prayer, enfolded by luminous clouds below Him).

Did not much of what Mary was claimed to have said in Ohio to the nun (*"There must be much more good than evil prevailing in order to prevent the holocaust that is so near approaching"*) parallel apparitions in Heede, Germany, where, as one author said, "Our Lord's messages are reported in summary that mankind had ignored the Fatima messages and it was for this reason that Jesus Himself was now coming in person, in this last hour, to warn and exhort mankind. People must repent, turn away from sin, appease God's anger, especially by reciting the Rosary. Pleasure parties and entertainment must come to an end"?

A warning of nuclear holocaust if mankind continued to stray?

That was the era now entered: a world where there was the possibility, if Russia, China, and America fought, of global annihilation, or at least the destruction of entire nations, as mentioned in the messages of Fatima in 1917. Avoiding it relied on the collective moral goodness—especially purity—of *everyone.* At Montichiari she had even used the term *"sins against holy purity."* Could a single leader change this? Maybe. Probably not. At Fatima Mary had told seer Jacinta Marto that God was particularly offended by fashion and sins of the flesh. It was curious how the great sign of Fatima (an aurora borealis in 1938) was said to have mimicked the atmospheric luminosities at a nuclear detonation, especially in the way of two giant red spots. One scientist worried that a massive nuclear blast would one day eat up our atmosphere, creating a magnetic dynamo that set off fusion of air particles (*"annihilating nations"*). It could also take down electronics. It was hardly just abortion. A reversal of *Roe* would certainly go a long way. But would that be enough to counterbalance the many other ways of offending Heaven—the lasciviousness, the adulteries, the pornography, the abuse of children, the trafficking of humans, the divorce, the hatred, the vile public discourse, the disrespect for God, the materialism?

The world was *"approaching ruin,"* the times had grown *"dark, full of confusion and horror,"* the Montichiari seer said (quoting Mary), and the Lord already wanted *"to send another flood of punishments,"* Mary intoned, *"but if people pray and do penance, this heart of the mother will once more get light, love, and peace for the whole world from the Lord."* The Church too was *"in great danger"*—which it was; a scandal, germinating in these decades, and challenging the very foundation of institutional Catholicism (though never the spirit, the rock, of the Church itself), would one day erupt: About four thousand priests were to be accused of abusing nearly eleven thousand of the faithful (seventy-five percent of the incidents taking place between 1960 and 1984).

Woe. Great woe. Had there ever been a better example of wolves, hiding behind the Lamb, in sheep's clothing (*Matthew* 7:15)? And another question: Was this what Our Lady of LaSalette, speaking of clergy a century before, had warned would become a *"cesspool of impurity"*? It was a disaster of epic girth, a constant shock, costing the U.S. Church four billion dollars (enough to fund the Vatican's annual operating budget for nearly eighteen years, or build more than twenty cathedrals). To detail some cases was an exercise best left to the exorcist, for that was clearly operating here: either the devil inserting false vocations (inspiring homosexuals to use the Church as a safe haven, a place where being single was not questioned and with ready accessibility to the trusting young) or twisting the inclinations of priests who had started out right but had been overcome by temptations of the new era, there alone, in rectories.

Wasn't it the dawn of the age of liberation?

Wasn't everybody doing it?

Wasn't everyone called to shuck old standards and "open" oneself?

The abuse was even more rampant at public schools, where one in ten students would report it (more than twice the level among clergy). *"Things will get so bad that people will think all is lost, but I am after all a mother who has a living heart for her children and would save them,"* the Montichiari *apparition, before rejection, had claimed. "As you can observe for yourself, human pride has resulted in confusing those in the highest offices of the Church. The prayer, offering, and penance of so many people prevent true judgment of God falling upon mankind. In my love I am always pleading with my Son Jesus Christ. The times grow more calamitous through the effect of a satanic and godless delusion, which strives to undermine and destroy the world of the Divine Redeemer, the Lord of the whole universe. The world ought to have been visited by a great judgment because of its hardening sin. His great and endless Mercy has triumphed once again."*

It was curious, how the messages that reflected poorly on the clergy found rejection, whether LaSalette (which went through decades of acceptance/rejection), Montichiari, where that *noticia* was inside the church, or one during the early 1950s at Sabana Grande, Puerto Rico, where Mary allegedly had appeared to a seven-year-old boy named Juan Angel Collado and then two girls (one eight and the other nine), dressed in white and stepping out of what he described as a whirlwind.

Did she really appear?

There were strange elements, and I adhere to a determination by the bishop, who ruled negatively.

It was the hour, Mary supposedly said, in which all men needed to unite, supplicating mercy along with the Holy Father, bishops, and priests. Prayer was urged for the *"transformation"* of humanity, on this island that had been declared by Christopher Columbus in 1493 (and was now part of the U.S.). That change was especially important *"for those who are isolated and far away from God, especially the leaders of the Church."* A great danger threatened. The *"hour and time,"* the kids insisted they heard, were *"very near."* She wanted a daily minimum—claimed the kids—of five Rosary decades. That would allow her to shelter mankind with her mantle. In April 1953 she added, "[There will be] *difficult times of spiritual deterioration. Men's selfishness will reign. Those consecrated to my beloved Son Jesus, through my call to promulgate a new breed of true Christians, will be persecuted. Some new children, consecrated to my small reign, will thrust my heart with the sword of treason and the deterioration of their promise to Our Lord Jesus Christ. Nevertheless, the message of restitution will be accepted and promulgated beyond the sea, where I have set my right foot. In the moments of greater tribulation and persecution, I will send the angel who will show you the way again."*

The "sign" that the time was near?

When social, moral, and spiritual deterioration darkened humanity, when the world was plunged into a crisis of faith, when *"some priests, ministers of my Son as shepherds of the flock, are irreverent in the celebration of the Holy Sacraments"* and became enemies through their *"attachment to money"* and their *"search for recognition"* and *"pleasures"* (all themes Pope Francis would later take up, in warning). *"It is the hour in which, because you have not responded to my warnings, the prophecies will start to come true,"* a message supposedly said. *"My children, protect yourselves under my mantle and live in my virtues. I warn you that one day the vault of heaven will be totally orange and dark, there will be intense cold and a great tribulation and desperation will fall over mankind. It will be as if hell settled upon earth. Parents, children, and all human beings will fight among themselves and will want to kill each other. They will hurt each other till death. All that I have warned can be avoided and the crisis of faith could come to an end if the chosen ones become converted and start living a life of intense prayer, dedicating themselves to penance, subjecting themselves to fasting and abstinence, practicing mortification of the senses, and paying special attention to the participation of the sacraments."* One last *"word of advice,"* said "Mary," was that *"the devil will try to destroy my work and my manifestation to the world. There will be such a relaxation for the Divine that vain and superficial messages will be spoken of everywhere. Many will the alleged apparitions be. Some will be genuine and others will be the work of the evil one . . . Some of these apparitions that will not be my manifestations will be supported by shepherds and hierarchs of the Church of my Son Jesus. Others, where I am present, will be persecuted and repressed, but this should not be cause of frustrations and loss of faith; so much the better. Then, stay firm in the Church of my Son, love it more intensely, love your shepherds and priests, make an effort to live in harmony and common union with the shepherds. This will be a sign that you are with me and belong to my Son Jesus the Christ.*

"I will give you a sign; there where I will be, I will ask for prayer, I will ask for penance, with special attention to fasting, and I will ask for much sacrifice. Above all, I will ask a special love for my large star, my Son, the Eucharist.

"I am the major angel, envoy of these times, the Virgin of Light, the Virgin Mary, the spouse of God."

And so it went.

One had no trouble seeing why the Church would take issue with it!

Respect the Church, the messages said through one side of the mouth—while through the other taking issue with the shepherds—including negative pronouncements, as happened with Sabana itself.

We knew, from one of the most famous scriptures, the warning that Satan could come as an "angel of light" (2 *Corinthians* 11:14), and here was Mary calling herself an "angel" and also "the Virgin of Light."

Time stood still. Water looked like a rainbow. A cop in attendance cut his finger and it was healed instantly.

Chapter 26

Whatever did or didn't happen at Sabana Grande (the negative judgment upon which was recently affirmed), no one could deny the descent into darkness. It was 1953 and camera in hand, Hugh Hefner, seeking fresh, aspiring models/starlets (call them now "bunnies"), set in motion what can only be described as one of the most devastating trends in American history.

Never could Columbus, DeLeon, nor Father Lopez (to be certain) have imagined a country that would one day not only remove prohibitions against lewd talk and public nakedness but flaunt it—nudity, or ribald themes—in magazines at every drug store counter, or at least at newsstands and gas stations. Can anyone imagine the reaction of pilgrims, of Puritans, to *Playboy* or *Cosmopolitan*? Move over, Margaret Sanger: when it came to sociological nuclear bombs, when it came to saturnalia, nothing could compare to what Hefner launched. For in large part *Playboy* decimated puritan America and set in motion a "sexual revolution" that would cause a generation of men (and then another, and another) to treat women as objects and bring pornography (first the soft version, then hardcore) into the mainstream (all in the name of "liberation").

He became an image, did Hefner, an icon to which men, young and old alike, aspired: this randy bachelor with a gorgeous, statuesque brunette or blonde on each arm or in the pool and with a harem in the anteroom. Harsh as it could sound, the devil himself, in the flesh, would have struggled to play a better role of Mephisto, bringing Crowley's dictum of "do what thou wilt" into full relief—and soon, with the help of contraception (going full circle back to Sanger), making it the standard of American sexual life.

Love was suddenly sex. Sex was suddenly cheap. And not just sex but adultery and fornication. Anything went!

Soon mainstream did the magazine become that one day it could boast among its subjects for monthly interviews, or its contributors, Jimmy Carter, Bill Clinton, Donald Trump, and Martin Luther King Jr. Trump would proudly display the cover of his appearance in his Manhattan office and even make short video clips for Playboy. There were Truman Capote, Isaac Bashevis Singer, The Beatles. A Supreme Court justice wrote for it! And of course the hottest movie stars. A church-going relative once gave me a subscription for a Christmas present.

And so had begun—in the 1950s, as Elvis rocked the stage, as Ray Kroc founded McDonald's, and as Disney started Disneyland; as stocks soared; as movies took over; as "beatniks" entered the picture—the descent of a culture.

This was the decade—and 1953 the year—that secrets of genetic material began to unfold, revealing what scientists, in their new, skyrocketing hubris, decided was the key to life: DNA, the true design of life (no longer requiring, henceforth, the notion of a Creator). It was biology. It was *chemistry* (which went back to alchemy). No wonder the molecule was serpentine! (Now, two snakes—the "double helix," not just one—were on the "tree of life.")

Soon, man would launch up satellites, further breaching the fables of Heaven.

Back on earth, there was Marilyn Monroe, not just as a new "sex goddess" but a pivotal player in the movement she and other "goddesses," along with Hefner, helped to foment—a "liberation" that furthered the breakdown of taboos (didn't Satan always promise freedom, while causing bondage?). Knowingly or unknowingly, poor Marilyn, herself a product of a broken home, brought into our mainstream the idea of free sex and multiple marriages. Remember, this was the Fifties; June Cleaver was still on the scene. So were Ozzie and Harriet (their home in Los Angeles near a seismic fault). Marriage was still one man and one woman—and for the most part, intimacy waited for the wedding night. There was not even yet the term "living together." But that was shifting. Soon the change would be radical. Actually Marilyn predated Hefner, posing without clothes for a calendar that had been issued in 1949, a photograph deployed, in fact, to launch the first issue of *Playboy*. (One day, Hefner would buy a crypt, at Westwood Village Memorial Park Cemetery, next to hers.) Monroe's first big billing, her first lead role on the big magic screen, came in 1953 (*Niagara*). The titles of other movies said it all: *Monkey Business, We're Not Married!, Love Nest, Let's Make It Legal, The Girl In Pink Tights, Diamonds Are A Girl's Best Friend,* and *Gentlemen Prefer Blondes* (her hair was dyed that color—foreshadowing another major trend). In skin-taut dress and the bathing suits was the stereotypical pin-up girl-turn-Hollywood-star-turned-icon, a symbol for (and symptomatic of) a generation poised for tremendous change. There were not only her divorces but also Monroe's addiction to drugs. She was a genius at new sexual stunts that captured and enraptured the nation, such as her iconic pose with dress flapping up on the subway grate while filming *The Seven-*

Year Itch. Now let's look deeper. What spirit moved? As Monroe's own drama coach told her, "My dear, you haven't yet any idea of the importance of your position in the world. You are the greatest woman of your time, the greatest human being of your time, of any time—you name it. You can't think of anybody. I mean—no, not even Jesus..." and she was said (again by that drama coach) to be "engulfed in a mystical-like flame, like when you see Jesus at the Last Supper and there's a halo around Him. There was this great white light surrounding Marilyn."

Unbeknownst to such folks, that aura—charisma—could also come from the devil. In Hollywood, most of it did.

In fact, surrounding oneself with a "white light" was a ritual used in satanism—by Crowley.

Monroe frequently attended séances and psychic readings and before each scene meditated herself into a deep trance to get in touch with spirits.

It's not like she always indulged in evil intentionally. Like the rest of us, she could be deceived.

Deceived and a deceiver.

Or at least, that's what it seemed.

To this day, towering statues of her with dress blowing up from the classic scene have been in downtowns like Chicago.

She was hardly alone. There was Sinatra. There was the glitz of the Strip. There was this *explosion* of cultural-Vegas-Bohemian power. Hundreds of musicians ("one-hit wonders") became famous overnight. A wellspring, a gusher, exploded.

From whence did it come?

"Mankind is obscured by a thick fog, as a result of many grievous sins, which are well-nigh covering the whole earth," a nun in Consenga, Italy, quoted the Blessed Virgin as saying. *"Today, more than ever, men are resisting the calls from*

Heaven, and are blaspheming God, while wallowing in the mire of sin."

Already, warned the Virgin, there were *"many iniquitous and wicked leaders of the people."* Rapacious wolves, in the guise of sheep. *"Once there was the chastisement by water, but if there is not a return to God, there will come the chastisement by fire, which will cover the streets of the world with blood,"* said Mary, to reiterate—during a decade when seventy-five percent of Catholics still attended at least weekly Mass.

Three out of four: the good old days (seeing what it is now)!

Were there two sources—light and dark—or did fruits indicate only the latter?

Wasn't there "Let It Be"? Wouldn't there be "Lady Madonna"?

But also wasn't there Crowley in the crowd on the cover of *Sergeant Pepper*?

Wouldn't this be the decade during which a *Time* cover asked, "Is God Dead?"

Wouldn't John Lennon of The Beatles soon say The Beatles were also more popular than Christ?

Wouldn't he die on December 8—feast of the Immaculate Conception?

And wasn't the same day as the comet Ikeya was spotted (in 1965) the day Lennon's band released their album *Help*?

A big band out there had been "Bill Haley and the Comets."

Would fire from Heaven one day figure into the timeline?

It did if one subscribed to apparitions reported in nations such as Ukraine (where Mary (appearing the year of

Stalin's death) had said, *"Never have people fallen so low since the beginning of the world as at this time. This is the age of the Kingdom of Satan."*

This was Seredne, where she first appeared during Mass to a seer named Hanya just before Consecration.

"Whoever comes in the spirit of penance for his sins and drinks this water with faith will be strengthened in body and soul and he shall not die when catastrophe strikes," said the Blessed Virgin. *"I greatly desire to help sinners, because disaster is at hand, just as the time of Noah people will be destroyed not by flood but by fire, because they have sinned against God."*

Soon after she had appeared in Turzovka, Czechoslovakia, to a fellow named Matous Lasuta, once more behind the Iron Curtain, once more atop a rounded mountain, once more in a villatic, campestral setting, a pine bearing the image of Our Lady of Perpetual Help: it was here, where she had been honored, that Mary came, her expression majestic but serious, eyes azure, tall, slim of body, on a cloud that put one in mind of Fatima.

"Our Lady signaled Matous to look in the direction of the pine," noted Peter Heintz in *A Guide to Apparitions*. "He looked and saw a tableaux showing the globe; then all the different countries on earth were displayed. Different colors now appeared on the map, some green and some yellow. The water was blue. An inscription explained that the green spots indicated countries where the population is good and the yellow spots denoted countries marked for destruction owing to the bad behavior of the people. The high country was more green and the flat land more yellow. Matous saw the yellow invading and covering more countries while the green was retreating. The message was that the world was getting worse and worse. Then an inscription emerged forming the words: *'Do penance.'* By and large the yellow color invaded all lands. Then powerful explosions burst forth over the water and land. A dense rain of small leaves fell to earth, and upon reaching the ground, these turned into flames. Soon all the touched soil was covered with fire."

Wormwood? Radiation? The earth torched, as in the Third Secret? "And the name of the star is called Wormwood: and the third part of the waters became wormwood; and many men died of the waters, because they were made bitter" (*Revelation* 8:11).

Matous claimed that if things continued, two-thirds of mankind would be struck.

And this was before Woodstock, the Rolling Stones, the banning of school prayer, punk, heavy metal, *Deep Throat*, and legal abortion.

The seer had also claimed that the sun would cease to warm, causing cold summers that would prevent agriculture—while at other stages there would be terrible floods; earthquakes; mountains would *"move."*

"These days," Mary was quoted as saying, *"will start with rolling thunder and trembling of the earth. Then close well your habitation, pray, cross yourselves with the Sign of the Cross, repent your sins, call upon the Mother of God for help, and she will take you under her protection."*

For—she further told him (let us again say "allegedly," for the bishop initially halted pilgrims from going there, then allowed it)—*"the angels who are entrusted with the work of destruction are ready, but the wrath of God can be stayed by praying the Rosary, by penance and sincere repentance."*

All her children, said Mary, would carry the sign of the Cross on their foreheads. Others would not. *"This sign only my chosen ones will see,"* she said. *"These chosen ones will be instructed by my angels how to conduct themselves.*

"My faithful will be without any fear during the most difficult hours. They will be protected by the good spirits and will

be fed by Heaven; from there they will receive further instructions. They will fall in to a deathlike sleep, but they will be protected by angels."

What to make of such drama?

The Catholic version of the "rapture"?

And how was it that the angels of chastisement were at the ready in 1958—and yet still, in our day, without a climax?

Did Mary's appearances (about to spread exponentially) hold back her Son's Arm, as she so often put it?

When Communists destroyed the pine, and incarcerated Matous (he ended up three years behind bars), the wood was used for a Cross that as in America—during those early explorer times—was planted firmly in the ground.

God warned and *warned* and warned, and showed mercy, and responded to prayers, and warned anew, and was merciful again, due to the Rosary and penance among a small flock.

Their numbers dwindled.

So did sand in the hourglass.

Mary saw what humans—with microscopes, with telescopes—could not:

Evil was not only creeping in—very soon to inundate—but becoming institutionalized.

It had been said in the 1880s during Pope Leo's vision that the devil had been granted fifty to sixty years.

That was eighty years before.

Had he been given additional decades?

The young disappeared from church as homilies dragged—now more philosophical than inspirational. Academia had taken the reins—tossing that Prayer to Saint Michael and replacing the exorcist with the therapist.

In convents, what would soon be known as the New Age ("Asmodeus," in the warning of LaSalette) planted seeds while confessionals were turned into closets and statues banished to the basement (or trash heap).

In Rome a nun named Elena Patriarca Leonardi (whose alleged visions began during the 1950s and extended into the 1980s) would proclaim that if men did not stop offending God, there would fall upon earth an *"unforeseen fire," "the worst punishment ever seen in human history,"* covering *"the whole earth, and a great part of humanity . . . destroyed."*

Such drastic warnings could be relegated to the dustbin of supernatural eschatology but for their similarities.

Serious times were likewise indicated at a controversial apparition called Garabandal, which had begun at the very onset of the Sixties.

Located far up in the Cantabrian Mountains (a gorgeous but harrowing journey from Fatima, as I was to see first-hand), these Spanish apparitions crystallized previous prophecies into the drama of secrets arranged like those at Fatima but with more flare—proclaiming the coming of a huge "Warning," a "Great Miracle," and a chastisement (which from certain indications seemed to include indeed a comet or something hanging as a terrifying spectacle in the sky, events that, claimed the seers, would sear consciences and reveal the state of every person's soul).

In 1995, the overseeing bishop sent me a letter saying he had rejected the supernaturality of Garabandal—upon the recommendation of the Vatican—although since then there seemed to be a softening in the diocesan stance.

Still, it remained in limbo.

Something paranormal had occurred.

The question was what.

The warning, indicated these seers, would be "like two stars . . . that crash," though not like two stars actually falling; a loud noise as everything in the world seemed to stand still.

It would be visible everywhere.

An event would come, they were claiming, one that would cause everyone pause.

As for the Chastisement, that would be "far worse than if we were enveloped in fire," said a seer named Conchita González, "worse than if we had fire above us, and fire beneath."

Chapter 27

In obedience, one did not dwell at more length upon what the bishops felt was questionable.

But it was haunting stuff.

Whatever was or was not coming, it could be known that protection came through faith, prayer, and our angels.

Mostly, protection was there when we are doing His Will.

And protection—personal and societal—was urgent.

The drama and warnings of Garabandal may have been linked, spiritually or emotionally, to the great threat of nuclear holocaust that with Khrushchev (who ruled at this time) hung like the "Sword of Damocles."

Fire.

As for the timeline: we were now well into the Sixties.

Prayer and the Bible would be stripped from schools—starting a fall of dominoes that would relentlessly seek to remove crosses and the Name of Jesus not just from public classrooms but every government property and even Catholic schools like Georgetown (where, one day—to its great shame—Crucifixes would be removed).

My own alma mater Fordham would allow "yippie" Jerry Rubin to speak at its student center, smoking a joint.

But as for that removal of prayer: this was largely the handiwork of the man who helped found the American Civil Liberties Union, bringing the first lawsuit opposing school supplication to the Supreme Court in 1962. He was closely followed by atheist Madalyn Murray O'Hair, who successfully challenged Bible-reading, leading to what would become a cascade against any religious involvement (save for the New Age) in the public square, including prayer at high school football games and during graduation ceremonies.

One day, teachers would cite students for wearing crosses or any other representation of Christianity—even seek to expel those who handed out biblical tracts (as if it were pornography, which actually was more to their liking!). A poor soul, was O'Hair, who met a violent end decades later, slain by a criminal she employed.

But by then the tide against Christianity was becoming a tsunami and would see concerted attempts not just to erase God from public buildings but likewise the historical role of Christopher Columbus, who was charged by ACLU types with racism (for his alleged treatment of Indians) when the real motive lay in secular resistance to his Franciscan aura, to the Mariology that permeated his missions.

The fruit of secularization: rampant sex, crime, and drug abuse at the nation's schools.

Discipline was tossed out the window (see *Proverbs* 13:24).

At Christmastime—during these 1960s—the vogue was now "Merry Xmas," taking "Christ" out of post offices and off store windows and even greeting cards (His own birthday!). A dirt route in my city known as St. Joe's Road would become "Palm Coast Parkway," as Christian names were paved over.

In the West—where Haight-Asbury was in bloom—the move would be to smear the name of Junipero Serra.

At LaSalette, we may recall, the Blessed Mother had warned that *"all civil governments will have one and the same plan, which will be to abolish and do away with every religious principle, to make way for materialism, atheism, spiritualism, and vice of all kinds."*

Yes, "spiritualism"—psychic phenomena, soon to be called "New Age"—was another great fashion of the Sixties. *"The demon of magic,"* as she'd put it. And it fit with drugs like a glove (see: Timothy Leary).

No decade would be more pivotal.

No decade would be pervaded and embossed, even formed, with more darkness.

Society had left the era of Elvis and was wandering blindly—trying anything and shrugging as God was cast away.

One had only to look at the litany:

Invention of the Pill (1960).

The introduction of Bob Dylan.

Alfred Hitchcock's *Psycho.*

Depiction of TV as a "vast wasteland."

The election of Kennedy.

The Cuban Missile Crisis.

The Berlin Wall.

Viet Nam.

The assassination of JFK.

The Beatles on Ed Sullivan.

The first Super Bowl.

The Summer of Love.

The Rolling Stones ("Satisfaction").

Woodstock.

The feminist movement.

The Watts riots.

Campus uprisings.

Vatican Two.

The Martin Luther King assassination.

Neil Armstrong.

Launch of the Gay Rights Movement (see Stonewall riots).

There was an explosion of "cultural" force. But where did it come from?

Why was the Ikeya comet spotted on the same day (September 18, 1965) that the new hot song was "Help"?

And why—if it was simply a cultural phenomenon, the Sixties, not a spiritual one—did men like Leary (great advocate of hallucinogenics, which Indians used to contact spirits) also profess Luciferianism?

Lastly, was not free sex, a part of the pagan culture ("Saturnalia"), now joined by another tactic of witchcraft: use of drugs (*pharmakeia*)?

Chemicals for everything.

The Pill. LSD. DDT.

Could anyone be surprised to read that both Lennon and McCartney felt as if the songs often came from somewhere else, and that their songwriting sessions had aspects of a séance?

Oh, yes, some of the songs were beautiful, and perhaps even good (I was a Beatles fan).

But what a time. What a decade.

Soon, we would need *The Exorcist*!

In 1966 the official Church of Satan (established on the teachings of Crowley) was born in San Francisco. That was also the year—from *Pet Sounds*, to Frank Zappa, to *Revolver—of* rock's greatest explosion.)

No one could judge another but one could say that we are all deceived. We all have good and evil. Everyone has good and evil. Every waking moment, we all struggle against the prince of darkness. Marilyn Monroe was a friend of Anton LaVey, founder of the satanic "church," as was sex "siren" Jayne Mansfield.

And that, apparently, came to no good end: Mansfield decapitated in a car crash after a falling out with LaVey while Monroe died from an overdose in mysterious circumstances (and was linked romantically to both John and Robert Kennedy, who also found themselves in tragic circumstances, Robert clutching a Rosary).

When JFK was killed, something died in America, something that went beyond the death of a leader, more momentous even than the death of Lincoln: something (perhaps because of rumored CIA involvement) that scored the death of American innocence.

This sense of loss went beyond losing a glamorous White House; it seemed like a mourning over the end of an era—started by Columbus—in U.S. history.

Perhaps it was a feeling of unsettlement, impossible to extinguish, deep in the psyche, that something very dark and complicated was behind the assassination, that segments of government had turned on each other, and that one faction, the intelligence-military-industrial complex, had so much power it may have engineered the president's death (miffed at the president's vow, after Bay of Pigs, "to splinter the CIA in a thousand pieces and scatter it to the winds").

There was plenty of evidence (see Catholic author James W. Douglass' *JFK and the Unspeakable*, the "unspeakable" being evil) that before Dallas, conspirators had sought to kill him first in a Washington suburb and then in Chicago.

The interweaving of motive as well as the testimony (and often peculiar deaths) of many witnesses in Dallas, including a deaf man who claimed to have seen a second gunman dressed as a rail worker, and a woman who said she saw Jack Ruby, who had connections to Cuban gun runners, disembarking from a truck at Dealey Plaza shortly before the assassination, as well as those who swore they saw other suspicious men and heard shots from the area of the notorious grassy knoll, and then the odd killing of Oswald (by Ruby) and Ruby's own death (as well as that of so many others connected to the case) formed a compelling and astonishing argument, one that hardly faded when, soon after, also during the Sixties, Bobby and then Martin Luther King Junior—likewise threats to the status quo—were assassinated. There were those who claimed the CIA was even using mind-control techniques, under a program called MK-Ultra, to engineer assassins. (I believed this to be a possibility.)

Who was in charge—the elected or the intelligence-military-defense industry?

And if Oswald was a Russian agent, why was he escorted, upon arrival from Russia, and settled in Dallas, by people with CIA links?

"The 'unspeakable' that rules us now took power on November 22, 1963, and was confirmed by the Warren Report," wrote a reviewer of Douglass' book.

"By denying the void at the heart of our system, we have allowed it to undermine everything."

Very dark, was the void. There were questions everywhere—conspiracy theories.

But the real conspiracies were at a spiritual level, devised by "forces of darkness in high places," as *Ephesians* put it, not by a cabal in Geneva or Washington.

Did anything signify the orchestration of evil more than Charles Manson (Man-son; Son of Man reversed), who killed the actress Sharon Tate while her husband was directing a movie about the devil's baby at the Dakota apartments near

Central Park in New York—the same building where Lennon and his wife were to hold seances, spot UFOs, and where the great singer-composer was killed by a man listening to "little people."

All this: really, happenstance?

These were only a few of endless examples, Marilyn once saying to a reporter tellingly that she was a "Jekyll and Hyde, two in one, more than two. I'm so many people. They shock me sometimes. I wish it was just me."

Indeed.

Was this not also the decade that immediately followed the famous 1957 movie on "multiple personality" called *The Three Faces of Eve*?

The darkness fell like a curtain: Bart Simpson replaced Fred Flintstone, the Grinch elbowed out Popeye; then the carnality: *Sex in the City* instead of *Mayberry*. Carnality? In short order, Marilyn would be replaced by Linda Lovelace and female vampires would take the place of the *Flying Nun*.

Betty Boop?

Replaced by Beavis and Butthead.

And so from the Sixties into the Seventies and subsequent decades went the culture like a runaway rollercoaster while very, very few—a truly precious few—listened to the Blessed Mother, though she certainly seemed to know, at the cusp of the Sixties, what was germinating and how at first subtly and then at times not so subtly would turn evil. *"The world will have to drain the cup of wrath to the dregs because of the countless sins through which His Heart is offended,"* she had said during four apparitions at Marienfield, Germany (to a twelve-year-old girl that had no diocesan prohibitions against them).

"The Star of the infernal regions will rage more violently than ever and will cause frightful destruction, because he knows that his time is short, and because he sees that already many have gathered around my sign.

"Over these he has no spiritual power, although he will kill the bodies of many.

"Some have already allowed my sign to be impressed on them; their number will increase. But I want to tell you, my children, not to forget that the very cross of those bloody days is a grace.

"Pray, make sacrifices for sinners. Offer yourselves and your works to the Father through me, and put yourselves at my disposal without reserve. Pray the Rosary. Pray not so much for external things—weightier things are at stake in these times.

"After this, the Devil will be possessed of such power that those who are not firmly established in me will be deceived. There is a time coming when you will stand in this place all alone and will be frightfully calumniated. Because the Devil knows how to deceive men, they permit themselves to be completely blinded to the higher things. But you should establish everything with confidence (in my Immaculate Heart). The devil has power over all people who do not trust in my Heart. Wherever people substitute my Immaculate Heart for their sinful hearts, the devil has no power. But he will persecute my children. They will be despised, but he can do them no harm. Expect no signs or wonders.

"I shall be active as the powerful mediatrix in secret."

Chapter 28

And so it was that there were two major developments right after the Sixties: first, Satan's massive ritual—the pulse of music with a voodoo beat, the *pharmakeia* so dear to witchcraft, the *Saturnalia*. And next: the most damaging jurisprudence in the history of the United States, a decision that would have made those in Lincoln's time, those who fought slavery, those around George Washington, those aboard the *Santa Maria* appalled beyond tears.

This was the Supreme Court decision in 1973 that legalized the termination of unborn human babies.

It was the culmination: a blood sacrifice.

Unless this was quickly undone—along with all the other rampant evil—the nation had met its fate.

And that fate was spelled out this very same year halfway around the globe at a convent in Akita, Japan, where a deaf nun "heard" Mary warn not specifically about abortion (curiously, few approved apparitions did), but about the general sins of mankind, sins that, yes, would result in fire. *"Many men in this world afflict the world,"* Mary said, speaking through a statue at the convent that wept on 101 occasions. *"I desire souls to console Him to soften the anger of the Heavenly Father. I wish, with my Son, for souls who will by their suffering and their poverty enact reparation for the sinners and ingrates. In order that the world might know His anger, the Heavenly Father is preparing to inflict a great chastisement on all mankind."*

This was at the Institute of the Handmaids of the Eucharist. Later, as usual, controversies would swirl and one day, the nun, Sister Agnes Sasagawa, would find herself all but stripped of religious veneer and banished to an apartment near Tokyo, there under the protection of a priest.

It was hostile territory—the world, including often the ecclesiastic sector—for those who claimed to see the Virgin!

Was it a true revelation?

One bishop said yes, *his* successor no, his successor not quite sure. I was sent material from the diocese saying what was substantiated were the tears: analyzed in a laboratory, it was confirmed that the statue had inexplicably wept human ones.

When I checked with the Most Reverend Francis Keiichi Sato (at the time Bishop of Niigata), he faxed me a letter saying, "As you may know, opinions are divided on both sides of the question. As pastor of the people on both sides of the question, I have tried to maintain a delicate balance between giving freedom to devotions at Akita and leaving it to time to clarify the nature of the events." With his letter was an official statement affirming that the statue did indeed exhibit supernaturality.

"The fact that the wooden statue of Our Lady shed tears is undeniable; it is something that occurred over and over between 1975 and 1981, with a great number of eyewitnesses," wrote Bishop Sato, affirming a predecessor, Most Reverend John Shojiro Ito, who in a pastoral letter had said, "The scientific examination of Professor Sagisaka, specialist in legal medicine in the faculty of medicine at the University of Akita, has proved that this liquid is indeed identical to human tears. It is beyond human powers to produce water where there is none, and I believe that to do this the intervention of a non-human force is necessary. Moreover, it is not the question of pure water, but of a liquid identical to liquid secreted by a human body. It flowed only from the eyes of the statue, as tears flow, and that more than 100 times over a period of several years and before many numerous witnesses. It has been established that it could not have been by trickery or human maneuvers."

That meant tentative—but not final—approval.

There would still be confusion. There would be animadversaries. The archbishop of Tokyo opposed it, as did a commission and at least two papal nuncios (ambassadors from the Vatican). Communiqués originating out of the Vatican's Congregation for the Doctrine of the Faith also cast doubt on the situation, though that dubiousness seemed to soften when Bishop Shojiro sent a larger dossier to Rome and met with the Congregation's head, Cardinal Joseph Ratzinger, who (it was widely reported) gave no objection to the bishop's supportive pastoral letter, which authorized devotion at the site.

Meanwhile, the secular ambassador to the Vatican from the Philippines, Howard Dee, with whom I had some communication, related that once, when he pressed Cardinal Ratzinger (of course, now Benedict XVI) about the third Fatima secret, which Ratzinger had read, but which at that point had not yet been publicly dispensed, Benedict told him that if he wanted to know what was in the secret he should read the messages of Akita.

Another of those messages (recorded by Sister Sasagawa on October 13, 1973, *anniversary* of the great Fatima sun miracle), said: *"As I told you, if men do not repent and better themselves, the Father will inflict a terrible punishment on all humanity. It will be a punishment greater than the Deluge, such as one will have never seen before. Fire will fall from the sky and will wipe out a great part of humanity, the good as well as the bad, sparing neither priests nor faithful. The survivors will find themselves so desolate that they will envy the dead. The only arms which will remain for you will be the Rosary and the Sign left by My Son. Each day recite the prayers of the Rosary. With the Rosary, pray for the Pope, the bishops and priests.*

"The work of the devil will infiltrate even into the Church in such a way that one will see cardinals opposing cardinals, bishops against bishops. The priests who venerate me will be scorned and opposed by their confreres . . . churches and altars sacked; the Church will be full of those who accept compromises and the demon will press many priests and consecrated souls to leave the service of the Lord.

"The demon will be especially implacable against souls consecrated to God. The thought of the loss of so many souls is the cause of my sadness. If sins increase in number and gravity, there will be no longer pardon for them.

"With courage, speak to your superior. He will know how to encourage each one of you to pray and to accomplish works of reparation.

"It is Bishop Ito, who directs your community."

The Blessed Mother reputedly smiled and then said: *"Today is the last time that I will speak to you in living voice. From now on you will obey the one sent to you and your superior.*

"Pray very much the prayers of the Rosary. I alone am able still to save you from the calamities which approach. Those who place their confidence in me will be saved."

This was electrifying because indeed there was a link: when the third secret was revealed in June of 2000, it turned out to be the image of an angel ready to torch the world, but for a luminosity that came from the Blessed Mother and drowned out the flaming sword. I was astonished because a book I had penned, *Prayer of the Warrior*, one I had dedicated to Sister Lucia (and sent to her in 1993, seven years before the secret was revealed), had, as "luck" would have it, a flaming sword on the cover.

Also of note was the fact that the Akita statue was fashioned after a design given to Ida in Holland during those apocalyptic apparitions in the 1950s. Further, the message at Akita sounded awfully similar to what during the 1960s an obscure German publication, *Neues Europa*, had claimed was text of the third secret.

Had Sister Sasagawa simply read about the alleged secret, as presented by that periodical (widely denounced as fraudulent, including by Sister Lucia), or were there words attached to the image in the secret, text hidden from public view, because of their apocalyptic nature and also because, again, they reflected poorly on the clergy? Like Akita, it had spoken of great calamities, in the world and the Church, of cardinal versus cardinal, bishop versus bishop). Or was it a third possibility: that, as rumored, a copy or summary of the secret had been sent to JFK and Khrushchev at the height of nuclear tensions and during such transmissions someone who'd glimpsed the secret spoke about it?

I don't believe two popes (Saint John Paul II and Benedict XVI, both of whom were involved with the eventual release of the secret and said the image, unaccompanied by words, was all there was), along with Sister Lucia (who also said the image was the whole of it), would lie. The pertinent point: both Fatima and Akita indicated a world set ablaze as punishment (or cleansing, if you prefer), a holocaust that would mimic but dwarf the event a century before in the blazing hinterlands of Wisconsin.

Obviously, taking place as it did in Japan, the cause for potential chastisement had more to do than with only the U.S. and *Roe versus Wade*. No, it wasn't just abortion. That was clear. But the killing of unborn had to weigh mightily. Soon fifty million would be killed via abortion each year around the world, nearly a million and a half in the increasingly de-Christianized states.

This was like destroying the population of San Antonio, Texas, each year.

The Chicago Seven, Kent State, attacks by the Viet Cong, Watergate, Legionnaires' Disease, *Star Wars*, Ted Bundy, Son of Sam, a blackout in New York, Three-Mile Island, Khomeini, a singer named Madonna, set to take the reins from Marilyn, performing lasciviously on a stage designed to mimic a Catholic church (but with black candles).

Oh, raise that Cross! Chastisement seemed to approach, fade back, approach, fade back, each though a bit closer. Four hundred years now since St. Augustine and Menendez. Whenever you went back to that founding, you felt the juice. Woe! So long ago. Much water under the dam. A new nation rising. Not a better one. America had reached and was ready to pass its peak as measured in wholesomeness, along with progress, along with real human prosperity. Kennedy was dead, and the stage had been taken over by the rancor of rock and soon heavy and heavier rock until it reached Goth proportions. Boom boxes would soon blare defiant rap. The air was to be saturated with noise and beat. It throbbed. Ritual-like. You could hear it from cars through closed windows. It was coming up and down the streets. Spirits marched. It was an unleashing. Something very good in America had died and was now at Arlington. No one had yet noticed its death. There was comfort only in the presence of Mary, who, it was said, around this same time as Akita, was also appearing down in deepest Africa.

That involved fifteen alleged apparitions in the state of Orlu Imo, Nigeria, to a fellow in his mid-thirties named Innocent Okorie, which started in 1972 and stretched (again, reputedly) until 1985.

In Peter Heintz's summary, the messages addressed how the world had failed to serve God and thus had fallen "to evil influences in the world."

If mankind continued and ignored the messages, said the Blessed Virgin, that evil would be met with events (beginning in 1980). Catastrophes and natural disasters would take place. Christians would suffer greatly. (Such materialized precisely in Nigeria, with Muslim radicals kidnapping, torturing, and slaying Christians—thousands, including priests). *"Faithful Christians will suffer greatly,"* the Blessed Mother had accurately predicted.

She also foresaw epidemics—uncontrollable ones—saying on July 13, 1982, such sicknesses would come from *"the murder of the unborn that your country and America, particularly the USA"* allow. She said these countries would *"receive disaster,"* alluding also to an *"increase in earthquakes"* and further adding (allegedly): *"I am sorry for Canada and California."*

Indeed, the West Coast, terrain of Father Serra, where so many very holy Franciscan missions were, where the cities—San Francisco, Los Angeles (full name: Our Lady of the Angels)—had borne holy names, now denigrated by rampant entertainments, fornications, drug use, crime, homosexuality. To view photos of gay-pride events in the Castro District was to see a display of anti-Catholicism at its very most vile, detestable, and demonized (half-naked men in "nun's" habits, "priests" in jock straps or with sexual toys, blasphemous posters of Christ and the Blessed Mother). *This* wasn't a "hate crime"? It was okay to besmirch Christianity but say not a thing about gay marriage—about transsexuals, about lesbians (and the poor children they now were allowed to adopt)? The "Golden State" was now a bastion of the occult, of Wicca, of magic; the wands of holly had cast their spells—and of course it went right up the coast and settled with particular sinew in Oregon and Washington, frontrunners when it came to legalized suicide, which would also take hold in California. In Portland would even be a new trend called "polyamory": official tolerance and encouragement for threesomes living as man and wives or wife and men. Never mind cohabitation! Never mind gay marriage! Now we were making little orgies into marriage. Can you imagine the look in the eyes between George Washington's perfect locks of reddish hair, or as Ben Franklin peered at this over his bifocals? Maybe it *was* "bye-bye Miss American pie." Perhaps the Holy Ghost *had* caught the last train for the coast—the day not just music but goodness—and idyllic America—died, or at least began to grow startlingly ill. Gonorrhea would soon be replaced by HIV. San Francisco's fog was not just meteorological! No. And of course San Jose and Seattle would become hotbeds for hyper-technology, including firms that wanted to clone first animals and, one day, humans. Algorithms. Robots. Dehumanization. With Google Earth, everyone was now the all-seeing eye; everyone had the vantage point of God (or so they acted, at times). With search engines, instant information was no longer in the sole province of Heaven. Men were re-creating Creation and making earth into a Godless paradise—or so was the goal. In Arizona a firm froze bodies in the hope they one day could be brought back to life (a dastardly place that was more hoax than reality but a real attempt at immortality on *human* terms).

Oh, the hubris! The arrogance! There were some messages in Nigeria that seemed very strange. The Church did not rule on it. I'm not sure what to make of it. But who could deny the poignancy of messages that said things such as, *"You have transgressed all the Commandments of God; idolatry, profanation of Sundays and Holy Days of Obligation, and adultery-fornication.*

"Go around the world," she allegedly told Innocent, a father of nine and a stigmatic (his bleeding had begun on the first Friday of Lent and stopped on Holy Saturday), *"and learn that my Son Jesus Christ is no longer respected. Most serious are the insults heaped upon Him in the Blessed Sacrament."*

There were now different forms of idolatry, said Mary. It was no longer those snakes as in Pharaonic times near Cairo, no longer those multi-limb gods, or the earth-fire-wind force of Greece and Rome—the Jupiters, the Zeuses.

No.

Now we revered other idols among them Ayn Rand, money, and lust—lust at every turn, including the lust for food and drink and celebrity. Appearing just once on the silver screen, or even television, conferred a magical aura. "Stars" were far more respected than bishops. Wearing a collar was nearly like wearing a scarlet letter. Ostracism. That led many men to shy away from seminaries, while those who entered too often found them dominated by classmates with a homosexual proclivity. It is where the devil tempted good men or planted those who were never meant to be priests and were simply hiding their disposition behind Church walls. Clearly, the priesthood—so precious to Mary (she called clergy her "beloved sons")—was Satan's main target of attack. The culture of academic pretension also invaded, turning homilies into pleonastic lectures. Philosophy. Humanism. Scientism. There were even apparitions—and warnings—in Vietnam, which was such a flashpoint during both the Sixties and Seventies; there at Binh Loi in February 1974 an imprisoned paratrooper named Stephen Ho Ngoc Anh who had been reduced to a state of complete disability saw a pilgrim statue of the Fatima Virgin (brought to an American hospital) shed tears—a claim at first dismissed, of course, by the aporetic chaplain. The following October, while praying a Rosary, Mary appeared to him in white, promising that one day he would be cured and then reappearing on December 21, when she asked Anh to go into the yard so he could receive a "sign" and where Anh spotted *a large comet* along with the Blessed Mother. (At one point, it was said, Our Lady miraculously caused the young man to be transported inside a shrine, surrounded by her blaze of light and listening as she emphasized the importance of special devotions to the Sacred and Immaculate Hearts—messages that fell on deaf intellectualized ears.) Philosophy. Scientism. Had we forgotten what Thomas á Kempis had once said: "What, therefore, have we to do with questions of philosophy? He to whom the Eternal Word speaks is free from theorizing. For from this Word are all things and of Him all things speak—the Beginning Who also speaks to us. Without this Word no man understands or judges aright."

What happened to Bible study?

False gods. No question. Men were cluttering their souls with things of the world. Praying the fifteen decades daily was critical, said the presumed apparitions in Nigeria; with each Rosary, the power of Satan "diminished." Instead of criticism, priests needed novenas. They were on the front lines. And they were wounded, falling. *"You are required to pray and do penance for [priests] instead of degrading them,"* Mary supposedly said. *"Avoid slandering priests who are servants of my Son."* A great *"period of penance"* had set in, she supposedly added. A light was sometimes witnessed coming from the seer's chest. That's where prayer needed to originate. A sun miracle was seen on July 18, 1975. She predicted a non-Roman Pope after Paul VI. She predicted quakes would proliferate not just in the U.S., but globally. There would be terrible lightning storms. Great flashes. There would be famine, hunger, landslides, great heat. She predicted rainy and dry seasons would be altered. Governments would collapse. Countries fall. War: widespread. Russia would cause conflict. When the *"cup"* was filled, Innocent quoted Heaven as saying, *"fire rains down and consumes the whole world."* One took the germ, the essence, from such messages: tested the spirits, kept what seemed good (especially as far as personal devotions), and left the rest (*1 John* 4:1). The sun would radiate great heat toward the earth, before darkening.

I was most interested in the emphasis on disease, strife, and unsettled geology, for the same was said during this same time (on the same continent) in Rwanda, where—during apparitions that were to meet with full Church approval (the approbation announced from Rome), seers would likewise be shown images of the future in which entire hamlets and villages were abandoned and a *"river of blood"* would course through that nation. In fact, during these apparitions, which began in 1981, at Kibeho, several hours west of Kigali (in one of the poorest spots on earth, which is why—the purity of poverty—Mary said she chose it), young Catholic schoolchildren fell one by one into ecstasy (there would be seven main seers, three named in the official approval) and said, one day, in 1982, they'd been shown horrifying images of countless bodies, headless, stacked up during a coming genocide that would pit Hutus against Tutsis, even though both tribes were largely Catholic. She warned this would come due to the nation's turn toward materialism, Godlessness, and the rampant abuse of bodies in fornication, including prostitution. As in Wisconsin, this prophecy, which was recorded, and even delivered directly to the prime minister of Rwanda (as directed by Mary), materialized precisely twelve years later: in 1994, when Rwanda was torn asunder by what stands as the greatest daily rate of genocide in recorded history. Between eight hundred thousand and one million Tutsis would be slain—many in rabid decapitations that left bodies stacked like cordwood as roadblocks or tossed into the Kagera River—turning it into what *The New York Times* (as if to quote Mary) would later term a "river of blood." According to Father Gabriel Andiron (who wrote the first widely-circulated book on the apparitions, titled simply *Kibeho*), "the visionaries sometimes cried, their teeth chattered, they trembled. They collapsed several times with the full weight of their bodies during the apparitions, which lasted nearly eight hours without interruption. The crowd of about 20,000 present on that day was given an impression of fear—indeed, panic and sadness." Recounted a more recent book (*Our Lady of Kibeho*), "The tone and energy of the apparitions that day seemed different from the start. When [seer] Alphonsine Mumureke entered her state of ecstasy, her heart opened to Our Lady by offering her the song of welcome: *'Tune None Kugushima Mubeyi Udahemuka'* ('We Come Here to Thank You, Faithful Mother'). Yet she was cut off by the Holy Mother after just three words. *'I am too sad to hear my children sing,'* the Blessed Mother told her.

"Suddenly Alphonsine let out a gut-wrenching scream that cut through the startled crowd like a razor," said the book.

"'I see a river of blood! What does that mean? No, please! Why did you show me so much blood [she asked Mary]? Show me a clear stream of water, not this river of blood!'" One horrifying vision after another. During the apparitions, her voice (though not Mary's) was recorded. "Stop, stop, please stop! Why are those people killing each other? Why do they chop each other?" Tears gushed from the visionary's eyes as she trembled uncontrollably. The grotesque sights worsened still as Our Lady expanded Alphonsine's vision until she beheld a panoramic view of a vast valley piled high with the remains of a million rotting, headless corpses, and not a single soul left to bury the dead."

This was indeed to occur. A truer and more detailed prophecy I have never seen, not even from Fatima.

For blood flowed not only with the waters of the country's main river but also down the aisles of churches where Tutsis had desperately sought refuge in the tragically mistaken hope that Hutus would not kill them in a holy place.

Many years later I stood at the very site of these apparitions and peered toward a large brick church less than half a mile away where an estimated three to five thousand Tutsis had succumbed. Until recently, many bones still poked from the earth. I was told by one of the seers—who happened to be inside during the massacre, and said she had been assured by Jesus that she would escape (which miraculously she did, disguised as a nun)—that a Polish missionary celebrated Mass as Hutus surrounded the church, telling the many huddled there—the utterly terrified villagers—that they were all soon to die together but that Heaven awaited, as he then bravely proceeded with Mass and met with his own execution.

Less than half a mile from where Mary had appeared, part of her prophecy had specifically, dramatically, and indisputably materialized.

Three seers would die in the holocaust. Another, hiding under the altar in a school chapel, barely escaped.

The visionaries also reported that they had been shown abandoned villages, and besides Tutsis fleeing Hutus—even before that, right after 1982—a mysterious disease later called AIDS would empty communities and kill tens of millions.

One suspected source: prostitutes plying their trade along the Kinshasa Highway (north of Rwanda).

More sobering, Alphonsine (now cloistered in Rome) was quoted as saying that not only Rwanda but the world faced catastrophe (an "abyss," in her words).

As that vision of holocaust began to fade in 1982, it was noted, Mary had "asked the stricken Alphonsine to sing another song, this time repeating two lines of verse seven times each."

First:

"There will be fire that will come from beneath the earth and consume everything on earth . . .

And then:

"The day will come to take those who have served You, God, we beg you to have mercy on us . . ."

Chapter 29

When I asked one of the surviving seers, Anathalie Mukamazimpaka, what *she* was told of the future, she replied, "I saw mountains crashing into each other, stones coming out of the earth, nearly as if they were angry. I saw storms crashing against each other and fire coming from them. I don't know what this means. I was told that people are causing this [headed for an "abyss," due to sins of impurity and materialism] and that it is coming." That was in 2010.

Other seers said the same, and there were always questions when a person was sole witness to seeing something as extraordinary as an apparition of the Virgin Mary, there had also been copious signs during the apparitions at Kibeho and they were seen not just by a handful of kids but by thousands: In addition to striking sun miracles—observed by the throngs—witnesses insisted there were instances during which half the sky had turned eerily dark. On one occasion, when villagers asked for a sign, according to author Immaculée Ilibagiza, Jesus appeared and said if He were to give a sign, it might be similar to what then followed: as thousands gaped, the moon and stars suddenly receded into a backdrop that was pitch-black (to the point where they had trouble finding their way home from the apparition).

Remember, this is a Church-sanctioned apparition. Was it a preview of coming events? I noted that at Kibeho there were indications fire would come from below and in fact as the genocide ended and millions who'd hidden or fled to Zaire gathered at a refuge, a volcano overlooking the camp (Nyirogongo) glowed ominously. *"If you don't take refuge in God,"* the Blessed Mother was quoted by another Kibeho visionary, Vestine Salima, as saying, *"where will you go when fire will spread everywhere?"*

Anathalie said she was also told that the Church "would go through many trials" and that she wasn't sure if the trials involved the recent abuse crisis or future crises.

The priest close to the seers, Father Maindron, wrote that "Alphonsine tells us that Our Lady came to Kibeho in order to prepare us for the coming of her Son"; equally apocalyptic (and jarring, considering that it was Church-sanctioned) was the third approved seer, Marie-Claire Mukangango, who was quoted as saying that "humans' time on earth is nearing the end."

Repent, repent, repent, urged the Virgin, who Marie-Claire quoted as saying, *"I am not addressing myself strictly to you, child, but I am making this appeal to all the world. Today, man empties all things of their true value. Those who are continually committing sins are doing so without any acceptance that what they are doing is wrong."*

It was serious stuff, hard to discern, and had started just months after the famous apparitions at Medjugorje, where earth was portrayed as *"covered with darkness"* and on the brink of secrets that involved warnings to the world and a great miracle that would lead to healings, conversions, and an indestructible sign (shades of Garabandal), followed by a series of "chastisements"—truly momentous global events, by all indications. I had interviewed all six seers on their secrets, and while finding them sincere, convivial, and convincing, could glean few hints about these secrets (the number of which was uncertain, for they each had nine or ten and some may have differed). For more than three decades they had not only avoided revelation of details but also had held together as a unit with no dissension and not a single one doubting (unlike Garabandal) that they had seen what they had first reported in 1981 and in some cases were still seeing (there were three who still received daily visitations). I was able to get a visionary named Vicka Ivankovic to address the possibility of the end of the world, the Second Coming, and the antichrist. Was any of this in her messages, I asked? No, she said, while another named Mirjana Dragićević, offering the most in the way of hints, said events sent as "warnings" were in her first several secrets.

During a private interview with her spiritual director, Father Petar Ljubicic, in 1985, pressed on the serious nature of her first two secrets, Mirjana said, "There never was an age such as this one, never before was God honored and respected less than now, never before have so few prayed to Him; everything seems to be more important than God. This is the reason why [Mary] cries so much. The number of unbelievers is becoming greater and greater. As they endeavor for a better life, God Himself, to such people, God Himself is superfluous and dispensable. This is why I feel deeply sorry for them and for the world. They have no idea what awaits them. If they could only take a tiny peek at these secrets, they would convert in time. Certainly, God always forgives all those who genuinely convert."

She added that the time between the first and second secrets would be different than the time between the second and third. "For example, and I stress: for example," she said, "the first secret may take place today and the second one already tomorrow."

On October 25, 1985, according to Father René Laurentin, one of history's most noted Mariologists, Mirjana had spoken about a coming event or events which she said she'd been shown as in a supernatural video. One of her secrets, he quoted her as saying, involved *"the upheaval of a region of the world."* Curious it was that here, too, it was related the devil was in a period of special power, as if the time mentioned by Pope Leo had been extended (the claim now was that Satan had been given a century).

The notion of upheaval (some disputed she said this), and the remark, by a priest there, that after the secrets played out there would be more a "pleasant" lifestyle (among those still alive), was interesting insomuch as that same year (1985), a professor named Dr. Howard Storm (at the time chairman of the art department at Northern Kentucky University, now Reverend Storm, a minister) had a near-death brush during which he said he'd been shown the state of the world and its future. Storm said he was told there would be no third world war—no utter destruction by nuclear weapons, because God simply wouldn't permit that—but was shown the future of earth as a beautiful natural wooded place devoid of artificial devices and human intrusion but not humans themselves.

They were there, but in gardens they tended in close harmony with plants and animals, eating what they grew without cooking it.

This was beyond a peasant's lifestyle! He claimed they "communed" with nature (angels supposedly showed Storm this) and also saw them spiritually healing the sick and living in small communities the world over. It was like the Indian culture that had been quashed soon after the early explorers, though with none of the violence: everybody a student and partner of nature, instead of seeking to transform, re-create, or annihilate it.

Dr. Storm said he was astonished because when he'd thought of the future, he'd always thought of something out of science fiction.

This was far different. Man had been brought back to God's original Plan, he said. When he asked when this would come about, he said he was told in a century or two. "This is the future God wants for humanity," he quoted the angels as saying. "And it will happen. This is the world God has created for us to live in."

How would it happen?

The Lord, he was supposedly told, would awaken each human to the person he or she was meant to be, and those who accepted His Will in their hearts would flourish while those who did not would perish.

Would the United States still be the leader of the world, asked Storm?

"The United States has been given the opportunity to be the teacher for the world, but much is expected of those to whom much has been given. The United States has been given more of everything than any country in the history of the world and it has failed to be generous with the gifts. If the United States continues to exploit the rest of the world by greedily consuming the world's resources, the United States will have God's blessing withdrawn. Your country will collapse economically which will result in civil chaos. Because of the greedy nature of the people, you will have people killing people for a cup of gasoline. The world will watch in horror as your country is obliterated by strife. The rest of the world will not intervene because they have been victims of your exploitation. They will welcome the annihilation of such selfish people. The United States must change immediately and become the teachers of goodness and generosity to the rest of the world. Today the United States is the primary merchant of war and the culture of violence that you export to the world. This will come to an end because you have the seeds of your own destruction within you. Either you destroy yourselves or God will bring it to an end if there isn't a change. The United States has been given the opportunity to be the peacemaker of the world. With medical, agricultural, manufacturing, and scientific knowledge, the United States could teach less fortunate countries how to give every person food, clothing, housing, medical care, education, and economic prosperity. The United States has the power to help every person in the world access clean water and hygienic waste disposal. There are millions of people in the world dying for lack of things people in the United States take for granted. This is not God's Will. God wants you to know that every person is your brother and sister. God sees the United States becoming increasingly greedy, self-centered, and uncaring. There must be a turning to God or the reign of the United States will end."

A third-world country.

Major, major change.

Was *this* the upheaval to which Mirjana alluded?

Was this what the priest meant by "peasant"?

Remember again that this was 1985. Wall Street was the focus of American life. It was even the big movie (*Wall Street*, starring Charlie Sheen—whose father had been to Medjugorje, and had even narrated a video about it).

"Greed is good," was the mantra of a main character in that Wall Street film, and this was still being preached! Talk-show hosts scoffed at anything that was "anti-capitalism" or against the interests of corporations and the rich and I had to admit this despite my own conservative politics.

A Protestant named John W. Johnston, who moved to the mountains (from a beach area in Virginia), said, "Around 1981 God gave me a prophetic word of knowledge that has been partially fulfilled. These events are time markers and very soon we will see the fulfillment of the rest of this word. The Lord told me the following: *'When you see that the Berlin wall comes down and when you see the Soviet Union take a severe blow then it makes a recovery, and then you see the death of Fidel Castro; then shall come the collapse of the economic system of the United States.'*

"The Berlin wall separated East Germany from West Germany for more than twenty-five years. The construction began on August 13, 1961. The wall was opened and many sections of it literally knocked down on November 9th, 1989. The Soviet Union is considered to have officially dissolved on December 31, 1991. This is when all official Soviet institutions had stopped to function in the different 'republics' of the Soviet Union. The individual governments of these republics started functioning separately. The Soviet flag flew for the last time over the Kremlin. As you know Fidel Castro is now a very old man in his 80's [this written a couple years before his death] and his health is not well. Cuba could very soon see the death of its long time Dictator. When you see Castro's death then you will see the complete collapse of the economic system of America!"

The 1980s: a warning had been issued. In 1987 the stock market fell more than twenty percent. But no one saw this as a sign. Perhaps it wasn't. I thought at the time it was. But America—and Wall Street—went on from there. The market would not only recover but hit a feverish pitch, going on the index from 1,700 points in the 1980s to 20,000 (by 2016)!

The *opposite* of what God wanted, it seemed, had prevailed. There was more greed than ever. There were more Mercedes-Benzes than ever—despite the next swoon in 2008 (which, like natural disasters, was more intense than the previous event). There would be countless private jets. There were people "worth" eighty billion. There were nearly two *thousand* billionaires—a quarter of them in the United States.

The wealthiest one percent of the population controlled ninety percent of world wealth.

They met at places like the Club of Rome and Bilderberg meetings or at Bohemian Grove in California to socialize and strategize (more on that in a moment).

Them against the rest.

This was what God planned?

A thousand dollars could buy 27,000 meals in dirt-poor and dirt-eating Haiti (according to the relief organization, Love A Child) and a thousand bucks to someone with $80 billion was like less than half a penny is to someone with a worth of $50,000.

You could buy everyone in Haiti a meal for $400,000.

Someone with a billion dollars thus could keep $200 million and with the rest purchase a meal for everyone in Haiti for five and a half years (albeit, a dirt poor one, and a child's portion).

Yet you saw very little of this. We exalted selfishness. We glamorized it. We voted for it. Our politicians made millions giving speeches or turning into lobbyists. By one estimate the number of lobbyists at all levels was 100,000. Oil men minted money. There were private ranches that spread across 75,000 acres. I knew a woman whose family owned one. (After Hurricane Katrina, she had entered the first floor of her home to find everything gone and an alligator that looked like it had just eaten a small deer, along with a large water moccasin, where her lavish living room had been.

These were signs! We had embraced selfishness as an American value and those who argued against selfishness were labeled as socialists.

This flew in the face of the Church—which basically had been saying what Storm was now saying and would continue to do so under "green" popes like Benedict XVI and Francis—who in their admonitions on selfishness often sounded like those angels. In fact, both Benedict and Saint John Paul II both stated that capitalism and socialism could both be good or could equally be evil. It depended on how much God was involved with each.

Socialism without Him had been horrid (Communism). Our Lady had vanquished it (after the 1984 Consecration of Russia, according to Lucia).

But neither did we want a society so hyper-capitalistic it allowed the use of non-degradable plastics that were filling the oceans or use of a plastic bottle for a sip or two of water—a Styrofoam cup for a quick soda— and then throwing it away. At Medjugorje the Blessed Mother warned that *"Satan is strong and wishes not only to destroy human life but also nature and the planet on which you live."*

I won't go on longer with this. I have written about it extensively in *Tower of Light*. The point was that society had pirouetted from capitalism to unfettered capitalism and even toward pure libertarianism, which had been popularized by a writer named Ayn Rand who openly detested the Catholic Church and was candid in her promotion of selfishness and atheism. Survival of the fittest. Survival of whoever grabbed most, and first. Accumulation of things had become the American dream.

Would it soon become the American nightmare?

Lennon assassinated. Mount St. Helens. A new plague called AIDS identified. Michael Jackson's *Thriller* (laden with demonic imagery). Afghanistan. Assassination attempts on President Reagan and the Pope. Terrorists in Lebanon. The *Challenger* explosion. The Chernobyl nightmare. The *Valdez* oil spill. Tiananmen Square.

These were the 1980s. In 1990 came an alleged prophecy I have frequently written about. It foresaw genetic abominations—and chastisement—predicting regional events and saying, *"Your era is ending. Soon the world will not be the world you know. I am not speaking of a barren world, or one depopulated, but of the end of your technological era. Many inventions of mankind will be broken down and there will be more of a peasant attitude and way of life everywhere. After this breakdown of false society will come persecution of Christians and also a new world order. The antichrist will be on earth trying to affect the new world order. Hardly anyone will notice the extent of his influence until afterwards."*

In 1993 came a historic flooding of the Mississippi as well as Hurricane Andrew—after which, sorting through the rubble of his home, Howard Kleinberg, former editor of *The Miami News*, found a damaged Bible turned to *Genesis*: "And God said unto Noah, the end of all flesh is come before me; for the earth is filled with violence through them; and behold, I will destroy them with the earth."

Whirlwinds everywhere.

The entire society was in a tourbillion.

Heaven groaned. Tears fell from statues of Mary. A Pope died after just thirty days on the throne.

If people did not repent of their sins, Mary had intoned to Stephen Anh (in Viet Nam), *"The world will suffer great disasters."* According to Anh, the Blessed Mother expressed grief over priests who didn't follow her words and had warned in 1976, as in Akita, that mankind faced unprecedented tragedy without repentance. In her last message she had used the verb "urgent" not once or twice but four times. (Soon after Anh, who was miraculously healed on two occasions, including of a badly disfigured face, disappeared in the prison system.) The Church did not rule one way or another on such events: An archbishop who had been invited to witness one of the healings declined the invitation. By 1977, there were also reports of a woman who was married to a lieutenant in the South Vietnamese army receiving apparitions, warning again of chastisements and in need of prayers that she said were like flowers from the heart that were used for redemption. *"Fulfill the three messages of Fatima so that the destruction does not happen to mankind,"* the Blessed Mother supposedly told the woman, whose name was Theresa, and who said Our Lady also urged—as did Our Lady of America—devotion to Saint Joseph. *"My work on earth is to prepare for the Kingdom of God to come, but the closer the end approaches, the more terribly the work of Satan emerges, which is why, once again, I command the world to venerate my heart,"* the Virgin allegedly said in the messages, so rife with the prospect of chastisement.

A *"great purification"* was coming, a *"new deluge,"* a purification that would begin *"stormily,"* devils all around, as evil inundated mankind—and as time began *"running out"*; in one message mankind was referred to as being *"in the final hour."*

Chapter 30

When I wrote a book called *The Final Hour* in 1992—a book about the apparitions of the Virgin Mary since the Miraculous Medal up to the present—I was not aware of the occurrences in Viet Nam, nor did I have any intention, initially, of a title that sounded so apocalyptic. It was simply a compilation of her alleged as well as Church-approved appearances along with the messages. Yet in the midst of writing it, I had an inflected thought that said, *"You shall call this book 'The Final Hour.'"* It was a very strange "thought," for that title had never come to mind and I wasn't even at the stage yet of contemplating a title. Yet there was the interior prompt, which I immediately dismissed as too reminiscent of pitied, ridiculed folks who parade around places like Times Square with sandwich boards that proclaimed that "The End is Near."

None of that for me. It was enough that I'd jeopardized my career as a secular journalist by even delving into Catholic writing (I thought I was only doing so temporarily, as a "thank you" to the Blessed Mother), and such a title would obliterate my reputation. But I "heard" it again: *"You shall call this book 'The Final Hour.'"* I thought, "I shall not call this book 'The Final Hour'!" And that—or so I thought—was that. I heard the "voice" a third time and again managed to dismiss it before heading out for daily Mass ay eight a.m. at Our Lady of Mount Carmel in Niagara Falls.

There, to my shock, the Mass reading that day, not half an hour after that "voice," was from *1 John* 2: 18: "Children, it is the final hour; just as you heard that the antichrist was coming, so now many such antichrists have appeared. This makes us certain that it is the final hour."

And so the book, which, with virtually no publicity, became successful way beyond my expectations (selling far more than secular books of mine that had been on shows such as *Today, Phil Donahue, Nightline,* and *McNeil-Lehrer*), was called *The Final Hour.*

I still don't know what that means, nor do I pretend to understand Heaven's time frame. It didn't feel imminent. It was the final hour, not the final minute.

But those chastisements loomed, faded, loomed again, before lessening, then seemed threatening—more than ever, more perhaps than before Hitler—again. It was like Nineveh, where Jonah felt like a false prophet when punishment was put off (due to fasting), as well as Sodom and Gomorrah, where God held back His Hand because fifty, then forty, then just twenty were interceding.

The numbers varied: down, up, down—further than before. Were we doomed to that "twenty" or "ten"?

This reckoning with Nineveh and Sodom shed light on how, through the decades, the Virgin, the Lord, or an angel could issue dire messages of imminent chastisement yet nothing arrived, nothing, at any rate, apocalyptic, nothing on the scale that had been implied. It was not because the Blessed Mother was wrong, nor necessarily that an apparition was false. In some cases, I believed, it was because she had marshaled those "ten" figurative faithful to pray, do penance, make sacrifices. It was why there were seers like Anh who were stigmatic, victim souls: folks had offered up prayers and sufferings. They had committed themselves to devotions such as First Saturdays (requested at Fatima). This was seen when the third secret was released, Mary radiating a light that quenched the torch with which an angel was about to punish the earth, her overpowering radiance due to all the prayer and sacrifice she'd gathered. On October 11, 1993, Sister Lucia made an astounding assertion that "the Consecration of 1984 prevented an atomic war *that would have occurred in 1985*" [my italics]. That was the year of Dr. Storm's near-death experience, in which he was told there would be no nuclear holocaust, and that God would not allow men to destroy the entire planet. The remark by Lucia, made to a contingent headed by Cardinal Ricardo Vidal of the Philippines, all but confirmed that such a war was what was indicated by the famous third secret and the *"angel with a flaming sword in his left hand; flashing, it gave out flames that looked as though they would set the world on fire; but they died out in contact with the splendor that Our Lady radiated towards him from her right hand."*

A nuclear warhead would come with flames flashing and an all-out war would indeed seem to "set the world on fire."

On May 13, 1984, one of the largest crowds in the history of Fatima gathered to pray the Rosary and that very day an explosion at the Severomorsk Naval Base destroyed more than half of all the missiles stockpiled for the Soviets' Northern Fleet in what Western military experts called the worst naval disaster the Soviets had suffered since World War Two. In December, a Soviet defense minister, mastermind of the invasion plans for Western Europe, suddenly and mysteriously died, followed soon after by hard-line Soviet leader Konstantin Chernenko, who was succeeded by

Mikhail Gorbachev. A "period of peace"—as promised in the Fatima secrets—had been granted and incredibly, on November 9, 1989, came the astounding fall of the Berlin Wall, followed by the independence of Poland, Czechoslovakia, Romania, Bulgaria, Albania, and East Germany (which was reunited with West).

No geopolitical expert, no ambassador, and no intelligence agency predicted this was going to happen or even that it *could* occur.

By Christmas, 1991, the Union of Soviet Socialist Republics was falling apart, with freedom for heavily Marian Ukraine. I was in Rome when Lech Walesa was elected president and vividly recall a large photograph on the front page of a newspaper that showed the victorious freedom fighter smiling, next to a Fatima statue.

War—atomic war—had been averted. Communism, at least for now, had fallen. It was beyond astonishing.

But it had been a close call. *"At these moments all humanity is hanging by a thread,"* Mary had said in 1983 to Gladys Quiroga de Motta, a seer at the authenticated site of San Nicolás in Argentina. *"If the thread breaks, many will be those who do not reach salvation. That is why I call you to reflection. Hurry because time is running out; there will be no room for those who delay in coming!"*

"Today the Sacred Heart of Jesus is beside you to be your guide and to ward off the evil one who is attacking with all his fury," added Mary in a subsequent message. The enemy attacks *"like a violent tempest,"* she said, and *"in all places . . ."*

Gladys had a vision in which she saw a street and found herself standing there as "some enormous monsters come toward me; it is like an avalanche. They are horrible, some like dinosaurs and others seem to be people, but very ugly, with large heads and ears. When they are very near me, there appears a blue wall and it is interposed between the monsters and me. Then I see the Virgin."

The wall, Mary explained, *"is my protecting cloak. The Lord places me like a shield, like a guardian.*

"I will defend you, my children [she said]."

Chapter 31

That protection was crucial because though there were victories—such as the fall of Communism—a tempest already had *"broken out,"* said Mary, *"a terrible tempest, the work of the devil* (April 6, 1986). *The enemy is challenging me pitilessly; he is tempting my children openly. It is a war between light and darkness, a constant persecution of my dear Church* (May 22, 1986).

"My children," she said, *"do not live in the easy way as is done these days, to the rhythms of madness, of violence, believing that man alone can provide himself with everything he may want,"* added Mary on July 17 1984. *"All is falsehood, because it is a mistaken way of living."*

"Pray for those lost souls [and] the materialism they want to impose on the weak—for the hollow world in which so many children fall and that offers nothing," was the timeless message.

She said two-thirds of the world was *"lost"* and the remainder *"must make reparation"*—extraordinary, sobering, if not shocking words.

On March 21, 1988 had said: "I have a vision: I see the earth divided into two parts. One part represents two-thirds and the other one-third, in which I see the Blessed Virgin.

She is with the Child and from her breast rays of light go towards the part that represents two-thirds of the earth. Immediately she says to me: *'Gladys, you are seeing the world half-destroyed. These rays of light are sent from my heart that wants to save as many hearts as it can. My heart is all-powerful, but it can do nothing if hearts are unwilling. The means to save souls are prayer and conversion. Every soul must prepare so as not to be imprisoned eternally by darkness. Amen, Amen!'"*

Meanwhile, at Cuapa, Nicaragua, in a nation that was still recovering from a devastating quake, Mary told a seer who would later enter seminary and become Father Bernardo Martinez, *"Pray, pray, my son, for all the world. Pray the Rosary. Meditate on the mysteries. Listen to the Word of God spoken in them. Forgive each other. Make peace. Don't ask for peace without making peace. Tell believers and nonbelievers that the world is threatened by grave dangers.*

"I ask the Lord to appease His justice, but if you don't change you will hasten the arrival of a third world war," she had added.

Prayer fed her luminosity—her power to persuade Jesus, Who had intervened. No global disaster, at least for now.

So the dire warnings, the threats, had worked: they had marshalled prayer.

But for how long would this be the case?

Came a word of knowledge: "Pray, for the deception comes when all is 'good' as in times of old and when there is only revelry—relief that a great evil has passed, when in fact the events will pour upon mankind with little warning, but for rumblings and a luminosity in the east that will draw scant attention. There will be no surplus and in the throes of desperation many will seek God as they rush to encampments formed by those who are of like spirit."

Sometimes it was gripping: the similarities and the simple air about them. At Itaparinga, Brazil, seer Edson

Glauber would receive initial diocesan support and would claim to receive a message that said: *"Behold your Immaculate Mother who comes from Heaven to tell you that the hour has arrived for the immediate conversion of humanity, which will be shaken by great and painful events. My maternal heart is apprehensive and embittered by swords of pain. My children, many of you are doing little and laugh at my messages, scorning them and leaving them aside. What will become of you when the great chastisement comes from the sky and befalls you? Who will be able to defend you when Divine justice touches humanity with such force?*

"Very soon Italy and the United States will be punished in a way never seen [before]. A great light, like fire, will be visible in the sky of Italy. Pain and sorrow will be great, and when this happens only the Rosary and my maternal heart will provide hope, refuge, and protection for many. Italy will be shaken because men did not respect what is owed to God, did not honor His Holy Name, did not obey his Holy Laws. Enormous pain will also come quickly in the United States, causing a particular region to be practically destroyed."

How much was actually Mary?

I knew only that starting in the late 1980s, the "quickening," every year, was getting a bit quicker.

Striking was the stridency: how drastic prophecies are though from sources that were impressively widespread as to all but guarantee they have not heard of each other.

In Hartesbeespoort, South Africa, a young boy who is said to have encountered Jesus when he lost consciousness (and virtually died), suffering brain damage during a serious accident, returned to say, "Jesus loves you so much, believe me. You are the reason why He sent me back. I didn't want to come back, but He sent me back so that you can be ready for His return."

"Together we will proclaim God's Word because He has chosen us for the end time," the boy, Aldo, told his mother,

Retha McPherson, who wrote a book about him. "I have to be a prophet who warns people that Jesus is coming back for us. We will experience the Power of the God we serve through floods and earthquakes. Mom, will you warn everyone that the floods are coming?"

Truly disparate regions and situations.

Mother Angelica used to say the same thing—about Jesus returning. A Catholic from Louisiana named Sondra Abrahams long ago was featured in a video during which she discussed her own death "crossover" and the future she had beheld (replete again with a series of unfortunate earthly events).

Some saw invasions and nuclear and natural disasters ahead for the West. One saw uprisings in South America and tremendous destruction in the middle and Western parts of the U.S. There would, some claimed, be small "cities" of refuge, where people pray, share with each other, and protect themselves from those marauders who will all but take over the land. This was remarkably similar to a book by a woman named Julie Rowe of California, who "saw" a number of places where Christians would congregate to protect each other and live through events in mutual prayer for one another. "I saw that we must not delay getting our lives in order," Julie wrote. "The time has come to get our houses in order and prepare for the days ahead. Time is short and we must do all in our power to prepare for every needful way. I was shown upcoming natural disasters on a scale unlike anything the earth has ever experienced. Earthquakes, hurricanes, tornados, tsunamis, plagues, droughts, famines, pestilence, and all manner of disease will be upon the earth in such a deep and broadened scale that mankind cannot even imagine what it will be like."

She emphasized problems along the "Ring of Fire," where she believed a big quake would be like the first "firecracker"—perhaps better said, a blasting cap—in a series of them, as the world beneath our feet (at least near the Pacific) is "jostled." This will trigger volcanoes in many places, she believed.

Take heed, she said, when an event occurs along the Wasatch Range (near Idaho and Utah).

Was it true? Or what is meant by "tickling the ears" (*2 Timothy* 4:3)?

"I have been contacted by several people who have seen many of the same things that I saw concerning the future," Julie wrote. "Some were shown these things during their own near-death experiences, while others have been shown in dreams and visions. Many people have been given some of this knowledge through other forms of personal revelation, such as thoughts and impressions that have come to their minds. People from all walks of life have felt prompted to prepare both spiritually and temporally. The Lord is warning in many ways."

To whatever extent, and in whatever way, events did seem to be coalescing—if not a quickening in a grinding way. Refuges? A mystical priest I knew kept getting "Angel Fire" (New Mexico).

In Arizona, Hopi or "Pueblo" Indians had that ancient prophecy. After destruction would come return of the Great White Spirit and a society of peace. There would be new, wondrous means of architecture that would make current ways of building obsolete (innovative materials) and "new types of power from the magnetic fields of the earth"—a prediction remarkably like one that Venezuelan mystic Maria Esperanza made.

Truth? Fable?

Chapter 32

Let's cut to the chase.

There could be positive developments on the world stage—John Paul II—and sometimes in politics (Reagan), in the economy—but that was the world stage. More relevant—much—was what transpired in every heart, in every human thought, in every bedroom, and though we could be certain that in totality it wasn't very good, only God could calculate it in its entirety.

At Medjugorje, in the early 1980s, she had described a *"darkness"* that *"reigns over the whole world,"* a *"great struggle"* about to unfold, the *"present hour"* as the *"hour of Satan,"* when *"the demon is authorized to act with all his force and power."*

That darkness, that deception, was seen everywhere from a cuddly E.T. (making us comfortable with aliens) to the blackened eyes of radical Muslims to outright ritualism on the musical stage, with fantastic displays in the way of Madonna, as the new Monroe (but worse), and Marilyn Manson (an actual Satanist, according to reports). If the Seventies thought it had seen enough of a cultural descent—enough bad societal examples—with the glamour of *The*

Godfather, the sadistic violence of *A Clockwork Orange*, the casual sex of *Saturday Night Fever*—disco stuff—there was AC/DC and Gun n' Roses: really hard stuff, now, *really* straightforward. No hiding it. No wonder another big movie was *The Exorcist*. It was coming right out of the box—Pandora's. Noted Peter Bebergal in *Season of the Witch*, writing of the music: "I think Led Zeppelin and Black Sabbath actually transformed pop culture. That's real magick. A band's adherence to some occult idea, be it LaVeyan Satanism or the Norns, is fine for making a certain kind of music that might have its own dark power, but that doesn't make them any more 'authentically' occult. But what Led Zeppelin and Black Sabbath both did so brilliantly was find the perfect balance between mythology and marketing. What is the occult if not a kind of transmission between the audience and the musician, whereby there is a kind of unspoken agreement to suspend disbelief, just as when we watch a stage magician. Black metal bands have a powerful pact with their audience and sometimes the media likes to make hay of it all, but that transmission rarely reaches beyond their subculture."

There was Ozzie Osbourne, his family soon a reality show, as if he'd never also sung an ode to Crowley—though he had—and led a band called Black Sabbath, as well as released a song called "Speak of the Devil."

Speak—or sing his songs?

There was David Bowie, looking like an alien, with a past that included songs and a video giving what was tantamount to devotion for Crowley. "As I say . . . I believe Bowie [was] true magician in the story of rock and roll, the artist who most perfectly realized the definition of magic, both Crowley's original ('The science and art of causing change to occur in conformity with Will') and Dion Fortune's modification ('Magick is the art of causing changes in consciousness in conformity with the Will')," wrote Bebergal.

"The thing I wanted to emphasize is that the occult imagination is not simply about belief or practice, it's about how the application of the occult became the very method by which rock-and-roll was often realized. Bowie's music and performance were a magical practice, maybe even more potent than if he sat by himself in his room and tried to conjure a demon. I think this goes to the heart with my frustration with the occult merely as a belief system. Without art, without some expression of those experiences and those interactions with the unconscious, I lose interest . . . The story of David Bowie drawing the Kabalistic tree of life in the studio when he was recording 'Station To Station' resonates because of *Station To Station,* the album. It's a masterpiece, and it is partly a result of what was going on in his head as he tried to manage a psyche fractured by cocaine and occultism."

No wonder a teen committed suicide after listening to an Osbourne "hit" (called "Suicide Solutions"), and no wonder that Columbine was soon to occur: the kids were listening to these dark heavy-metal "gothic" Bohemian artists whose charisma and fame and wealth were ordained by darkness.

We excused even pedophilia!

Unbeknown to us, even priests were venturing onto this hideous terrain.

While recording their first album, a member of Osbourne's band read an occult book, according to Wikipedia, "and woke up to a dark figure at the end of his bed."

Did it surprise us that many such folks like Osbourne were born into homes where a parent was a non-practicing Catholic?

"Madonna" was the singer's actual given name! (She would later name a daughter "Lourdes.")

This was a poor girl from an auto town in Michigan whose mother had tragically died of breast cancer when Madonna was young and who took her hurts and the rebellious streak to cosmic lengths, dressing herself in lurid fashion (soon to be imitated by her many teen followers), singing about the joys of being a "material girl, and penning what was nothing less than a pornographic book called *Sex*.

Whose heart didn't break for her? There was something in her Catholic roots, her Catholic upbringing, her Catholic education (St. Andrew's Elementary) that she was in touch and struggling with: connected at the same time she was disconnected—cognitive dissonance—her name seeming at too many junctures like a joke prescribed by the evil one. For no one since Marilyn Monroe—whom she openly adulated—had been so counter-Virgin, so anti-Madonna—born the same year (1958) that Sister Mildred was being told by Our Lady of America of a coming crisis of youthful purity while across the Atlantic deep in Communist territory the real Madonna appeared in Turzovka, Czechoslovakia, the words, *"Do penance."*

For blasphemy had been dragged to a new depth, a whirlpool in a caldron, seen now simultaneously by millions, especially the most impressionable. The lines between male and female were being blurred. Pop. Dance. Rock. This stuff counted. Electronic.

Fishnet stockings. Bracelets bearing the Crucifix. Sadomasochism and homosexuality were the anthem, along with premarital heterosexual sex.

Madonna's "greatest" hits? Those were in an album called "Immaculate Collection."

Oh, the devil. Pity us. It was the dawn of those who, on census forms, could soon check a box for "no religion."

What a curtain of darkness! What an "hour."

But there was the sweet Virgin Mary: after Medjugorje, an explosion of alleged manifestations, so many it defied synopsis.

I visited sites from Ukraine to Ecuador, from Ireland to California. Just in the United States, according to one list of apparitions (any list was by definition incomplete, perhaps even very incomplete), there were twenty-seven during the 1980s, and one hundred and sixty-nine worldwide. The figure would jump in just the U.S. to fifty-seven the following decade—and this was according to incomplete lists: Ohio, Georgia, Colorado, Louisiana, Arizona, New Jersey, Iowa, Minnesota, Wisconsin, Pennsylvania, New York, Connecticut, Michigan, Illinois, Missouri, Texas, Florida.

As I said, most were problematic—at least partly questionable, some entirely so. Many were doctrinaire and cultic: if you didn't believe in it lock, stock, and barrel, you weren't a real Catholic. It was as if, in the wake of Medjugorje, the devil was trying to do what he had at Lourdes. There he had diluted Bernadette's authentic experiences with a flood of about fifty false or demonic seers, almost causing Bernadette herself (and another woman who was eventually approved, named Mary Corresh) to be condemned by the bishop.

For a prelate, a hard task was this! In most cases dioceses ignored the claims, or declared that there was "no evidence of the supernatural," when in reality it was more the case that phenomena was difficult or impossible to explain but a diocese had serious questions about the seer or mystic, and so decided to discard the entire matter as "non-supernatural."

In point of fact, a weeping statue or stigmata *could* be supernatural—and an entity asomatous—but from darkness.

Perhaps best said, it was an hour of the preternatural.

Such were the times. The dynamics were intense. They would reach a fevered pitch. Everywhere I spoke, I met a local alleged seer or locutionist: by and large good, sincere Catholics but often leaving a concern about deception. Even the most well-intentioned could be deceived.

Was the Marian scene being ensorcelled?

Bishops had a right—a duty—to be cautious. Thank God for them.

But had the skepticism gone too far? Were officials in America headed too far in the direction of psychology and scientism? Many dioceses wanted therapists to sit on commissions investigating apparitions, though many psychologists didn't even *believe* in the possibility of the supernormal.

All such claims were archetypes, in the lingo of Carl Jung, who believed that universal, mythic characters (see sea monsters, perhaps) resided in the "collective [global] unconscious," which might explain an eruption of apparitions that bore astonishing similarities with each other in far corners of the world, though there was no practical way, back when I was traveling worldwide, studying this, for these folks to know of each other. We're talking about apparitions in places like Hrushiw, Ukraine, where there were not even telephones or radios in most homes and where during brutal winters farm animals were granted stable in a room in the house.

Few and far between were automobiles.

Of course, there was no internet, as yet.

Yet startling similarities abounded.

Rare was the apparition—whether in Ireland or Ecuador—that did *not* have strikingly familiar messages, summed up at places like Belpasso, Italy, where, it was asserted, by a fellow named Rosario Toscano, the Virgin granted confidential prophecies first conveyed in January of 1987. "That the contents of the secrets are grave and serious is a fact we can gather from several points," noted a website dedicated to the event. These, it said, were "the worried, excited tone of the entire message given by Our Lady on January 3, 1987; the revelation delivered the next month, that 'there are most serious chastisements for mankind;' the attitude and expressions of the visionary after the apparition, and in the further accounts given by him. The words used by the Blessed Virgin leave no room for doubt. They are especially *'unpleasant events'* (01/05/89), *'most serious chastisements'* (01/04/87), *'purification'* (01/10/87).

"Many have asked themselves whether these disagreeable events are to be very sorrowful," Rosario reportedly remarked on November 5, 1987.

"Just know that I cried for weeks, and maybe I wouldn't have peace any more if the Heart of our Mother hadn't consoled me and the Grace of Our Lord hadn't assisted me."

Could we ignore such words?

They were puissant ones from an apparition that had attained a degree of diocesan favor (allowed to be a shrine by the bishop). Yet, it was noted, at least some of the secrets could be lessened. However—it was also noted—they could not be erased. "The messages as a whole let us understand that God has made a decision and fixed time limits: therefore the secrets are to be realized and can only be attenuated (Rosario said *'mitigati,'* mitigated)," reported the website. "Sins that draw chastisement are *'superficiality'* (01/02/88), 'spiritual idleness' (01/05/88), *'to have sold themselves consciously to worldly gratifications'* (01/02/88), *'forgetfulness of God and His laws'* (01/05/88), and *'indifference to Jesus and His sacrifice'* as well (01/06/87)," continued a description of events.

Extra attention was paid to Rosario's seventh secret, which seemed especially momentous but in 1991 was said still to be *"in the distant future."*

That seventh secret would allegedly revolve around an event that will display "the glory of the Church to the world." It was likewise said that Rosario indicated it would involve "something that was forgotten" that will now be restored.

Rosario was quoted as saying. "I'm full of hope in the goodness of the Lord. In fact, the Lord doesn't intend to terrify his children, but only put them on their guard. Just think of Our Lady girded by a white sash: it's a symbol that means we must always be ready. The Lord never abandons his creatures; His love for them is limitless. When the world is afflicted by unpleasant events near their point of culmination, a lighthouse will shine in the night: the seventh secret. About this secret the Queen of Peace has stated *'it will be replaced by another event, which will be pleasing for all the people of God scattered all over the earth.'"*

Chapter 33

Mysteries everywhere. This was near Mount Etna, an active volcano that had recently spewed ash. Was there any real significance in that? There were certainly amazements: A cardinal in the Philippines deemed it a supernatural occurrence when, during the overthrow of Ferdinand Marcos, soldiers pressing into civilian crowds to quell revolution saw a Cross in the sky and then (when that didn't deter the armored cars and tanks), a beautiful woman dressed in blue with heavenly eyes who appeared in front of the troops and said, *"Dear soldiers, stop! Do not proceed, do not harm my children."*

The soldiers dropped their weapons and joined the throngs opposing the corrupt Marcos.

I don't say "alleged" here because the Church has approved this as an authentic miracle. A major prelate, Cardinal Jamie Sin, vouched for it.

Where was *this* in Western homilies? Certainly, it was an inspiration to those struggling now in another kind of suppression: the intensifying secularism. As that increased, so did reports of Mary. And the U.S. became "ground zero."

Many times would Maria Esperanza visit dioceses in the U.S. (with the formal invitation of local bishops), and she too spoke of the future, albeit with an encouraging twist—calling events that she saw occurring—including great quakes ("the earth's core, it is out of balance"), a sexually-transmitted epidemic, and an attack on America's own soil—culminating, however, in a "new dawn." She called anything sent as chastisement more a "good test" than Divine rage. I knew for a fact, having interviewed him in person, that her bishop not only approved of Maria's mysticism, but visited her once a week, and I recalled a message given at her Church-approved site (Betania, near Caracas), that, like so many others, said, *"If there is no change and improvement of life, mankind will succumb under fire, war, and death. We want to stop the evil that suffocates you; the evil of rebellion; and overcome the darkness of oppression by the enemy. This is why, again, in this century, my Divine Son arises, so that you will follow His steps, as a shepherd of souls, and obtain the alliance of peace among people, and preserve your hearts as clean temples."*

She'd also come, the Virgin told Maria, *"to ease the burden of my sons and priests. It is they who in answer to my call will have to make my place chosen for these times of great calamities."*

The justice was coming, said Maria, adding cryptically that "it will start here" (implying Venezuela) and guessed that major events would occur by 2020 (only a guess, not a revelation). I heard a similar speculation from Ukrainian mystic Josyp Terelya, although I put the time-frame through to about 2035).

The great mystic added that "Jesus will have a great surprise."

We would see Him, she said, "with rays of light. He will brighten the whole world with His rays.

"The last messages are beautiful—it's incredible the way He will come in glory."

Did I think that everything Maria said was gospel?

Only God is perfect. Humans heard the same thing in different ways. Humans had their own inklings. But I also knew that Esperanza was soon to make an astonishing prediction that was fulfilled, and as for that remark about it "starting here": by 2016 Venezuela (and specifically her hometown of Caracas) would face an uproar of rebellion and shortages, stores stripped of groceries as economic and political crises, due to socialism, gripped the land, causing tens of thousands to eat cats and dogs or even seek refuge across the nation's borders.

There was a social meltdown. There was *upheaval.* Hyperinflation. Riots. Murder over resources. And alarmingly similar to what Howard Storm was told would one day occur in the United States.

There was an unraveling of governmental control in Venezuela. The military had to step in, and a plan was set in place to make citizens work at least two months of the year on farms; basic items like bread, milk, and eggs had vanished from stores and warehouses, or were about to.

"Venezuela On the Brink of Total Collapse" was the headline in a newspaper in 2016.

Would this scenario one day visit North America—when it was least expected?

Chapter 34

Was it a case that angels drew close, then drew back, close and back, at any number of points—not just in the Fatima secret but now these others?

We knew from *Revelation* that under orders angels could bring forth a smoking censer (reminiscent of a torch) or sprinkle epidemics or sound the trumpets—a shofar—which was peculiar because soon folks around the world would claim to have heard rumblings, booms, and unexplained elongated reverberations resembling precisely a trumpet.

We know from Scripture that angels are at the four corners of the earth, that they fight evil, that they restrain the winds or let them go. They harvest, they bind Satan, they announce the fall of Babylon.

It was an angel who first appeared at Fatima, and angels were claimed at most sites of apparition, accompanying Mary.

When they sounded trumpets it could mean an announcement, a message, protection, a call to arms, or hail and fire, mixed with blood, a third of all the trees and grass—destroyed.

Would nuclear war one day rise again as a threat?

"Wormwood" translated in Ukrainian as "Chernobyl" (a bitter local herb).

Days might be shortened, and the sun dark for a third of the day. Time could be quickened. One day, might a massive army (*Revelation* said two hundred million) be commanded from China (or a caliphate of Islam?).

Striking—startling—was the focus in so many revelations on materialism.

It was mentioned as much as abortion.

Kibeho. Medjugorje. Belpasso. San Nicolás. (*"All is falsehood, because it is a mistaken way of living."*)

There was the glory to look forward to but also those "good tests."

Life was a test! Once we acknowledged that, we transcended it.

There would be suffering. There'd be challenges. Never would there be utopia. That was for later. That was in Heaven. But Heaven there was.

And so fear was not in the equation—not for believers who knew there would be protection with Mary and a way out of situations that seemed to have no exit.

It was the devil who planted despair—although also the devil who planted the notion that all was okay when all was not okay.

He played all sides.

He was a man—a spirit—of extremes.

Extreme tolerance had, as its opposite, extreme judgmentalism while an approach that was Pollyannic had, as its counter, a Cassandric, dystopian one.

The voices of seers were cacophonic. I could hardly keep up with them. I met five at just one stop in Denver. Was there room for caution—with "private revelations"? There was an urgent *need*. Many fell into the orbit of self-styled mystics and all but waged war on those who discerned differently. When this was around—hostility and exclusion, along with confusion—it was a first sign of Satan: divide and conquer, was his stratagem. There were those who suffered mental issues and were so swayed as even to leave families for communes that were announced as "refuges." I knew of situations where land that seemed anointed (with healings, spinning sun, and conversions, even leading young men to vocations)—were taken over by questionable seers. A major American one was known to rave and rant (out of earshot of pilgrims). Oh, clever, was Satan! There weren't dozens of mystics, but *hundreds*, some reeling off booklet after booklet (of "messages"). One priest who oversaw a major American site was later defrocked for abusing youngsters. I met another who had done time for armed robbery (though that hardly precluded an authentic experience, rather showed the variety). In most cases, bishops kept a distance. Often, one could appreciate why. My intuition was that many locutionists were quoting a mixture of inspiration, their own subconscious thoughts, and deception by spirits playing games with them (demons or deceased). This could also occur with weeping pictures or miraculous photos, which were in tremendous abundance. At apparition sites, where such photos were standard, I was uncomfortable with ones that captured squiggly neon lightning. An especially troublesome case was in Queens, New York—prudently condemned by the bishop—while likewise disapproved was another that generated countless photos of a Virgin statue lighting up or Saint Padre Pio illuminating. In Arizona, I watched the face of one seer transfigure into awful visages (including that of a hag) during ecstasy.

Yet, was it right to throw the baby out with the bathwater?

As mentioned: didn't Scripture say to test the spirits and *keep what was good*—which could be taken to be not only discerning one mystic from another, but discerning alleged phenomena and messages from the same circumstance and separating the chaff from the wheat? For, clearly, there *was* a legitimate prophetic pulse: remarkably similar themes recorded not only in the U.S. but from far abroad, most notably the phenomena around a young Syrian woman, Myrna Nazzour, now in her fifties, who, it was asserted—and affirmed by various Church authorities—experienced a rare phenomenon whereby pure olive oil not only exuded from an icon of Mary in her proximity but also from Myrna herself, causing consternation and wonderment to Catholics, Greek Orthodox, and Muslims.

Myrna herself was from a household that was both Catholic—her father—and Orthodox—her mother—breathing with what John Paul II called "both lungs" of Christianity (the phenomena approved by the papal nuncio at the time, Bishop Luigi Accogli, the Melkite Catholic prelate, Isidore Battikha, and an Orthodox Patriarch), a gathering of denominations (perhaps unique in Mariology) all the more poignant by her message of religious unity. (In fact, some of her phenomena only occurred at times when Orthodox and Catholic holidays coincided, including Easter and Christmas—which on their differing calendars are often days or weeks apart).

Mary was known here as "Our Lady of Soufanieh." Her husband told me she'd had 37 ecstasies, five experiences of stigmata, and five full-fledged apparitions of Mary, her messages concluding in 2007.

The oil had caused pain as it exited from Myrna's eyes, and more befuddling, the exudations left no "oily" mark. "Several oil samples from Soufanieh have been analyzed: from the icon and from Myrna's hands," noted a book about it by Christian Ravaz. "The results of these analyses made by specialists have revealed the presence of hundred-percent pure olive oil. However, pure olive oil is nearly impossible to trace in its natural form. Basically, all olive oils include, in addition to the basic components, a minimal quantity of external ingredients. When oil oozes from Myrna's body, it evaporates slowly without leaving any trace on the [skin]. This oil doesn't stain."

She was a jovial woman, Myrna, who lived a *quarter of a mile* from where Saint Paul had escaped from jail and closer yet to the spot where Anaias had baptized (then) Saul.

This was a dramatic location, for when I spoke to her husband in 2016 (Myrna did not speak English), their city was surrounded by radical Islamists—ISIS—bent on Christian ruin. He told me they and their two children were doing well in Damascus, but that ISIS had caused huge disruptions in surrounding vicinities. A jewelry shop he'd owned had closed.

Mary had come, said Myrna, in a globe of light resembling the reflection of a diamond and left in three flashes.

As the halves of the globe fell away, Myrna had testified, a bow of light appeared above and inside was the beautiful lady.

And then there was Jesus.

Among His later messages: *"The act of Adoration, meditation, thanksgiving, and spiritual guidance cause me to rejoice. But the whole is incomplete without your unity at the altar. I am giving you My Body and My Blood as a proof of My fidelity and love. Receive from Me this sacrament with trust and faith, because this sacrament comforts you, provides you with strength and wisdom, and increases you in grace. Difficult days are coming. Turmoil within the Church."*

Indeed: churches were to be leveled (you have seen this on the news) and Christians beheaded.

In December 2016, a strange storm cloud made the news when it lingered eerily and exactly above the border with Israel.

Still more remarkably, the same had occurred—apparitions—in neighboring Iraq.

There too—in Mosul—they seemed to foretell disturbance. Galvanizing it was that the city had been the *site of ancient Nineveh,* where Jonah issued his warnings (of coming chastisement: *Jonah* 1)—warnings that were initially heeded, resulting in the Lord sparing Nineveh, which for fifty years had been the biggest city in the known world, a hub of activity for the entire Mideast, but warnings that were later ignored (with resultant devastation).

Fast-forward two thousand six hundred years and here, in Mosul, once Nineveh, the seer had been a young woman named Dina Basher.

Of Dina there was no longer a trace. Despite several attempts, I was unable to locate her.

Had she survived in this city that had taken repeated direct hits—relentless hits—by ISIS?

Like Myrna—astonishingly similar to the Syrian—Dina also exuded oil from her skin, in her case directly from the stigmatic wounds. *"Dina, tell them,"* she quoted Jesus as saying. *"Announce this, my message, to all the churches. Bear all. You will be exposed to many pains and dangers, but I beg of you to bear it so that you may be with Me always and I will help you in everything and I am with all of you. Tell My people I suffer like you; tell My dear ones I suffer so much. My daughter, obey your priests and obey your deacons and obey all who tell you something good. Pray with your priests and all the people. Unite, unite, My brothers. Unite and you will receive the power to fight those who oppose Me."* Dina had claimed the Second Coming was drawing nigh and however that prediction may pan out, her Patriarch issued a decree referring to the happenings as "astounding miracles and wonders," while the Bishop of Baghdad described her phenomena as a manifestation of God's living power.

If nothing else, no one could deny, already, a microcosm, the localized version of an apocalypse.

For virtually every major Catholic church in Mosul would be dynamited or badly damaged, including a monastery, St. Elijah's, that had stood for 1,400 years.

Priests, nuns, and faithful were murdered.

Persecution was in the wind and the wind was beginning to howl—a whirlwind, in Iraq, Syria, Iran, Turkey; short of all-out war (perhaps nuclear), no leader—not Obama, not Trump—was going to *permanently* stop it. The wind had been foreseen by mystics—the "watchmen"—who began to have their visions in the Eighties (in the case of Dina, 1990), as society started to list like an injured ocean liner—or perhaps like the *Santa Maria*, as it neared the inner rings of a *hurucan*.

Much had to do with the egoism touted now by writers who declared the baby boomers coming of age this decade as the "Me Generation." "Ego! It is the great word of the twentieth century," said a famous writer.

Few things could be more devastating.

Alcoholism was nothing next to it.

Drugs weren't as addictive.

Many, many sins came from it.

For ego was pride and pride was a superiority that lacked love and sought material things and sex—and fame—avidly—and wanted to assume the Throne of God; it was a self-focus that thought so much of itself that in its ivy towers and laboratories it figured it would one day extinguish even human mortality. We'd live—and sin—forever! Truly, the credos of Crowley, set to music—in ritual—had materialized. Few had listened to the Virgin, who even had appeared in Bethlehem.

What devastation would come of it—self-centeredness—and not just here on earth: for other revelations, older revelations, spoke of how exquisitely dangerous it was when it came to an eternal destination.

"Oh, how different are the decisions of this Divine Judge compared to our own!" said an anonymous revelation called the *Secrets of Purgatory*. "Often we think: 'This soul is surely lost, or at least deeply buried in purgatory—and for a long time this particular soul already has been in Heaven. Or again we think: 'This soul surely is in Heaven—it was so holy'—but it is still in purgatory.

"Yes, God alone knows the hearts of His creatures. God alone judges correctly. Yet God is wondrously gentle and kind in His judgments while we, on the contrary, are so hard and blunt. The Lord is unjust to no one. As Judge, He is so tender, so loving, so righteous! Everyone who is of good will is dealt with most kindly.

"The souls in purgatory are enveloped, as it were, in a thick shroud into which they have wound themselves while living here on earth. It is the garment of their own egoism. Their main care in this life was themselves, just as the world's highest ideal is self-glorification and honor. It is this which fashions that coarse garment through which the Light of God can hardly penetrate. Many souls on earth do not seriously ask themselves the question: 'Does my way of living please God?' Instead they think without anxiety that their life is upright and most praiseworthy, but they are mistaken. Indeed, there are even people who gladly go to church, who pray and perform works of mercy—but a thin hard crust forms around their souls. They think that everything they undertake is very pleasing to God. But they never truly seek God's wishes. They perform all their actions without love, without holy fear of God. They dull their conscience through the fulfillment of external duties only. If someone calls their attention to a fault, immediately they endeavor to pardon and justify their actions. There are many such souls in purgatory; these are even now not entirely susceptible to the truth. It comes only gradually, so that only after a long while does the Grace of God break through the shroud and arouse the soul from sleep.

"There are also souls in purgatory," it went on, "who had great wisdom and learning in this life, who were famous, who did much good for their fellow men, who upheld all righteousness and justice. However, they performed these actions because of ambitious motives. They were entirely permeated with the spirit of the world, living a selfish and independent life, while completely ignoring their Lord and Creator. These souls enter eternity with the least knowledge of God. On earth they were well-versed in everything; now they find themselves in the greatest quandaries. Formerly they were so high educated and now they know nothing, for God reveals the truly great things only to the humble. Such 'wise' men often have shallow souls. They frequently remain a long time in purgatory—until they have been liberated from their ego, until they are aroused from their slumber, until they lose all concern for themselves. They lie, dead and lifeless, in their shroud until Light Everlasting finally penetrates through their windings to the interior. These are the most helpless souls, for they have so much of the world and self in them.

"There are in purgatory wise men who stood in great repute among the worldlings, but now they find themselves greatly perplexed. For there the smallest and poorest child is often wiser than they. Again this truth comes to light: God reveals great things to the humble."

A child sees the world through wisdom, instead of the prism of man-made knowledge—sees as the Child saw.

It is why Mary came to peasants. It is why she appeared in campestral settings. It is why she chose Kibeho and Fatima and Lourdes and Guadalupe and San Nicolás: quaint spots devoid of worldliness, complications, and braggadocio. How true it had held! When Medjugorje first began, the seers lived in hovels constructed with rough-hewn stone from the fields. They farmed, did seers, at other places of apparition. Wisdom was given—Lourdes, Fatima—to poor children whose simplicity allowed direct communication. Now she was coming again. And no seer was in Manhattan. Skeptics asked why she didn't prove herself by appearing in a city like New York, right downtown, in Times Square. Do we not have the answer? She revealed great things only to the humble. It is why I stayed away from seers who had ego. It is also why I questioned myself: where was my pride, where did it reside and *hide*? How was it blinding me? What was I missing? Was I as humble as Heaven would require, simple enough? Was every motive pure, all done solely for love of God?

This had to be the case, for direct entry into Heaven.

Purity of intention.

And Mary was giving us the way—at the authentic sites.

She was also indicating much to her sons the priests.

Too many of these—said the Pope—were worldly and afflicted with pride: unbeknown to their conscious selves, feeling superior to laity.

Only with humility could love be accomplished, all day, all the way. Pride hated. Humility loved. Thus was ego (not money, which was a subcategory of pride) the root of all evil. Money was the root of "all kinds" of evil (as certain translations put it), but not every evil. No: for that—for the root of all sin—we had to look toward lack of love.

That was the opposite of Heaven. It was the opposite of God. Important it was to eliminate every thought that was critical, that was less than charitable, that demeaned, that lacked empathy, that saw negativity first. This was best done by simply praying a *Hail Mary* every time someone popped into our heads, especially if that person had what we perceived as faults. God's Mercy was such that all we had to do was start this now—praying for everyone who popped into our minds, feeling empathy—and the countless times we had failed to do so in the past would be erased from the scorecard of Heaven.

Chapter 35

That was the critical thing (where one ended up as far as eternity) and for all the obsession with entertainment, politics, and pop culture, which maintained a steady descent, it was the personal state of a soul that mattered. This is where, one day, the most troublesome "chastisement" would occur: in the afterlife. Few focused on this. The technology of "infotainment" dominated and diverted attention.

I spoke to a woman named Valentina Papagna from Sydney, Australia (originally from Slovenia) who claimed to have been visited since childhood by souls in purgatory—often, famous ones (in dreadful states). She saw a rock star. She saw a princess (stripped of all glamour). She saw the leader of a country. She saw a comedian who had committed suicide: begging her, claimed Valentina, to offer prayers. Some looked monstrous, ghastly, forlorn, lonely. No more adoring fans! A beauty it was, to watch souls freed. For purgatory was just that: a place of dinginess, of shackles, even palpable darkness.

She told me she had been seeing Mary and Jesus since April 4, 1988 (while still grieving over a husband who'd been killed in a head-on collision).

"I hardly slept at all because I was still very much grieving for my late husband but I was also praying," said Valentina. "My son went to work, I tried to do a bit of housework and chores, but then I saw rain and all that I thought, what was the point to do all that when it is raining. So, I went back to my bedroom and I opened the shades on my window and I sat on my bed and I said my morning prayers and then I said the Sorrowful Mysteries of the Holy Rosary. I should have said the Glorious Mysteries because Jesus had resurrected and it was Tuesday after Easter, but to me I find comfort in the Sorrowful Mysteries. I found myself looking through the window from my bed. I was sitting there and I was watching the rain that was pouring, gray sky, very depressing. All of a sudden, I noticed it was quarter past eight and I thought to myself, what am I doing wasting time here; I should be up, I was supposed to meet my friend in Merrylands. I put my legs down on the floor but I was still sitting on the bed when I heard this very strong sound of wind. It was really a harsh wind that was coming close to me I placed my hands over my ears as it was so loud! Yet when I looked towards the window, I couldn't see any trees moving; everything was standing still. The wind was coming closer and closer and closer."

A moment later, the tumult caused Valentina to fall halfway off the bed.

"It came like a wind, not in my room, the sound of wind, and when I looked out the window I didn't see any leaves moving or anything and when I blocked my ears it was so loud and I realized it was the Holy Spirit," she told me. "A minute after, a great round light appeared, almost like a balloon, and it came down like a flash of lightning and it was Our Blessed Mother. White dress, blue mantle, like Lourdes. When she came I felt so good. I was in ecstasy and could not move."

Mary had her hands held together in prayer (this is the most effective way to speak with God, she told Valentina), and they prayed together (though Mary did not say words such as "Hail Mary," only "full of Grace"). On the second *Hail Mary* the Blessed Mother rose from where she was standing, revealing, presumably, a golden veil or "curtain" that she drew like drapes and Jesus was there, surrounded by "little baby angels."

The wind, she later discerned, had been the Holy Spirit sweeping away evil before Mary came.

When the Blessed Mother left, Valentina noted that the gray day of rain instantly turned gorgeous.

"She consoled and healed me, told me death wasn't the end of days but the beginning of new life—spent about thirty minutes with me. It was the new beginning of taking away all the sadness. Then Jesus turned to me and said, *'Listen to my mother. She will teach you. She will guide you.'* I thought that would be it but they continued to come. They said the world was really bad, very sinful, and had to convert, had to go back to God."

In fact, claimed Valentina, the state of the world was worse than at any time in history, even the Roman era.

Regarding an upcoming Mardi Gras, Our Lord said, *"The city that accepts filth and sin and promotes it, that city cannot receive blessings from Me."* (I would later write about the occultism, lust, and storms in another city that had Mardi Gras, New Orleans: It was here, during a Super Bowl, as a half-naked rock star named Beyoncé pranced onstage, and as commercials even featured the devil, that the stadium lights went completely, inexplicably dark.)

"The Lord said in the past people were bad but not as bad as now," said the seer. "If people would pray—even a quarter of the people—it would get better. And it is getting worse: Year by year, it's going really bad. The Lord appeared to me and told me we are living in the worst time.

It's about sin and darkness that reaches all the way to Heaven. God cannot tolerate it anymore, so there is going to be chastisement if we don't pray enough, and it's happening anyway."

When I asked her the worst transgression, she immediately cited homosexuality.

"How can homosexuals marry?" she said. "That could never be. God is so holy. I feel embarrassed at how He feels. Broken marriages: Blessed Mother said they will destroy marriage. When two men marry, we cannot get worse than that."

Valentina insisted that without dramatic change, the devil would "take over the world." She believed events would begin unfolding after 2020 and said she was warned about nuclear weapons (in the "wrong hands").

For the time being, however—she claimed—"[Jesus] has had His Hands on it. The Lord told me America will be given a *'very hard test.'* Could be a comet falling down, could be anything. God spoke to me many times about America. He told me He will *'visit'* every nation until there is conversion."

Valentina explained that at one point, during her apparitions (which allegedly continue): "The Lord stopped right in front of me and said, *'Can you tell me what country you come from?'* I said, 'But you already know.' He said *'Yes, Slovenia; I will visit your country very soon.'* And I said, 'Lord you will like my country! It is a very beautiful country.' But added Valentina: "The next week there was a tremendous storm, like a cyclone. The Lord told me the heat [climate change] is a punishment—not [a matter of] science, like they think. *'Tell people that many storms will happen all over the world such as you have never experienced.'*" With alacrity she described Him as wearing a brilliant white tunic and over the tunic a "very pale-cream vest, all the way to the ground."

"My children," she quoted Him as saying, *"I am very sorry that you all had to go through a lot of suffering through this heat wave that came. My children, if you think that the heat wave was due to the scientific environment, then you are all very wrong. You can see that signs are given to you all over the world, the changes are coming everywhere. The city of Sydney is no exception, it is a very, very sinful city."*

Speculated this reputed visionary, on what might occur, "It will probably be the economy and then natural disasters. One time the Lord took me into a supermarket and said, 'Take a close look, my child.' The next minute it was completely empty—nothing on the shelves. He said, 'This is what will happen.'

"There was damage to crops. Some parts [of the world looked] like desert, others a deluge. It's not just India or Africa but also America and Australia, where there will be a shortage of things—famine and so forth. We have to go through this. I said, 'Can't You do this a different way?' He said, *'How else can I purify the world of all the evil?'"* She said she was warned by the Lord that *"there is much confusion in the world today. They make up dates of My coming. These dates are false."* Yet Valentina herself said a "holy person" who appeared to her in January 2016 prophesied a huge event for that year—"something great and big" that will happen in the world, an event that have not yet occurred.

Time frames.

Very precarious.

For if a prediction was inaccurate, it tended to call into question a seer's entire collection of locutions (though once more this could be throwing the baby out with the bathwater). "When a prophet speaks in the name of the Lord, if the thing does not come about or come true, that is the thing which the Lord has not spoken. The prophet has spoken it presumptuously," is how the Old Testament put it (*Deuteronomy* 18:22).

"Every human will experience this; no one will be capable of refusing it," she insisted of the aforesaid event.

Chapter 36

Was it only the time frame she got wrong? Did it not sound like other predictions of a sign? As Scripture said, we were not to despise prophecy; we were to test it, and keep what was good. What—how much—was good?

I faced that question constantly.

Where were the events mentioned so passionately since the 1980s—this chastisement or that one? Where was the "great sign"? Where was what so many had warned about?

To repeat, most locutions seemed like an admixture of inspiration, subconscious speculation (here we find the presumptions), and spiritual mischief (by forces around us, forces that sought, perhaps, to dilute or discredit real mystical pulsation, along with causing unnecessary fear).

That was always my advice: Take what seemed good. So many of these folks in the 1980s and soon 1990s—and then the twenty-first century, so very many—would repeat the same template: there was going to be a great warning or warnings (Medjugorje said *several*, initially regional rather than "the-day-the-earth-stood-still"), severe natural disasters, war, a strange darkness, a great miracle or sign (even

Fatima had that), stirrings in the ocean (see LaSalette), economic crises, all the fire (Kibeho, Akita), economic crises, sundry uprisings, and in some cases a threat from the sun or space or due to the earth wobbling on its axis and acting in an way unprecedented in all of human record-keeping.

When I thought about the Eighties, I thought not only about the godlessness portrayed in movies like *Wall Street*, the reptilian selfishness, but also the spirit of games, the fantastic energy that was now focused not on God, not on spiritual development, but on Pac-Man and television and boom boxes and soon Walkmans and then iPods—until came the cell phone, wrapping everything together in such a neat little automagical package that it seemed like alien technology. ET was released. The *Challenger* crash. Chernobyl. Oh, 1986: Halley's again passes! Good news: the Berlin Walls falls. Yes. Were there now different clouds on the horizon?

In Agoo, Philippines, where apparitions supposedly began in 1989, and where events were investigated both by the diocese and a national commission, a seer named Judiel Nieva quoted Mary as warning that *"the earth will shake, the sun will spin with a big explosion and the moon will appear in the morning; the sun at night.*

"The miraculous phenomenon will be visible all over the earth and all will happen within half an hour.

"Big storms, floods, volcanic eruptions, earthquakes, and changing weather conditions are already on the way."

It was tempting to discount it as sensationalistic (on the order of unfulfilled apocalyptic presentiments in Columbus' time), but at the same moment intriguing because a similar scenario had been indicated at Fatima, whose central seer, Sister Lucia had confided to colleagues before she died in 2005 that although the entire "third secret" had been fully revealed by the Vatican five years before (in 2000), many years before that, in 1944 (while praying about writing down the secret for her bishop)—toward the end of World War Two—she had been granted an additional "enlightenment" (to do with the vision of that angel touching the earth with a flaming sword). Recalled Sister Lucia, "The tip of the spear as a flame unlatches and touches the axis of the earth. It shudders. Mountains, cities, towns, and villages with their inhabitants are buried. The sea, the rivers, and the clouds emerge from their limits, overflowing and bringing with them in a whirlwind houses and people in numbers that are not possible to count. It is the purification of the world as it plunges into sin. Hatred and ambition cause the destructive war!"

A tip of a spear that touched the axis of the earth.
Mountains and cities buried?
The sea and rivers, overflowing?

That sounded astonishingly similar to the *Neues Europa* "secret" and also what was said at places such as Akita and now a multitude of more recently alleged and dramatic apparitions. *The axis of the earth.* How could one dismiss it as morbid fantasy, as sensationalism, as footle, when it was coming from a visionary who ranked with saints Bernadette, Catherine Labouré, and Juan Diego?

While potential nuclear war remained a very likely component of aforesaid warned events—and while, with Russia and China flexing muscles, the threat of a gigantic nuclear holocaust, as I write, in 2016 and 2017, has hardly vanished (more on that in a moment)—the additional enlightenment of 1944, revealed in a book by Sister Lucia's fellow nuns called *A Pathway Under the Gaze of Mary*, raised the question not only of whether the legendary secret had yet to play itself out (as so many, though not the Vatican, believed), but whether it pertained to the possibility of war *and* an extraordinary natural event—one that would involve both "fire" and a massive geological effect ("everyone experiencing it").

Might there one day be a tectonic upthrust in the Atlantic Ocean off the shore of Lucia's own homeland of Portugal—as there had been on All Saints Day in 1755, an offshore quake that destroyed much of Lisbon as buildings crashed, fires erupted, and a tsunami had washed against Western Europe, even raising the ocean levels in North America, not to mention Ireland, the reverberations stirring wells in Scandinavia?

I knew this: under the waters of the ocean was the "Gorringe Strait," a seismic region amid submerged mountains that could cause giant quakes and commotion of water.

Put more directly, would a massive tsunami one day take the same route that Columbus had?

The combination of *"fire"* with *"sea, the rivers, and the clouds* [emerging] *from their limits, overflowing and bringing with them in a whirlwind houses,"* along with specific mention of the earth's *"axis,"* opened up a myriad of scenarios, none comforting, leading me to wonder if nuclear war and a great geophysical upheaval were both implied, or if an event such as an asteroid or comet would fit the bill as both causing fire to fall (touching the earth, as with a fiery sword) and affecting the earth's axis in such a way as to disturb the oceans.

Whether a comet of the size necessary to affect the earth's tilt would leave survivors was a question for astronomers. It seemed impossible that anything would be left, even if the comet were large enough to cause only a minor change in the planet's rotation or orbit. One expert said it would take a force the equivalent of a hundred *million* times the world's entire nuclear arsenal. Only an asteroid or comet more than four times the size of the moon, striking a glancing blow at the earth's equator—call it Planetoid X—would change the earth's rotation, according to an expert who added that there is no known asteroid that size.

Of such mass is our planet that a comet the size of what some believe lead to the extinction of dinosaurs would change the length of the day—the earth's rotation—by a mere .004 seconds.

That's minuscule, but thousands of times the effect of the 2004 quake that caused the great Asian tsunami. The earth's axis, its tilt, is the cause for seasons. Any change in it alters climate. While it varies slightly through the millennia, it is normally within a narrow range.

Whether a large planetoid-kind of any object coming from the outer zones of the solar system might cause fiery debris along with "precessional" or gravitational effects that would nudge the earth, without actually touching, was a more open question. Nor did we know what could be effected by a sudden shift in gravitation from the sun (which is 333,000 times the mass of earth). Was it not the sun that created the great miracle of Fatima—and now also at many other apparition sites?

One could also speculate about mega-volcanoes, which might cause fire to fall and perhaps provoke concomitant earthquakes that would disturb the "sea":

There were increasing signs that the interior of the earth might be unsettled, and as I said, strange rumblings or "booms," as well as seismic events, have been recorded during the past several years in many parts of the world.

Might something inside of the earth—the theoretical molten core (scientists aren't even really sure what the core is like)—shift in a way that would tilt the earth or affect its rotation, even by just a mite, at the same time shaking loose lava and causing tremendous quakes? It would take a relatively minuscule change in the planet's axis to have profound effects on climate, which already, in the late 1980s, and 1990s, had been poised to change in most parts of the world, with some wrongly assuming it must all be due to human input while others denied that the change has taken place despite extensive evidence from governments around the world.

Both were wrong. Climate had changed, but it was largely natural (from changes in the sun); not all of it was from human input.

Stuff already was occurring, and if Jesus could mention such change as signs, it was hardly outside the perimeter of Catholic doctrine to look for the same—perhaps in accordance with *Matthew* 16:3.

A time when a singular event would galvanize consciences of all those on earth had been bandied about, as we have seen, for decades (with special fervor in Spain in the 1930s through the 1960s, when indeed we were on the brink of a nuclear holocaust, one that may also have been warned about at Fatima). The same was true with the matter—with the prophecies—of darkness. Three days of darkness occurred, of course, in the time of Moses, and a repeat had been foreseen by many cloistered nuns in France since the 18th century. Recorded in the diary of Saint Faustina were these words (allegedly from Jesus): *"Before I come as a just judge, I am coming first as the King of Mercy. Before the day of justice arrives, there will be given to people a sign in the heavens of this sort: All light in the heavens will be extinguished, and there will be great darkness over the whole earth. Then the Sign of the Cross will be seen in the sky, and from the openings where the Hands and Feet of the Savior were nailed will come forth great lights which will light up the earth for a period of time. This will take place shortly before the last day."*

In Sydney, Valentina, speaking of Christ, had added: "He is still in Mercy when He [chastises]. It's just that He wants to correct us, like a father. Nothing is hidden. I think He is going to come and create a new world. It is not the end of the world, but probably chastisement. There will be earthquakes, really bad; hurricane winds, and total destruction in areas. I could see a few people coming out. People will think it is doomsday. Houses will be swallowed. The Blessed Mother showed me the moon will be dark and the sun black. They will think it is the end of the world but it will not be. The earth will go off its axis and there are all the disasters coming. I could see fire coming from the water and the sky, on the water. The angel said, 'Everything will be on fire.' There will be unbearable temperatures unless people convert and stop offending God."

And then, here and now, was the matter of spiritual warfare.

"The Blessed Mother warned me about that very early," said Valentina. "She said, no doubt the devil will come around you and trouble you. But I would know when Heaven appears; I will feel very, very peaceful; but the devil makes me edgy, nervous. He was dressed always like the Blessed Mother but his face was ugly like a lion. I asked [the Blessed Mother] why is he always behind her, and she said because one day she will crush him.

"He comes all the time, he tries to strangle me, he comes with a Doberman. He has dark hair and a pointy thin beard, thin, and beady eyes. One day he brought two devils with him. He said I must obey him because he rules the earth but finally left when I made the Sign of Cross (three times)."

Valentina believed a great evil entered our era around 1969—that capstone of the Sixties and the year LaVey penned the first satanic "bible." Demons? These, claimed Valentina, had manifested in different ways. "Their faces sometimes appear like animals: they look like monkeys. If you saw with naked eyes what is [mystically] going on in the world, you would die. It is like snakes hanging from the trees."

Were terrorists among the "snakes"?

"The Lord told me we will all be persecuted by Muslims," declared Valentina, with neither apology nor doubt.

Would Donald Trump now quash this threat? *Could* it be quashed?

They were a billion strong—Muslims—and their militant segments had long sought to conquer Christians. At one point in the seventh century, they had swarmed over all of Spain, much of France, and fought on the outskirts of Rome itself.

In fact, Muslims had just retreated from a great suppression in Europe when Columbus set out, and may have been what instigated his notion of apocalypse.

Historically, Muslims had reached as far north as Grenoble, France, and threatened Czechoslovakia and Poland (leading many Christians to convert to more neutral Judaism). For centuries, Christians had to bury or otherwise hide Crucifixes and statues of Mary across large swaths of southern Europe. If we recall, the very image of Mary that had been buried at Guadalupe in Spain and found by Gil Cordero had been hidden precisely due to Muslim terror (and later was credited with helping the Spanish in this region turn back Islamic jihadists).

So there had been a religious war, sometimes quiet, sometimes simmering, sometimes frothing over, for fourteen centuries.

Steam was coming out of the kettle once more—from the 1980s and 1990s on.

There was that first attack, in 1993, on the World Trade Center.

Already, there had been Munich and skyjackings.

A religious war was on the horizon.

Chapter 37

All this was only a distant scent in the wind in the 1980s.

So were the politicians who one day would cause great American commotion.

But in 1989, something seemed to shift. That year a quake in San Francisco, which shut down a World Series game and badly frightened the Bay Area, had reverberations far beyond. There was a graduation to a period of enhanced events in various locales—soon, a historic mudslide in Venezuela, a hurricane that washed bodies across borders in Central America, Asian typhoons, gargantuan floods in India, Hurricane Andrew, that historic flooding of the Mississippi in 1993, mayhem in Africa, and wildfire after wildfire. It was just as it said in the 1990 word of knowledge, which had foretold of chastisements that would "differ according to region" and not "always or usually be immediately noticeable for what they are," which certainly fit the bill for the storms, quakes, fires. In 1994, developments in government funding and scientific experimentation opened the door to genetic manipulation, including cloning, in a way they had never done before, as if to fulfill the part of the prophecy that said a "great new evil"—somehow similar to, and yet very different from, abortion—

would arise on the scene. Events had stepped up—not as they eventually would and will, but in a way that was significant too (noticed by those who had eyes to see and ears to hear, *Matthew* 13:16), in the world of politics as wars began to be fought over oil (an intervention in Kuwait, Iraq, and Saudi Arabia that directly drew the undying wrath of terrorists, who saw it as an invasion of Mecca, in turn leading to the Trade Center attacks, the first in 1993), but also in the way of politics, particularly with a presidency, overflowing with sexual scandal, that not only roiled political meteorology but introduced the notion to our young that certain intimate questionable acts were okay because they weren't really "sex."

It is hard to overstate the negative impact this had on an entire generation.

Another sexual floodgate opened—hook-ups—and as worrisome was the "new age," me-generation feel to this presidency. I'd had a brief phone run-in with the Clintons in 1986 and was astonished to watch such a couple first appear prominently (he as keynote) at a convention, and then, far more jarringly, soon become his party's nominee for president (and win). My trepidation, as much as anything, was a spiritual antipathy. I don't doubt there is good in them. We are told to see Christ in everyone; when we look, we can usually find Him. Sometimes it is harder than at other times. My chore was watching my own inner goodness—evaluating myself (the planks in my own eyes). It was only when we purified ourselves that we could see clearly, and judging others is a bad habit—left only for God. *But why did I have the reaction I did? Where did the darkness originate?* Was it my imagination? Did it matter that New Age enthusiasts were invited to Camp David and the White House. It reminded me of the seances Abraham Lincoln's wife held while he was in office. The Clintons were hardly alone in brushing up against the occult. Under Jimmy Carter our government had had contact with the famous Israeli psychic Uri Geller. Rosalind had him bend a spoon! He did an experiment with Henry Kissinger (at a social event), and hobnobbed with intelligence gurus, military brass, ambassadors. Nancy Reagan had a personal astrologer. It was not something that brought good "luck." But it went beyond a brush with the occult. She sung the praises, did Mrs. Clinton, of Margaret Sanger, a Rosicrucian who had founded Planned Parenthood and edited a feminist newspaper called *Woman Rebel* (the motto of which was "No gods, No masters"). Sanger had urged women to "look the whole world in the face with a go-to-hell" attitude. Unknowingly controlled by what famed occultist Aleister Crowley called the "secret chiefs," Sanger had been trying, in essence, to involve an entire society in an occult ritual of Saturnalia. If Spiritualism was the demon of magic, this was the demon of lust. For centuries witches had promoted just what Sanger later promoted, and as her organization still does: free extramarital sex and the sacrifice of innocents. Now this too was being done on a massive scale by Planned Parenthood (America's largest abortion-provider, and apparently also a supplier of baby parts, bringing us full circle back to Nazism).

The occult spirit engendered by Spiritualism and nurtured by the secret cults was integrating itself into society's mainstream through the 1980s under the guise of liberated sex and feminism—Sanger the Marx of illicit relationships, describing herself in a book called *My Fight For Birth Control* as part of a "secret society" of "agnostics and atheists" who were waiting for the "coming revolution."

Chapter 38

Wasn't this what Crowley celebrated—in 1900—when he'd proclaimed that "the Age of Horus is arisen by the Magick of the Master, the Great Beast"?

And so was evil in its final stage of refinement before attempting to assume control.

One day, would another Crowley, another Sanger, enter the stage, a "super-Crowley," fitting another prediction, in the 1990 word, that said an antichrist type would one day rise, not visible as a leader, but orchestrating profound trends in hidden ways—unknown "until he is accomplished"?

Was it wrong to watch constantly for evil?

Or, as Thomas Jefferson had said, was "eternal vigilance the price of liberty"?

We were called to love *everyone*. There were no exceptions. There was no one we could hate. We were called to pray for a person as soon as a negative thought entered. But we were also called to see and speak the truth if we wanted to remain free.

It couldn't be repeated enough: just about every single experience I'd studied that had to do with passing over to the "other side" during a near-death brush emphasized the extreme importance of not judging, of loving, of connecting with one another: emphasizing how everyone was in the same boat. Did we really want to see any person—any—descend into hell? Were we not called to bless every person we encountered or even passed in the course of a day? Did not uttering a *Hail Mary* whenever the mind hovered on negativity not release the flow of affection that would make up for past lacking in this critical regard, which God would judge?

Indeed.

But a roller-coaster, when it was on its descent, took away the breath, all but squelched verbal prayer, and it was where the country was: at the top of a roller-coaster and ready to be released downward, to a finale, whatever that finale was.

"We are at the end of Christendom," Archbishop Fulton Sheen said in the 1970s. "Not Christianity, not the Church, but [Christendom]. What is Christendom? Christendom is economic, political, social life as inspired by Christian principles. We're seeing it die. Look at the symptoms. Break up of the family, divorce. Abortion. Immorality. General dishonesty. About fifty years ago, in one of the big Protestant churches in New York, a Mrs. Vanderbilt came into this church after her divorce and all the Protestant people turned their backs on her. That would not happen today. There are two kinds of barbarians. The active barbarians from without and the passive barbarians from within. We are not in as much danger from the active ones as the passive ones. Anyone who has left this country for five years and then come back is shocked by what he sees.

"We get used to things. The air that we breathe, the press that we read, the television that we see, in no instance is inspired by Christian principles. There is a tendency to go down to meet the world, not to lift the world up. We are afraid to be unpopular. We are at the end of Christendom.

"What is the attack on the Church today? It's the world. The spirit of the world. Today we have to conform to the world or we are abandoned. Our Lord said 'I have taken you out of the world" and we say, 'No, we have to win the world. To win it, you have to be one with it. Our Lord said, 'I pray not for the world.' He's praying for the spirit of the world. And this is the easiest way to fall off the log. It's so simple. And it's justified by a thousand reasons. The Vatican Council said we have to go into the world. Indeed, but not to be *worldly*, which is quite a different matter.

"This is our attack today. There are three classes of people today. Wise men, knaves, and fools. Wise men mean to do good and they do it. Knaves mean to do evil and they do it. The fools will do right or wrong depending on which is the more popular. And they are divided into white fools and black fools. The white fools would rather do right but will do wrong if it's popular. And the black fools would rather do wrong but will do right if that's the more popular. Now this is the situation we're in today and this is one of the basic causes of our degeneration. We're dying."

In the end, actually, we know Who was going to triumph. There was no questioning that. But how long would the darkness linger? How steep would be the descent? Would we be able to recover our breath?

There were mysteries. There were the "Georgia Guidestones." These were monuments located nine miles north of a small city called Elberton (in the middle of a rural "nowhere," about ninety miles northeast of Atlanta) that they called America's Stonehenge. The granite megaliths, reaching as tall as nineteen feet, set in a paddle-wheel formation around a central stone surmounted by a capstone, actually had been contracted for in 1979. It was that year a well-dressed, educated man who went by the pseudonym of Robert C. (R. C.) Christian entered town and approached Joe

H. Fendley Sr., president of the Elberton Granite Finishing Company, saying he represented an unnamed group that wanted to erect monuments aligned with the sun at noon, the North Star at all times, the solstice, and the equinox. He explained that the plan had been in the works for twenty years with highly specific designs. At first treated as an eccentric, that changed when "Mr. Christian" next sought the assistance of a local banker, Wyatt Martin, president of Granite City Bank in Elberton, who became his intermediary and the only one allowed to know his true name (though not the group he represented). Mysterious? According to a plaque that was now at the site when I visited, "Christian" insisted that the banker sign a confidentiality agreement "for perpetuity," saying he and his group "wished to remain anonymous forever." He arrived in Georgia from various cities and wired money from different banks (his first down payment was $10,000 for a structure that cost in the six figures, a payment that had convinced Fendley he was serious). He chose Elberton, it is said, because it has excellent granite, a mild climate, and the heritage of a great-grandmother who was a native Georgian. The monuments were finished and dedicated in 1980 as four hundred locals looked on, although no one knew if Mr. Christian, who said he had chosen that pseudonym because he was a Christian, was among the onlookers. Just west of the stones is a larger plaque set in the ground above a time capsule that's buried six feet below.

It was one thing that these strange stone structures—the largest and most exquisite project in the history of Elberton, which is the "world's granite capital"—would be so precisely aligned with astronomical bodies, and so indestructible (Christian wanted them to survive any disaster), but what has captivated everyone from Yoko Ono to alarmed Christian fundamentalists were the messages. For etched in the capstone on all four sides (in classical Greek, hieroglyphics, Babylonian cuneiform, and Sanskrit) were the words *"Let These Be Guidestones to Reason,"* and on the supporting megaliths—this time in eight languages (English, Spanish, Arabic, Chinese, Hebrew, Russian, Hindi, and Swahili)—what some called New Age commandments for survivors of an unspecified future apocalypse.

What they said was:

"MAINTAIN HUMANITY UNDER 500,000,000 IN PERPETUAL BALANCE WITH NATURE

"GUIDE REPRODUCTION WISELY—IMPROVING FITNESS AND DIVERSITY

"RULE PASSION—FAITH—TRADITION—AND ALL THINGS WITH TEMPERED REASON

"PROTECT PEOPLE AND NATIONS WITH FAIR LAWS AND JUST COURTS. LET ALL NATIONS RULE INTERNALLY RESOLVING EXTERNAL DISPUTES IN A WORLD COURT. AVOID PETTY LAWS AND USELESS OFFICIALS.

"BALANCE PERSONAL RIGHTS WITH SOCIAL DUTIES

"PRIZE TRUTH—BEAUTY—LOVE—SEEKING HARMONY WITH THE INFINITE

"BE NOT A CANCER ON THE EARTH—LEAVE ROOM FOR NATURE—LEAVE ROOM FOR NATURE"

While one can easily see the benefits of some of those points (the Vatican itself—three Popes in a row—extolled preservation of God's Creation and the benefits, to a certain degree, of globalism), the messages had a distinct libertarian occult esthesis.

Some went so far as to fear that the monuments set forth the tenets of a new world order and that antichrist.

Perhaps most hauntingly, there was the plaque to the west engraved with the words, "Time capsule placed six feet below this spot on ______" (there is a blank space) and "To be opened on ______" (another blank space).

Who would fill in those blanks?

What disaster was prefigured in the guidestones?

Mysterious indeed.

But nothing was more mysterious than who built them.

Some claimed that Elberton was chosen because Indians for vague reasons had considered it to be the center of the world, conforming with occult "ley" lines (geographical tracks that link prehistoric monuments and carry spiritual power). "It is very probable that humankind now possesses the knowledge needed to establish an effective world government," the group was quoted as saying in a booklet produced by the granite company. "In some way that knowledge must be widely seeded in the consciousness of all mankind. Very soon the hearts of our human family must be touched and warmed so we will welcome a global rule of reason. We are entering a critical era. Population pressures will soon create political and economic crisis throughout the world. These will make more difficult and at the same time more needed the building of a rational world society. The approaching crisis may make mankind willing to accept a system of world law that will stress the responsibility of individual nations in managing internal affairs, and which will assist them in the peaceful management of external frictions. We, the sponsors of the Georgia Guidestones, are a small group of Americans who wish to focus attention on problems central to the present quandary of humanity. We have chosen to remain anonymous in order to avoid debate and contention which might confuse our meaning, and which might delay a considered review of our thoughts. The celestial alignments of the stones symbolize the need for humanity to be square with external principles which are manifest in our own nature, and the universe around us. We must live in harmony with the infinite. We profess no divine inspiration beyond that which can be found in all human minds."

Some speculated that R. C. Christian played on "Roman Catholic," but more convincing were those who argued there was a link between the name and Rosicrucianism, which some dated back to the first century (others somewhat later: to the ancient Druids, who were also linked to Stonehenge). Membership had included mathematicians, philosophers, alchemists, and astronomers. The order was said to have consisted "of no more than eight members, each a doctor and a sworn bachelor. Each member undertook an oath to heal the sick without payment, to maintain a secret fellowship, and to find a replacement for himself before he died," and according to Wikipedia, "holds a doctrine or theology 'built on esoteric truths of the ancient past' which, 'concealed from the average man, provide insight into nature, the physical universe and the spiritual realm.'"

There were those who asserted that Rosicrucianism was in fact the basis for Freemasonry and that only Rosicrucians knew the meaning of secret masonic symbols. (Rosicrucians also have been linked to an occult group known as the Golden Dawn—tied to Crowley. Their magazine was called *New Age*.)

So there we had these monuments in Georgia as if in opposition to the Cross in the state to the south.

Druids, ceremonial magicians, Indians, neo-pagans UFO cults, and witches were known to gather at the monument.

Ironically, this was deep "Bible Belt," saturated with Baptist churches (twenty-six in the small city), and from this presbytery, perhaps, came those who spray-painted the stones in protest (*"No one-world government,"* a slash of now erased graffiti once said; *"Jesus will beat u satanists,"* said another). Meanwhile, there was even a recipe for conducting rituals there.

Across the road from the monument, in a house owned by an impoverished 43-year-old grandmother named Linda Crew, I was told that folks nearby often have seen strange "UFO" lights at night in the middle of the monument. Her son, Jeffrey Allen, said it was like a "glow" coming from the center, and while at first he assumed it was from flashlights, the second time he observed them for five long minutes, driving up to see what they were and finding nothing and no one there. "I actually got in my car, drove there, got out, and walked up there," he told me, and I came to find out that a witch and warlock were even married at the monument. Linda claimed to have seen the KKK there. Strangely, there was a report in a secular magazine saying that one of the granite workers who etched the lettering for the moment, heard "strange music and disjointed voices" when he was working on the stones. An uncanny black cloud wafted directly overhead when I visited, though the rest of the sky was cloudless. Allen claimed there'd been times when folks witnessed other peculiar phenomena. "It can be hot and no wind and a lot of people say they can see hay hovering above the monuments," he asserted, indicating, in hand gestures, sort of a whirlwind. When I phoned a local expert, Phyllis Brooks, who was president of the Elberton Chamber of Commerce, she confirmed that there have been witches there but that her organization "looks at the monuments for the craftsmanship. We don't get caught up in the good or bad or evil or whatever." Within a dozen miles of the monument were at least six billboards (one a double) with a phone number to call if one wanted to advertise: in giant numerals were five "666s" (three in a row), standing out, did the billboards, on the mildly rolling terrain, and no doubt a coincidence, for those who believed in coincidence.

Chapter 39

A conspiracy or eccentricity?

I had no clue. No one did.

But that a spirit was moving and had been moving for centuries calling for a secretive engineering of a new world and single governmental order was beyond dispute. The guidestones were merely a manifesto. As we have seen, Masonry was even there at the swearing in of Washington, in construction of the first president's house and the Capitol. While its membership had greatly diminished in the U.S., it was again more the idea of a spirit—a secular spirituality that was transmogrifying. There was no single cabal of humans, huddled in a Geneva hotel.

It was an overarching spirit.

But secret groups were to be watched closely, for they figured into future events and were pawns in the hands of the evil that wanted to unite humans in the wrong way and conquer them (dividing them, of course, before unifying them; unifying them, perhaps, as we will shortly see, during the coming upheavals).

Did it all tie into organizations like the Club of Rome, the Bilderberg Group, and Bohemian Grove?

Were there really "Illuminati"?

Whatever they were called, there was a current "aflowing" and it touched disparate organizations. The eruptions seemed independent and remote. I interviewed Hanne Strong, wife of a multi-millionaire oilman and U.N. official named Maurice who had set up a New Age community in the Sangre Cristo ("Blood of Christ") Mountains of Colorado—an area long known for Indian mysticism and UFO sightings.

Do we not note, by now, a common thread?

There, in southern Colorado, an hour from Alamosa, this community known as "Baca" sought to "harmonize" the world's religions. It was near what Indians had called the "Sacred Mountain of the East," the place of "emergence." There were Buddhists, psychics, Hindu masters, channelers, monks, priests, retired hippies, astrologers, Indian ritualists, shamans, yogis, crystal shops, a Carmelite monastery, and a shrine to the earth mother. If that had been the extent of it, so be it; the matter would not be of more than passing interest—a nearly whimsical attempt at one-world spirituality. But Baca, at least for a while, had a reach that went far beyond Colorado. Maurice had served as the Undersecretary-General of the United Nations six times (he'd been there since 1947) and had been a member of the Club of Rome, chairman of the Earth Council, senior advisor to UN Secretary Kofi Annan, consultant to World Bank president James Wolfensohn, and Secretary General of the 1992 Earth Summit in Brazil—the largest gathering of world leaders in history for the cause of the environment.

While Strong and his wife may have had good intentions—and while their other causes of brotherhood, ecology, and religious harmony were noble (urged even by Rome)—the move toward a global religion and single world government was worrisome to those concerned that the reigns of the world could be assumed by personages who might then herd the world toward paganism.

I am not talking about black helicopters but a peril that was as real as it was subtle, and Strong, who had close ties with both Al Gore and former President George H. W. Bush, had been described as the "indispensable man," one who'd held meetings with the likes of Baron Edmond de Rothchild and David Rockefeller. Was he what some might call an "Illuminati"?

Critics asserted that programs Strong had pursued would allow a handful of international bankers to control huge tracts of land in the name of conservation, and their fears were hardly allayed when, during an interview with a Canadian reporter in 1990, Strong discussed the plot of a novel he wanted to write about a group of world leaders that, convinced the West would not clean up its environmental act, formed a secret cabal to bring about a financial panic.

As much of a concern: the U.N. had a program engineered to send suggestions for sermons and song to thousands of churches (under what was called the Environmental Sabbath project).

Chapter 40

That sounded fine, even laudable—in many ways was—but the backdrop included a spirituality that veered toward earth worship.

Hadn't Columbus come to dispel native paganism, and here were folks like the Strongs, at a place historically known for Indian "vision quests" and UFO sightings.

While I respected aspects of many religions, and admired the Native Americans' sensitivity to God's Creation, I was troubled by earth religions that sought to replace traditional worship.

In Manhattan was the Temple of Understanding which had consultative status with the U.N.'s Economic and Social Council and had a covert relationship with Lucis Trust, a foundation once known as Lucifer Publishing.

The Temple aspired to be a "global interfaith organization" and some board members were also associated, reportedly, with members of David Rockefeller's Trilateral Commission.

And so the Blessed Mother warned and instructed and not just in former Yugoslavia.

In Argentina, at San Nicolás (where, again, there was Church approval), she said, *"The Sacred Heart of Jesus will give you plentiful blessings."* In adding that the promises of the Lord *"are waiting to be fulfilled,"* she cited *Amos* 5:9-15. *"At these moments all humanity is hanging by a thread,"* said Mary. *"If the thread breaks, many will be those who do not reach salvation. That is why I call you to reflection. Hurry because time is running out; there will be no room for those who delay in coming!"* In words strikingly similar to those so often used by Pope Francis—who was from this region of Argentina—Mary, speaking to Gladys, strongly requested assistance for the *"poor"* and *"destitute"*—and intercession also for the rich, *"because they are lost in their faith."* The Lord, she warned, *"does not want anyone to fall into worldly temptations."* This she linked to *1 John* 2: 6,17. *"I give you biblical passages with my messages for the world to see that they are authentic, so as not to doubt you. Read the Holy Scripture and you will learn to know Him . . ."* And indeed there was no way the seer could feasibly have linked so much Scripture (from 1983 to the early 1990s—about 1,900 messages!) so instantly. *"Reread the passages and you will find answers you do not find now,"* Gladys quoted Mary as saying, emphasizing that the important goal of life was to multiply spiritual goods, not material ones—the latter, warned Mary again, a diversion of the devil. Such messages called to question modern ways of "growing money" (finance) that became all the rage. Wasn't the World Trade Center at the heart of it?

It was no doubt for this reason, as well as rampant lust, that the Blessed Mother in Argentina called reliance on what is man-made *"a mistaken way of living . . . The world is full of falsehood, of vain people,"* noting: *"Do not let yourself be pulled by them . . . Whenever you are tempted, seek the Savior's help and He will put you on the right road . . . Today the Sacred Heart of Jesus is beside you to be your guide and to ward off the evil one who is attacking with all his fury,"* said Mary, adding in a subsequent message that the enemy attacked *"like a violent tempest in all places . . . he knows he is unable before the Lord, and this makes him worse still. You are protected. Glory be to the Most Holy."*

Indeed, Gladys had a vision in which she saw a street and found herself standing there as "some enormous monsters come toward me; it is like an avalanche. They are horrible, some like dinosaurs and others seem to be people, but very ugly, with large heads and ears." But Mary had said, *"Stay with the Lord and fear no attack, fear nothing, because nothing can prevail against God. He gives safety to His beloved fold. Amen, amen. Read:* 2 Timothy *2:19."* There was that blue wall that Mary placed between Gladys and the enemy. There needed to be instilled in us nearness to God instead of fear of the devil. Love transported prayer to the highest heaven—summoning warrior angels. When perturbed or anguished, Mary told Gladys, *"invoke God, invoke Him at all times because He is the One Who reigns in the universe, only He."* Especially, said Mary, remember the Holy Spirit, Whose *"strength can do more than any other strength."* Walk, she advised, with assurance as well as surrender (see *Hebrews* 3:12-15).

Do not humble oneself before the enemy, but to God.

Avoid those who hate, she implored, to paraphrase.

These were Church-sanctioned words from Mary. Yet: also remedies. Could one really call it "gloom-and-doom," or was where mankind headed, in its spiritual blindness, actually the "gloomy" approach?

And were all the concerns about a "new world order" (an expression used by none other than George H. W. Bush) just paranoia, a part of the darkness—or an engineer of it?

At LaSalette, to reiterate, Mary had said, *"All the civil governments will have one and the same plan . . ."* And right there in Europe—which had generated Freemasonry, and was now filled with "nones" (when it came to religion)—the Bilderberg Group, the highly secretive group that met every summer at plush resorts (and occasionally in the U.S.), also had been born.

Did some go too far with it—and with other such groups? Yes. Certain of the claims were absurd. For the most part, the Bilderbergs afforded leaders of government, royalty, industry, media, and business (especially banking), the opportunity to put together their heads for global solutions. You could take the conspiracy stuff too far.

But it wasn't all paranoia.

For, behind the Bilderbergs—behind a guest list that could include Catholics like *Wall Street Journal* writer Peggy Noonan—one found the omnipresent Rothschild and Rockefeller names, as well as ones such as Henry Kissinger, who had deep ties with the Rockefellers, and England's Paul Blair, not to mention future U.S. presidential candidates, or billionaire Paul Thiel, who was to serve on the transition team for President Trump (though Trump himself was not a known member).

Was it just that they were public-spirited—trying to effect socio-economic solutions, without media intrusion?

One could see it like that.

But the extent of secrecy was alerting as the likes of Bill Gates, Warren Buffet, Hillary Clinton, Colin Powell, Condoleeza Rice, George Bush, Paul Volker, and Jeff Bezos entered the posh settings.

Were they preparing the stage for permanent globalism (as the Strongs so clearly exemplified)? Or now, with a nationalist president—albeit one with billionaires and a Bilderberg member on his team—would globalism be forestalled, perhaps even halted? A Bilderberg group founder named Denis Healey admitted that "to say we were striving for a one-world government is exaggerated, but not wholly unfair. Those of us in Bilderberg felt we couldn't go on forever fighting one another for nothing and killing people and rendering millions homeless. So we felt that a single community throughout the world would be a good thing."

No doubt, it was not nearly as dastardly as some sought to portray. But what about the spirit of arid, materialistic humanism behind it?

What stage was it erecting, knowingly or unknowingly? And more to the point, who might one day surmount that stage?

The task was differentiating dark imagination from *realpolitik*; but this could be known:

For decades, low-key and even secret elements of elite Western society had been planning ways of diminishing the number of humans populating a "stressed" planet, as implied in the Georgia Monuments.

This was documented in a book by F. William Engdahl called *Seeds of Destruction*, which detailed an incredible memorandum issued (as a top-secret federal policy proposal) under President Richard Nixon (back in April of 1974) and entitled "Implications of Worldwide Population Growth for U.S. Security and Overseas Interests."

Also known as National Security Study Memorandum 200, or "NSSM 200," and made official policy under President Gerald Ford, the memo—which was kept secret for fifteen years (until organizations affiliated with the Catholic Church forced its disclosure)—had been commissioned at the recommendation of John D. Rockefeller III, whose family had long been interwined with the cause of population control, as well as establishment of elite secret organizations.

It was written by Kissinger, who also implemented the strategy. Some see the results are rising all around us.

As Engdahl pointed out, the policy of the Rockefeller-Rothschild-Kissinger elite consisted of adopting a "world population plan of action" for drastic global population reduction policies in order to preserve resources and maintain order. Put another way, the goal—which became a Rockefeller obsession—was that certain elements of society, especially those with great wealth, be genetically nurtured while poor and less "desirable" elements were reduced, an idea known as "eugenics" and popular in Nazi Germany, as well as one that had been embraced by Sanger. In fact, the Rockefeller Foundation, the greatest force behind NSSM200, also had funded notorious German eugenics programs (until 1939, charged Engdahl).

"John D. Rockefeller III was appointed by President Nixon in July 1969 to head the Commission on Population Control," alleged the author. "Among his recommendations were the establishment of sex education programs in all schools, population education so that the public appreciated the supposed crisis, and the repeal of all laws that hindered contraceptive means to minors and adults. It proposed making voluntary sterilization easier and liberalizing state laws against abortion. Abortion had been regarded as a major vehicle for fertility control by the Rockefeller circles for decades, hindered by strong opposition from church and other groups. "A fierce resistance from the Catholic Church, from every Communist country except Romania, as well as from Latin American and Asian nations, convinced leading U.S. policy circles that covert means were needed to implement their project," said Engdahl.

The goals and implementation of the memorandum were also connected to organizations such as the Council on Foreign Relations, the Trilateral Commission, and the Bilderberg Group—all involving Kissinger and founded at least in part by the Rockefellers, whose interest in limiting world populations dated back to its patriarchs in the late 1800s.

Kissinger argued that the world population should be reduced by five hundred million by the year 2000 (echoes, again, of the Georgia megaliths, if falling short of its goal) and a global food supply controlled by the U.S.

"The secret Kissinger plan was implemented immediately," said Engdahl, a Princeton scholar, in his startling book (which mainly documented the global purveyance of genetically-modified seeds). "The priority countries for population reduction (India, Pakistan, Indonesia, Thailand, the Philippines, Turkey, Egypt, Mexico, Ethiopia, Colombia, and Brazil) were to undergo drastic changes in their affairs over the following thirty years. Most would not even be aware of what was happening. The Brazilian government [for example] was shocked to find that an estimated forty-four percent of all Brazilian women aged between fourteen and fifty-five had been permanently sterilized [under U.S. "charitable" efforts, similar to how Bill Gates would later enter this same arena]. Most of the older women had been sterilized when the program began in the mid-1970s."

Sterilizations carried out by organizations such as the International Planned Parenthood Federation were administered by the U.S. Agency for International Development.

Illuminati? The number of high-ranking officials who had been affiliated with or funded by the Rockefeller Foundation and other offshoot organizations (and the extent to which such hidden elements sought to reduce numbers—fearing a large global population would consume valuable natural resources and upset the balance of power—was shocking. There was a conspiracy to create a new order on a less populous planet and it reminded one of Sanger, Hitler, and the capstones in Elberton. Rockefeller programs were connected to everything from invention of RU-486, the abortion pill, to the intrauterine device, and as far back as the Roaring Twenties funded (with a fortune derived from oil) the American Eugenics Society and Planned Parenthood of

America, which became the largest abortion-provider in America, killing about 325,000 babies a year (the population of Buffalo, New York) and grossing more than a billion a year from it.

It sent shivers. It boggled the mind. It begged chastisement. No wonder statues of Mary like *Rosa Mystica* were weeping. One looked at what was transpiring and asked: Could men have really plotted something so nefarious? And if so, was it then less rational—less than paranoid—to ponder a flu bug, bio-warfare agents, or food that was genetically-modified to lessen fertility unleashed on the unknowing masses—fears stoked when swine-flu was found to have strange DNA components, and then with outbreaks of ebola and Zika?

Perhaps it was farfetched. There were always flu bugs. Their DNA naturally mutated. But the history of powerful men who sought to "cull the herd," coupled with the profound interest of foundations and corporations in genetic and viral research, along with evidence that some vaccines had been released despite a dearth of testing (and with secrecy) made one wonder if past policies were behind an undercurrent of public apprehension—picked up intuitively by those who were wary of everything from man-made viruses to euthanasia in health-care policies.

Fears could spiral out of control. One had to be cautious not to fall into a mindset that saw everything as conspiratorial. There was no reason to believe that any group had engineered influenza. But the anxiety was yet more understandable in light of certain researchers. Engdahl claimed the Rockefeller Foundation funded a program to develop a vaccine that caused abortions in the early 1990s "when, according to the Global Vaccine Institute, the World Health Organization oversaw massive vaccination campaigns against tetanus in Nicaragua, Mexico, and the Philippines." The vaccine reportedly included something called hCG—a hormone critical in maintaining a pregnancy. Investigated by *Comite Pro Vida de Mexico*, a Catholic lay organization, it was found that, combined with a tetanus vaccine, the hormone caused a woman's body to turn against both tetanus and the crucial hormone, rendering the woman incapable of maintaining an unborn child. (Suspiciously, the vaccine was given only to women of childbearing age.) That was in the early 1990s. Did it hearken to the *"great evil"* in that word of knowledge? "One of the more prominent members of the American Eugenics Society in the early 1920s was Dr. Paul Bowman Popenoe, a U.S. Army venereal disease specialist from World War One, who wrote a textbook entitled Applied Eugenics," Engdahl revealed. "In sum [Popenoe said], 'The first method which presents itself is execution . . . Its value in keeping up the standard of the race should not be underestimated.' He went on to eloquently advocate the 'destruction of the individual by some adverse feature of the environment, such as excessive cold, or by bacteria or by bodily deficiency.'"

To make matters worse, as a key participant in groups such as the Bilderbergers, Prince Philip of England had written (in the forward for a book, half-jokingly or not was difficult to tell) that if there were such a thing as reincarnation, he would come back as a virus to reduce the population.

Chapter 41

And so some fretted and wondered—not just about Bilderbergs but also central banks, the Club of Rome, the Council On Foreign Relations, and especially Bohemian Grove in California.

Spread over 2,700 acres of redwoods in Monte Rio, about seventy-five miles north of San Francisco, this secret club had been founded in 1872 by journalists who called themselves "bohemians" and innocently enough began a regular meeting of writers, artists, and musicians.

Soon enough, however, it had begun accepting businessmen, oil barons, entrepreneurs, politicians, university presidents, and military commanders.

Among those who had attended its annual retreat: Kissinger, Richard Nixon, Ronald Reagan, the Bushes (including Jeb), Joseph Coors, David Gergen, Jimmy Carter, William Henry Rhodes, Teddy Roosevelt, George Schultz, Caspar Weinberger, Donald Rumsfeld, Bill Clinton, the Koch brothers, Walter Cronkite, Malcolm Forbes, Alan Greenspan, Henry Kravis, David and Nelson Rockefeller, Karl Rove, Arnold Schwarzenegger, Herbert Hoover, and Mark Twain.

Did that mean these men were nefarious? It did not. It was mainly a social gathering and "the main point is that these are the men from corporate, governmental, and military segments who get drunk together every year," a woman named Mary Moore of the Bohemian Grove Action Network told me.

But major ideas and future policies found traction here. It was Bohemian Grove where the idea for the Manhattan Project germinated, and in 1967 it was where it was decided whether Nixon or Reagan would run for president (they were both in attendance).

Unknown to most members, and perhaps more troublesome, was the spirit that may have guided it, for like Freemasons, the Grove had arcane rituals, including an annual event called the "Burning of Cares." During it, as one writer (who infiltrated), Philip Weiss, recounted: "Everyone hushed as a column of hooded figures carrying torches emerged solemnly from the woods a hundred yards away, bearing a corpse down to the water. A forty-foot owl 'speaks' (it used to be the voice of Walter Cronkite) as the fake corpse, representing cares, is burned in effigy."

The towering owl's name? Moloch.

If nothing else, the name showed gross spiritual naiveté. Was it just a lack of knowledge? Spelled also "Molech," it dated back to pagan Canaanite "gods," an idol upon which babies were burned in ancient sacrifice, and may have been known too as "Astaroth": in demonology the grand duke of hell, part of a hierarchy with Beelzebub and Lucifer, part, if you will, of an evil trinity.

A local fire chief called most stories about the Grove "myth and legend," and a retired executive, responding on Facebook, said, "I happen to know a few Grove members who are wonderful people and care deeply for humanity and it's future."

But knowingly or not, and half-heartedly and perhaps intoxicated or not, attendees were partaking each summer in a Druidic ritual. At least for the moment, the masters of finance and government and military became wizards. Dangerous stuff. "Then the crypt of Care was poled slowly down the lake by a black-robed figure in a black gondola, accompanied by a great deal of special effects smoke," said Weiss. "Just as the priests set out to torch the crypt, a red light appeared high in a redwood and large speakers in the forest amplified the cackling voice of Care." That was just before the fire was lit. In magical circles, an owl is often a symbol of evil or omen of death, so this was troubling. ("Professing themselves to be wise, they became fools, and changed the glory of the incorruptible God into an image made like to corruptible man, and to birds, and four-footed beats, and creeping things," said *Romans* 3:22-23.)

It got worse. Use of the owl in occultism went back at least to ancient Babylon, and after that the Druids, and was associated, by some, not only with Molech, but a demonic female spirit, Lilith—goddess of towers—who likewise was known for the sacrifice of infants. She was cited in a book Crowley wrote (and was one of his daughter's middle names); was linked to feminism; and was depicted as a winged creature or an owl. In legend she gave birth to a demon-child named Baphomet.

Now, each summer, not a hundred miles north of the Bay Area, we had 1,500 movers-and-shakers from the top tiers of business and government reveling before a towering idol that was also (the owl) a symbol of "Illuminati" and depicted on buildings that housed Freemasons (whose first formal meeting site, in England, dated back to 1599—not long after the establishment, across the ocean, of St. Augustine and not, as commonly stated, in the eighteenth century). The spirit some cited as behind Masonry: Baphomet.

Not all owls represented evil. Monasteries had used them as a portrayal of solitude, meditation, and wisdom. It could even represent Christ.

But that was rare. Most often it reflected gods and goddesses (an owl was often on the shoulder of Athena), and some even believed a tiny owl hid in the right corner of the dollar bill (on that same currency that had the all-seeing pyramid eye).

The Grove, said Weiss, "boasts that the Cremation of Care ceremony derives from Druid rites, medieval Christian liturgy, the Book of Common Prayer, Shakespearean drama, and nineteenth-century American lodge rites."

That was "lodge" as in Freemasons.

Was any of it—were any secret groups—unknowingly setting the stage for a part of the 1990 word that had said, *"Many inventions of mankind will be broken down and there will be more of a peasant attitude and way of life everywhere. After this breakdown of false society will come persecution of Christians and also a new world order. The antichrist will be on earth trying to affect the new world order. Hardly anyone will notice the extent of his influence until afterwards. He will not be of tremendous visibility until he is accomplished. That is to say, he will not rule, control, and be at all obvious to the world at the peak of his influence. He will not be unlike a figure such as Marx, except his ideas will be more immediate"*—adding several paragraphs down, in what seemed like a non sequitur, however relevant or not:

"The seat of Satan in America is north of San Francisco . . ."

Chapter 42

Could Trump stop this? Might he be the one? Would it be dangerous? Had John Kennedy tried?

I'll get to the forty-fifth president in a moment.

Back in 1985, a deliverance minister who saw "three coming judgments" said, "God is saying that the judgment of persecution against the Church can be averted. In fact, all the judgments can be averted. The whole purpose of God's warning is to turn the wicked to repentance and obedience. There are enough righteous ones in Sodom-America to make the difference, but these must not remain passive. As they minister the truth in boldness of faith, many will be turned to righteousness, and the powers of coming judgments will be turned aside."

At Medjugorje, the Virgin said, *"The devil tries to impose his power on you, but you must remain strong and persevere in your faith. You have to pray and fast. I will always be close to you."*

She also said, *"The devil is trying to conquer you. Do not permit him. Keep faith, fast, and pray. I will be with you every step."*

"The devil tries to reign over the people. He takes everything into his hands, but the force of God is more powerful and God will conquer."

Could America be reclaimed?

"Advance against Satan by means of prayer. Put on the armor for battle and with the Rosary in your hand defeat him!"

The disorientation was now across the board. This was in a decade that in startling fashion saw much of what was prophesied in 1990 crystallize; as the storms grew, as the climate began a dramatic flux, as thousands were injured—not yet killed, but injured—in the Trade Center, as a U.S. president was caught acting out the *Playboy* philosophy (and impeached), as the genocide—and AIDS—swept across a continent, as the "world wide web" was introduced, as a "perfect storm" blasted the Northeast, as "rap" music supplanted rock—sounds no longer simply backed by a vodoun beat, but now completely composed of the beat, of the pounding, angry, shouting noise—as the "new great evil" arrived stunningly not just with isolation of the first human embryonic stem cells, nor only "Dolly" the first cloned mammal, but an explosion of modified crops, right down to all the maize, the corn—such a foundational plant—at the same time that bird flu threatened and Hale-Bopp hung in the sky, a large comet only making a pass, only making itself unusually visible, for now.

Odds were an antichrist, if and when an antichrist arose (1 *John* said that through history there would be more than one), he or she would be too clever to spot. He would usurp influence in a way that was subtle, ingenious, unprecedented—obvious only in retrospect. He would be backstage or in the orchestra pit with a manner that resembled the way with which Bilderbergs got business done, but would not have to attend meetings, to set a public agenda, so innovative, so persuasive, so clever would he be. He would miche along the shadows. A "superstar," for sure! Not the antichrist but an antichrist—which was quite enough: a personage of evil, a major force of global influence, fighting against the spirit of God.

Not in a single place did the Bible mention "antichrist" in the singular (unless one used the imagery of the beast and dragon in *Revelation*. Instead, Scripture had phrased it in the plural because history was to see a number of men who from time to time would rise as the Roman emperors had, as Hitler and Mao did, as lesser ones such as Qaddafi or Khomeini or Bin Laden would, to cause global consternation.

This time, however—was the implication—there would be an adroitness, a level of control, a svelte stealth manner never seen before.

Had the "founders" anticipated such a threat?

Menendez had.

De Leon had.

Columbus had.

Columbus *expected* it.

Mary had—and did.

There continued to be a flurry of claimed apparitions, and hundreds of locutionists. What percent were real? Even if that percent was small, something big was being said and foretold. During incredible apparitions, the Blessed Mother appeared in a town called Litmanová in Slovakia the first week of August 1990 until the same month in 1995, experienced by two young girls from the mountainside hamlet named Katka Ceselkova and Ivetka Korcakova who heard Mary urge them to attend Mass and make reparation (for the region, as well as the world). She arrived under the title of "Untainted Purity." A message for our youth. And message for us all. Once more, a hillside (one could also describe it as a small mountain) and once more the Church declared it a place of prayer and pilgrimage and left it at that. Recalled the girls (in a statement about the first apparition, which started with loud, startling sounds): "We went up to the hillside—Katka, Ivetka, and Mikulas Ceselka. It was morning about seven o'clock. On the hill we played games all day long, we made a fire and we roasted some bacon and sang. The Liturgy was celebrated in the church at 5:00 p.m., but we did not want to go home to attend so we stayed up on the hill a little longer." Afraid of the sounds, they'd sought refuge in a hut. "We were sorry for our sins and at this moment there was a glow but we did not pay attention to this because we thought that it was from the sun. We did not say anything—because we thought it was something from our imagination, or out of fear. We made ourselves a pledge that during this week we would go to church every day! At this moment our fear left. We were sitting on the bed and suddenly a glow appeared in the middle of the room and we saw the Blessed Mother. We tried to see whether this was really her! She sat on the bench and she was listening to us. We were staring at the bench and Katka said 'I see the Blessed Mother.' 'I see her too,' said Ivetka. At this moment, we all ran out of the room. We left the place in a hurry, we did not even lock the door, we only ran home. The Blessed Mother followed us on the way, she stayed about two steps behind us. When we turned around, we saw her behind us. She accompanied us to the roadside Cross. There, she knelt down and prayed. Then, she went behind us and then she started to gradually disappear.

"On the way home we were still afraid. I turned to look and I saw the Blessed Mother in front of my house for the last time. Ivetka saw the Blessed Mother in front of her uncle's house. She did not speak to us at the time. She was dressed in a white dress, she had on a blue cloak, a blue transparent veil, and on her head she wore a crown and in her hand she held a rosary. We returned home frightened. I went to my room and was quiet. Ivetka went home and told her mother about everything. Her mother did not believe her and so they went to Katka's house to ask her whether it was true. We both started to cry because they did not believe us. Ivetka's mother believed a little bit."

When Katka's mother went to work the next day—according to the statement—she prayed: "Blessed Mother, give me some visible sign that the girls are not lying." And, said the statement: "That very evening she had a dream. 'I saw the Blessed Mother with a green garland. I asked her why she had a green garland. She replied, "Because I am a Virgin and I have a pure heart." 'Next I asked her whether it was true what the girls had said. The Blessed Mother relied, "Yes, do not doubt anything, but believe it all.'"

At the end of August, Ivetka, Katka, Mitko, and Ivetka's parents climbed the hill again and when they got to the hut, the three girls went into the room. "We asked our parents to leave us alone. We prayed *Our Father* and *Hail Mary* three times, *'Golden Our Father'* three times, and after that, *'O Mary, our Mother, protect us under your mantle'* three times. We sat on the bed and in a moment we saw a mist and in this we began to distinguish the outline of the Blessed Mother, but she was hardly visible. She did not speak to us and did not leave any message. She disappeared into the fog and we ran out to tell our parents what we had seen, that it was really the Blessed Mother! Mitko did not see the Blessed Mother, the two of us only saw her—Katka and Ivetka."

Soon the crowds gathered. That was now November and Mary appeared barefoot with Jesus. He, allegedly, was wrapped in a white cloth, weeping, the seers testified. "She gave us a message. She said that there are very few people that sacrifice, that Jesus made Himself a sacrifice for all nations. She gave us a proposal: 'Why don't men make sacrifices as Jesus did so many years ago?' She told us that people have many material things, they have everything they want and they would even kill each other for it. They only want to get more possessions. Jesus Himself taught us that we should love one another, that we should forgive one another."

Later Katka told me in an interview: "At first, she revealed herself every holiday and every Sunday; after six months she began to only show herself once a month, which was after the first Friday of the month. Mary's explanation for this change was that she came to us so many times, and very few people were living by her messages. After the first Friday, almost everyone would have gone to Confession, and so their hearts would be pure. This would allow them to take her words, incorporate them into their lives, and live by them."

"Do you still see or hear her?" I asked. "If so, when and under what circumstances? What does she say or indicate? What does she now appear like?"

"From the last time that Mary revealed herself, August 1995, I have not seen or heard Saint Mary, but I always feel that she is with me," responded Katka. "I feel her presence the most at Hora Zvir in Litmanová, where she revealed herself to us.

Q: What do you think was or is her most important message to us all?

A: I think that the most important thing that she asked for is to forgive and love each other, and prayer. She also asked that we would fast on Wednesdays and Fridays. In one revelation she told me this prayer: *'I love and therefore I repent, I love and therefore I forgive, I love and that is my peace.'*

Q: She seemed focused on purity. Would you consider purity the main message?

A: At the beginning of the revelations, we would ask Saint Mary what her name was and where she came from. She would respond, *'my name is the Immaculate Purity and I come from Heaven.'* That is why she would always urge us to have pure hearts and to protect ourselves from sin. It is not always easy, but we try to be better, and so we ask God for help, we repent, and walk on the right path.

Q: How do you think she feels about our current times—with all that is transpiring in the world, and has now for several decades?

A: I don't know exactly what I think, but when she came to us on this earth, she was not content with us. However, she did not come to judge us, but to help us. At the meetings with her, it was felt how much she loved us, like our mother.

Q: She had strong things to say about sin in your homeland of Slovakia. Has she mentioned the United States or elsewhere?

A: Saint Mary mentioned in her messages Slovakia, that Slovakia is awaiting a disaster, but if we pray it will move away. She did not mention any other countries or states, but she said that she came for everyone, not only Slovaks. She asked that many people come to Hora Zvir. The more people that would come and live by her message, the more happiness she would have.

Q: What sins in Slovakia do you think most troubled her? Where do you think things are headed in the world?

A: It is hard to say what I think. According to what we see that is happening around us, it is not going in the right direction, but if we believe in the power of God and the courage of Mary, there is nothing to fear.

On November 25, 1990, after a ceremony of consecration (for a new Cross), there were phenomena. "All present saw on the sun peculiar supernatural phenomena which brings to mind the sun miracle from Fatima," reported a website. "It was possible to look into, rotating, emitting concentrated circles in various colors of the rainbow; it was getting black and light again, it was shivering and changing its position. A ring of small 'satellite' suns was created around the main sun. These phenomena were observed by two to three thousand people, including the mayor and the local priest, later a vicar-general, Jan Zavacky. Phenomena were recorded also by the cameras."

And so it went.

In September of 2008 the Archbishop of Presov, Jan Babjak (a Jesuit), declared the Holy Mountain a place of pilgrimage (in the Greek Catholic Archepharchy). There was also a small, holy spring. "During 1991 another revelation was offered, at that time approximately five thousand people were making the pilgrimage to the Holy Mountain Zvir," reported a website called the Carpathian Connection. "On January 13th the children reported the Blessed Mother stated 'I bless the entire mountain.' Then the revelations came only every first Sunday of the month (after the first Friday). Mary explained they should go to Confession on the first Friday, and so will be able to realize her words more, take heart, and to contemplate them. Many revelations were given to the children with one being a secret on Sunday, April 7. On August 4, the first anniversary of the apparitions, the total number of pilgrims at the Holy Mountain Zvir was approximately one million people. On August 8 a Commission of Church hierarchy was established to investigate the events in Litmanová. They decided to continue to publish the messages of the Blessed Virgin Mary. The Blessed Virgin told the children many things to tell the people, some were: on September 8, *'God's visit is already close and therefore, search for love'*; on October 6, *'I Want to live in you and you in me,'* on November 3, *'Learn to thank,'* on December 8, *'I did all my life what God wanted.'*"

"On August 6th 1995, the last apparition of the Blessed Virgin Mary in Limanová on Holy Mountain Zvir took place," continued this website. "The Blessed Virgin Mary stated, *'For this time you need to repent! Please, please! You need to be more vigilant and simple; there is a time coming which is already here. You must have faith as a child and to accept God's Will for you.'* Ivetka said: 'This apparition was very special because the Virgin asked, "Touch the feet," and Ivetka kissed the foot of the Blessed Virgin Mary.'"

Chapter 43

Hale-Bopp was hardly the most spectacular "sign." For that we had to go back to the weather. And when one did, one wondered about all the signals from the sun.

At an observatory in Armagh, Ireland, I sat in a room refrigerated to preserve delicate hand-written weather records, among the oldest on earth, if not the oldest daily logs, and it was plain, away from all the political noise, that year by year, decade by decade, the temperatures had increased just as the European and United States climatologists said. The question was not what the temperatures were doing—they were heading up, at least for the time being—but what was causing the increase. I saw it as a sign of the times. I saw God's Hand in it. There was heating and that could swerve in the opposite direction—to global cooling—as had occurred in medieval times. The point was *extremes*: in many aspects—in nature, in society—we were headed for swerves.

There would be reprieves. There would be quiet "down" years, even short reversals. But it would continue—the signs that ran right alongside the warnings in Church-approved apparitions.

The sun was hanging bright and hot.

Sea levels were rising.

Permafrost in the Arctic was melting to the point where roads buckled and telephone poles had collapsed, in this same decade where "heavy metalers" tweedled our young (you can't say serenaded) with songs about violence (and even suicide), sometimes with horrible success (see again Columbine).

Did anyone know what to make of all the "apparitions" that continued to erupt?

Behind the scenes, I saw unnerving things.

Discernment.

Some seers drew Christ with eyes that were close to eerie, as in the case of a supposed apparition in Kenya to a nun who "saw" and photographed "Jesus" with eyes that glowed red at the witching hour of three a.m. (The visionary also wept tears of blood.) The apparitions had begun at the residence of a healing priest, Emmanuel Milingo, who became a bishop but was later laicized after calling for an end to celibacy and marrying a woman in a ceremony officiated by Sun Myung Moon (as in "Moonies").

In the far western reach of Brazil along the Amazon was visionary Edson Glauber, who (with his mother) began seeing the Blessed Mother in 1994 and whose messages from 1994 to 1998 (only those years) were approved by Archbishop Carillo Gritti of Itacoatiara, impressed as the bishop was by a prediction in the form of a drawing that ended up correctly foreseeing the Asian tsunami years later. "This drawing the Virgin asked Edson to put on the wall of his home in Itapiranga so people could see it, meditate, and pray that it not happen in the world, but many did not take seriously this request for intercessory prayer for the conversion of the world and saw these drawings and prophecies as nonsense and lies," noted a website devoted to him. "Many over time came to say: time has passed and nothing has happened. But people do not know God's timing."

A formal diocesan evaluation noted: "The signs of our times are dramatic. It is my sincere belief that devotion to Our Lady of the Holy Rosary, and Queen of Peace, can help us, in the drama of our time, to find the right path, the path towards a new and unique coming of the Holy Spirit, He Who alone can heal the great plagues of our time."

Many were the "plagues."

1991—The first Gulf War, which led to formation of al Qaeda under a radical Islamist named Bin Laden who was enraged that U.S. troops had dared set foot on the land of Mecca.

1992—U.S. presidential election (Bill Clinton defeats President George H. W. Bush). Riots in L.A.

1992—A category -five hurricane named "Andrew"—basically a gigantic tornado—kills sixty-five people and causes $26 billion in damage to Florida and other areas of the U.S. Gulf Coast, the costliest natural disaster until Hurricane Katrina.

1993—A truck bomb explodes in the parking garage, under the World Trade Center in New York City, killing six people and injuring thousands. (Months before, Maria Esperanza told a small audience that she saw two buildings in New York billowing smoke and collapsing; this prophecy would not fully materialize until 9/11.)

1993—In Texas a sect called Branch Davidians holes itself up near Waco.

1993—A "perfect storm," the "Storm of the Century," strikes the Eastern Seaboard, with blizzard conditions and other severe weather, killing three hundred people and causing six billion dollars in damage. I remember being in San Francisco and while waiting to speak (about signs of the times) reading about the storm in *The New York Times*, a confirmation that we were approaching a new stage of intensity (although that feeling was also there with "Andrew" and the following:)

1993—Massive flooding along the Mississippi and Missouri Rivers kill fifty and devastates the Midwest with $15 to $16 billion in damage.

1993—President Clinton signs "Don't ask, don't tell" into law which prohibits openly gay or bisexual people from serving in the military but looks the other way at homosexuality.

1994—North American Free Trade Agreement goes into effect, something many believed was favored by those secretive global groups.

1994—Northridge earthquake kills seventy-two and injures nine thousand in the Los Angeles area, causing $20 billion in damage and damaging virtually every x-rated company in the valley, which was the pornographic center of the world (on a seismic fault no one had recognized).

1995—Oklahoma City bombing kills 168 and wounds 800. The bombing is the worst domestic terrorist incident in U.S. history, soon to be outdone by:

1996—TWA Flight 800 explodes off Long Island, killing all 230 aboard; almost certainly a terrorist with a shoulder-to-air rocket, according to many witnesses.

Left out of this timeline, as presented, for example, by Wikipedia, was this same year of 1996 and how, at its conclusion, a week before Christmas, a towering likeness of Mary appeared in the oxidation of a reflective-glass office building in downtown Clearwater, Florida, precisely resembling the Virgin of Guadalupe in continuous colors and curves uninterrupted over ten large individual panes of glass (and out of reach of well-water sprinklers). A tremendous improbability. An impossibility. The feeling of Mary's presence, there outside, was palpable.

This image was to go dark the week before September 11.

The devil obviously disliked it. In 1997 it was the scene of a scuffle between police and a Polish immigrant who was acting strangely near the building, an episode that ended with the man's death.

And in a further representation of our time, was tragically smashed by a troubled youth with a slingshot in 2004.

Was there "warfare"? There was warfare! And no surprise: here in a striking way was the Guadalupe Virgin, the one that converted millions of Indians in Mexico, the one that bore the same name as the apparition site in Spain that was so dear to Columbus, occurring in Mexico shortly after Columbus's journey to the New World and now on a modern building in *La Florida*.

Regional events were expanding beyond count—and control.

Massive mudslides near Maria Esperanza's home.

Hurricanes that washed corpses from one Central American country to another—literally.

Floods in Africa that left villagers vying with lions (for bits of dry land).

Quakes in China (and even rattling in Europe).

It was remarkably similar to what had occurred around 540 A.D. as the evil Roman Empire was in its last throes. Weather flux? Again, extremes. Temperatures suddenly plummeted. It snowed in southern Europe. It snowed during summer in China. "The sun gave forth its light without brightness like the moon" from 535 to 536 A.D., according to a scribe named Procopius who was describing what happened in Rome itself.

From Sweden to Chile there had been savage storms and trees inexplicably stopped growing.

In Britain, hundreds of people had died in an awful tempest and hail like "pullet's eggs" fell in Scotland.

Suddenly, winters were so severe that birds allowed themselves to be taken by hand.

In those medieval times the southern part of the U.S. was battered by storms worse than any on the modern ledger, storms that according to one researcher with whom I spoke, Dr. Kam-biu Liu, of Louisiana State University (who has studied sand from ancient ocean surges), amounted to mega-hurricanes.

At the other extreme, drought had hit out west and affected the Indians—ravaging the Moche, Nasca, and Mayans in South America and causing the collapse of Teotihuacan.

According to Byzantine historians, many frightening comets appeared. Whether this was a coincidence, a sign of the times, or the cause itself (small comets can kick up enough dust to alter weather), there had been, in the Sixth Century, a major disruption in climate that was only now, in our day, with modern paleo-climatologic tools, becoming known to staid researchers.

"The trees are unequivocal that something quite terrible happened," asserted Dr. Michael Baillie, an archeologist at Queens College near Belfast. "Not only in Northern Ireland and Britain, but right across northern Siberia, North and South America—a global event of some kind [occurred]. We know from tree rings to the year exactly when this event happened. And some archeologists and historians are beginning to come around to the opinion that this was the date when the Dark Ages began in Northern Europe."

Were we at the entrance of another dark era?

The materialism, the paganism, the lust (which had been going on since the early emperors). It had been eerie. A dry fog hovered globally. The Justinian Plague began in 542. Less than two decades before (according to the later writings of astronomer E. F. Wilhelm Klinkerhaus), a comet appeared for twenty days "and after some time there occurred a running of the stars from evening till early, so that people said that all the stars were falling." (Was it Ikeya? Or Biela, as in Wisconsin?)

"There seem to have been comets, meteors, earthquakes, dimmed skies and inundations and, following the famines of the late 530s, plague arrived in Europe in the window A.D. 542-5," noted Dr. Baillie, with whom I consulted and who'd discovered that flooded bog oaks and archeological timber from this era displayed unmistakably narrow rings indicating trees that had suddenly and inexplicably stopped growing—just halted—around the world.

Promoted by unusually wet weather, bacteria spread from Africa through the Middle East and southern Europe and helping to end the Roman Empire in what we can clearly label a chastisement.

This was the plague that Pope Gregory the Great had halted by leading a procession with the image of Mary that was later installed at Guadalupe in Spain (Columbus's favorite place of devotion).

Speaking about the evil of that time, and the judgment of God, the Pope had said that "the scourges of heavenly justice have no end because even in their midst there is no correction of the faults of our actions."

Chapter 44

Now, fifteen centuries later, it was a natural disorder—the Asian tsunami—that convinced the bishop along the Amazon.

The prediction had occurred in 1996 and then again in 1997 and related, as it turned out, to the great earthquake seven years later.

There were also said to be "secrets."

And as always: that urgent plea to take up the Rosary.

"Sins are drawing great punishments upon the world," Glauber quoted Mary as saying at Itaparinga. *"If amends are not made for them and justice placated through prayers, fasts, and penance, the world will be struck terribly and not even dioceses and parishes will be spared, because they were places of terrible offenses, sacrileges, and profanations committed against God. The works of Heaven are not to be mixed with the works of the flesh and the world. But the Divine Light exposes darkness and combats it. Be God's Light in the lives of your brothers who are blind and in darkness. This is the time for the great work to be done, for the great battle against evil, in order that we might save the greatest number of souls possible for Heaven.*

"This battle is only won with prayer. Unite yourselves to your Heavenly Mother, always consecrating yourselves to my Immaculate Heart, and you will have strength, light and grace to overcome all evil and sin.

"I address all my children in the whole world: be converted without delay! The Justice of God will be strong/fierce, as great and terrible will be the day of the Lord, when He will cleanse the face of the earth with the power of His strong Arm. A great wave of pain and persecution will come in the Church and much blood will be shed. Many ministers of God will be delivered into the hands of rapacious wolves as easy prey. They will have no voice to speak and defend themselves: they will be silenced, but God sees everything!

"In Brazil, armed ambushes and conflicts are secretly being prepared that will make many of my children suffer. Brazil will be purified in pain and blood, because the sins of impurity are so many. I came to Itapiranga to receive in my maternal Heart those who wish to be saved, those who want to be within my Divine Son's Heart. Do not be deaf to my voice. Do not be unbelieving. Turn back, turn back to the Lord. Do not be attached to the world or material things. Money and power will not lead you to God, but to hell, because many have let themselves be corrupted by greed and selfishness."

Now came the year 2000 and fears of a computer breakdown and a year after the turn of the millennium—speaking of materialism—the World Trade Center.

When it fell, in its place was found a Cross, formed by twisted steel: as if Christ was reclaiming this land that once had been owned by a nearby church called St. Paul's Chapel, a Cross there, by the waters, in this very neighborhood where George Washington had taken his oath of office (at Federal Hall, which sustained a crack in its foundation) and where our first president had prayed (there at St. Paul's, with the first Congress).

In the smoke and fire were startling images. "There are quite a few photographs that the police officers from the 46th Precinct had taken, and how it started was during and after September 11 we were working 12-hour tours six or seven days a week, and a lot of guys were bringing in their pictures," Sergeant Ralph Sarchie, who had assisted at exorcisms and written a book about demonology, told me. "I said, 'Let me see some of the photographs,' because being down there, you couldn't believe what you'd just seen. I'd go into Ground Zero and have a security detail a block away and walk into the heart of Ground Zero and just stand there and look and leave and not believe what my eyes had just seen. I started looking at the photographs, and I saw hundreds and hundreds of spirit energies in the photographs. This just shows that hundreds of people who perished are still earthbound at that location, because they were picked up on film. And there was one particular photograph of smoke coming out of the building that has a *clear* demonic face on it. If you take photographs of smoke enough, you're going to get an image in there. But when you have different people taking different photographs at different locations and getting some kind of demonic face, you've got to really step back and take a look at that. Besides the one that was published in the newspaper and on TV, I had a cop here who took photographs, and it was pretty amazing. There was a demonic face in there. It was the devil somehow putting his paw print on it."

A chastisement of warning this was. "For the Lord of hosts will have a day of reckoning, against everyone who is proud and lofty and against everyone who is lifted up . . . against every high tower, against every fortified wall," says *Isaiah* 2:12-15. "Hyenas will howl in their fortified towers and jackals in their luxurious palaces; her fateful time also will soon come and her days will not be prolonged," says *Isaiah* 13:22. "On every lofty mountain and on every high hill there will be streams running with water on the day of the great slaughter, when the towers fall," states *Isaiah* 30:25. "I will set fire to the wall of Damascus; and he walked about among the lions; he became a young lion, he learned to tear his prey; he devoured men," says *Jeremiah* 45:27. "He destroyed their fortified towers and laid waste their cities," states *Ezekiel* 16:6-8, "and the land and its fullness were appalled because of the sound of his roaring."

When, immediately after September 11, I called mystic Maria Esperanza—who had warned me for close to a year that "enemies were on America's soil"—and asked her who was responsible for the terrorism (in the immediate aftermath, al Qaeda was not a household name—in fact was not immediately suspected or mentioned), she said, "a roaring lion is behind it."

The name Osama, it turns out, means "lion."

Chapter 45

It only continued through the 2000s and intensified: more drugs (half the population on prescriptions), more greed (*Wall Street* redux), more Madonna (the wrong one), more feminism (seeking to end masculinity), more war (another Bush, and another tragic war), more terrorism (soon the Boston, Fort Hood, and Virginia Tech; in Maryland, a sniper), more internet (sixty percent of men now viewing pornography), more revelations of clerical abuse, more blasphemy (destruction of statues, which also had occurred, back in the 1990s, just before the genocide in Rwanda), more sex (hook-ups), more homosexuality (far more, with *opposing* it now the crime), more militant atheism (billboards aimed at the young), more war on Christmas, more devil worship (a satanic "mass" at the Oklahoma City Civic Center), more abortion, more trans-sexuality, more technological dehumanism (no more personal contact), more medical profiteering ($85,000 for a hip replacement and $750 for a pill that was $13.50), more disputes over crosses in public areas (lawsuits against one in California, and even against lawn statues), more foul language (on TV and radio—and in every movie—the Name of God—*Nombre de Dios*—used in vain), more slaughter of defenseless wildlife (just eight percent of saltwater fish species not in some way endangered), more chemicals (some food was all but plastic), and as a result—a real chastisement here—more cancer (see *Deuteronomy* 28:27; the sinful and innocent, rained upon alike).

Another Scripture to study was 2 *Timothy* 3:11: "But realize this, that in the last days difficult times will come. For men will be lovers of self, lovers of money, boastful, arrogant, revilers, disobedient to parents, ungrateful, unholy, unloving, irreconcilable, malicious gossips, without self-control, brutal, haters of good, treacherous, reckless, conceited, lovers of pleasure rather than lovers of God, holding to a form of godliness, although they have denied its power; avoid these men. For among them are those who enter into households and captivate weak women weighed down with sins, led on by various impulses, always learning and never able to come to the knowledge of the truth."

That was where America was leading up to 9/11, with the consumer confidence index hitting a new high in August of 2001 (a level that would not be matched until the election of Trump, when it soared again).

So disconnected was the country that *after* 9/11, President Bush went out of his way to hold Ramadan commemoration at the White House—as if Muslims had been the victims.

Oh, America, did you really elect a man—a well-meaning man, in many ways a circumspect and decent man, but a disoriented man—whose brief career included a fight in his legislature for late-term abortion (and a hospital's right to allow an aborted child born alive to die alone, on the cold stainless-steel of a clinical wagon)? Would this fellow, with a Muslim name, not proclaim—yes, declare from the bully pulpit, of president—that contrary to what the

Spanish intended, what the Puritans set forth, what Washington and Lincoln professed, America was "not a Christian country"?

There was no judging a person on the basis of religion (he was also a Christian, with many fine points), but there was now a spirit pushing the nation closer to what many seers had said: persecution.

Men were marrying *men*—women betrothed to women—and in one of the most dastardly of all trends, they were now allowed to adopt children.

Soon, in order to have babies, men would have embryos implanted in them.

Where did you go Ward and June Cleaver?

Where were the descendants of John Winthrop?

They had taken away Columbus Day!

They had turned Easter into "spring break."

It was becoming illegal to hate evil: to proclaim what Scripture said.

If it was evil, you were legal.

Christian clerk, you must marry homosexuals. Catholic companies: you must fund contraception.

The cell phone was Scripture. Facebook—or was it now Snapchat?—was the Bible study. Everyone wired to "fame."

No longer to God.

No time to pray.

Noise (via electronics) was the devil's meditation.

Loud rap "music" blared defiantly at you.

You could hear the beat through car windows.

Oh, the reverberations!

This was America the beautiful, where God had shed His Grace, reduced to a secular heap.

Tens of thousands at rock concerts, while at the Cross in St. Augustine, you prayed alone.

God had planted a “cross” at Ground Zero and wanted a church built there but instead there was now a defiant tower.

There was something fundamentally different—or striving mightily in that direction.

Could a single candidate turn it all around?

Could that person be Donald Trump?

Might God use the imperfect for rectification?

Chapter 46

I didn't know. It would take a revolution. Otherwise—in reinstituting "Merry Christmas"—it was only a reprieve, a hiatus. Certainly, God had raised up David (Acts 13:22) and Cyrus (*Isaiah* 45). Was Trump like this?

If not, there would be war—perhaps on American soil.

Was not North Korea looking for a window of opportunity in making more nukes? And China entering the space race? And Russia re-arming Eastern Europe?

"My faithful one, if my warnings are taken seriously and enough of my children strive constantly and faithfully to renew and reform themselves in their inward and outward lives, then there will be no nuclear war," Sister Neuzil quoted "Our Lady of America" as telling her (to repeat). *"What happens to the world depends upon those who live in it. There must be more good than evil prevailing in order to prevent the holocaust that is so near approaching. Yet I tell you, my daughter, even should such a destruction happen because there were not enough souls who took my warnings seriously, there will remain a remnant—untouched by the chaos—who having been faithful in following me and spreading my warnings, will gradually inhabit the earth again with their dedicated and holy lives. These will renew the earth in the power and light of the Holy*

Spirit. These faithful ones of my children will be under my protection and that of the Holy Angels, and they will partake of the life of the Divine Trinity in a most remarkable way. Let my dear children know this, precious daughter, so that they will have no excuse if they fail to heed my warnings."

And the chaos would come how?

There would be riots.

There might be attempts at secession.

There could be civil war.

There were "red" states and "blue" ones.

Rhetoric already was extreme.

"Dear children!" she said at Medjugorje. *"Today I call you to accept and live my messages with seriousness. These days are the days when you need to decide for God, for peace, and for the good. May every hatred and jealousy disappear from your life and your thoughts, and may there only dwell love for God and for your neighbor. Thus, and only thus, shall you be able to discern the signs of the time."*

Some had it wrong: the new world order would come *after* disasters, after violence, after a breakdown of society and infrastructure, if America was not reclaimed, if it did not don sackcloth, if it did not repent Nineveh-like. That would be when an antichrist, if we accepted such "words," would rise.

Did we think Mary called herself "Queen of Peace" for nothing?

"I was told that these events would be acts of 'aggression, terrorism, and war,' performed by self-proclaimed radical groups, supposedly in the name of God," wrote a man who saw Mary as "Our Lady of Light" (before September 11), flatly predicting, in 1984, that "terrorist attacks and acts of war and aggression will continue to plague the Middle East, Africa, and Europe." However, he added, "a major terrorist attack may befall New York City or

Washington, D.C., severely impacting the way we live in the United States." He was shown a future in which violence would spread from the Middle East to Europe, and then to the former Soviet Union and Far East—particularly China.

The greatest threat, he was shown, would come from China and a "two hundred million army" (see *Revelation* 9:16).

"The Lady of Light specifically told me, *'Pray for the conversion of China,'*" he said. *"'The conversion of China to God is necessary for the salvation of the world.'"*

This was also claimed by the Georgia man named James Wilburn Chauncey, who believed he had been taken by angelic-looking beings into eternity, where he went "to the edge of paradise, like a cliff, and you could see the blue earth hanging there and when you wanted you could just zoom in on various places on earth. I could smell smoke and heard booming noises and it was like I was seeing over the Northeast toward Europe and I could see these armies moving from Russia over Syria and continuing southwest and southeast, bypassing Israel.

"They conquered all of Africa and Asia except for China, then they started across the rest of Europe and across to England.

"The English fought very hard. After England was decimated I saw missiles lobbed from boats at New York, Washington, Philadelphia, Cincinnati, Jacksonville, and Atlanta and some other place but at this point they weren't nuclear. That was followed by a landing of troops and I looked toward the other side of America when I heard some huge blasts and I looked toward Mexico and New Mexico. There were troops coming from Mexico and South America and they were Islamic. I kept 'getting' that Russia has a pact with the Islamic countries. After this, there were nuclear blasts. Atomic bombs started falling."

But both men also saw natural disasters, including a tsunami engulfing the entire East Coast (in the case of "Our Lady of Light"), and Chauncey believed he had been shown, as a youngster, during a near-death brush, quakes that would create a massive lake in the Midwest and a gulf of water between California and the mainland, along with volcanic eruptions and epidemics as unprecedented perturbations afflicted the planet (which, recalling Sister Lucia, he was shown would wobble before regaining equilibrium).

Was *everyone* who said these things—and had been, since the Sixties—simply suffering morbid imaginings?

"Mountains had fallen; canyons disappeared; the courses of rivers were changed, and much land disappeared," Chauncey claimed he had been shown as a child (actually in the 1940s). "Portions of Texas and Arizona were now lakes. What had been deserts of the west were now green and lush with trees and vegetation. Asia, Africa, Europe, and the world over became lush with vegetation, clear water, lakes, and rivers, and an abundance of fish, fowl, and animal life. My choice for six decades has been never to talk or write about the experiences. I am under great stressful pain thinking about the possibilities of persecution that may be heaped on my family. Because of this pain, on many occasions, I have repeatedly asked God to remove this burden from me. His answer is always the same: *'Remember Nineveh.'* One thing has been made perfectly clear to me. Humanity can cause delay or shifts within periods of time, but humanity cannot prevent them unless humanity totally rejects evil."

Chapter 47

Was it too preposterous to believe, or did we forget the tremendous changes that had occurred through earth's history?

There had been a time when Africa and South America had been joined.

There had been times—millennia—when flora and fauna on the Sahara had been like a garden of Eden.

In fact, there may have been a time when the earth's entire mass of land was a single continent.

Who could argue with the notion that major transitions were possible—perhaps sooner than commonly reckoned?

How these changes happened—how they affected humans—might be up to us: how much we participated in prayer, in Mass, in the holy heartfelt reception of the Eucharist (not just a ritual, but a life-changing contact with Jesus, with the Holy Spirit).

This is what was being asked: that everyone change *inwardly*, that in receiving the sacraments, in utilizing the Grace of Confession, and in praying the Rosary, or in tongues, we looked into our own souls before we looked at others, before we fretted over society at large, and purged the negative—all darkness to which demons could attach;

that we set our eyes on the final hour we were certain would come to every single person in the way of death.

This was what was being asked: that we fill ourselves with purity and love, which would outwardly radiate.

That effusion was enough to cause planetary effect. Had not Saint Faustina Kowalska through her own cloistered prayers staved off the chastisement of a major Polish city.

It was there in her diaries—which like so many apparitions, had met with initial rejection.

She also had seen the day when there would be that fantastic Cross in the sky, and from the holes where the nails had been, great light.

Was this the "sign" in secrets from places of apparition?

Had we heeded the requests of Mary (at Fatima) to practice the First Saturday devotion (which had been as much of a request of hers as consecration of Russia)?

Was there any jealousy left in us? Did we think of other negatively—even with animus? Was there still the habit of lust? Or materialism—warned about at Kibeho (as Mary spoke of fire)?

In Italy—where there was a supervolcano called Campi Flegrei, with twenty-four craters, most of them under the sea, the rest near or under the feet of millions—a volcanic field thought to have led to the deaths of most Neanderthal hominids forty thousand years ago, and a "volcanic winter" just several centuries ago—an alleged stigmatic relayed a presumed heavenly missive that said, *"Do not continue to be a threat to your earth. Soon all the elements will be unleashed upon you. Great chasms will open in the depths of the oceans and the earth will be disfigured, put out of harmony because of you, and everything will be terrible. The earth will emanate a red cloud like blood and with violence this cloud will ascend into heaven accompanied by a loud thunderclap. Everything will be made sterile, the air will be as unbreathable gas, springs will give out red water and it will be poison for those who want to quench their strong thirst. So many things essential for life will be missing. For ninety-one days you will experience darkness, everything will occur in a short time; when you are aware of these events everything will already be established, thus pray, pray, pray; be aware, be sober, be prepared, ponder, and do not underestimate the months of spring. Humanity is near to the abyss; try to be in agreement because you need to support yourselves; even if these events are [coming] soon, fix your hearts on my beloved Son Jesus and do not be afraid since you will be safe with him. My Son is at hand and is coming. Persevere in love, Jesus will cleanse everything and His Kingdom of Peace will be magnificent. I bless you in the Name of the Holy Trinity, Father, Son and Holy Spirit."*

There was fire on earth but the great threat was in the flames of the netherworld.

Did we pray for everyone we encountered, causing a domino effect, or were we besmudged with selfishness?

An election didn't purify the soul. It helped—yes. How much it would help, how critical, in the collective soul, to at least initiate an end to the horror of abortion, to draw back the climate for gay marriage, to lighten the clouds, meanwhile—at least in the U.S.—of religious persecution. There was going to be a great shaking and we had to position ourselves with that in mind, for if we did, it would be threatening only to God's enemies while it would be a promise—a challenge, but a promise—to His people (as one sermonizer put it).

We had to view a coming "great shaking" differently, he said. America was due for a shaking no matter who was elected president

Properly prepared, however, everything that shook out would be that which was militating against God, so that His people could *advance* in the midst of the shaking and recover lost ground.

We were simply due for it. There was no question that Hillary was a dangerous option—not acceptable, despite good qualities, and the excellent resumé, she possessed: like Obama, there was cognitive dissonance. How could one champion the welfare of children (*It Takes A Village*) while supporting abortion—even in the last month? This proved that wisdom was not in the measure of an I.Q. or S.A.T.

So yes, despite the public conduct, despite the rudeness, despite the terrible, hurtful insults, despite two divorces, despite a myriad of claims of business improprieties, despite shortchanging small businessmen, despite a bias in favor of the super-wealthy, despite lawsuits by students at a "university," despite tutorship by the notorious Roy Cohn, despite constant distortions of fact, and prevarication, despite an epically thrasonical personality, an ego larger than Ali's, an insensitivity that was breathtaking, a history of personal indiscretion, despite a materialism that was unsurpassed, a tower that rose in actual gold leaf (*towers*: he had built a number of them), despite an obsession with all that glittered, in direct contravention of what the Virgin said and Christ had preached (starting, silently, in the manger), and despite a frightening example of torrid consumerism that threatened to bring back the Roaring Twenties (and what came after), he was the preferable candidate with an opportunity to convert right in front of a nation—which is what it would take, conversion (though not through a prosperity minister)—and make historic change. True greatness this would be: the formation of a new Cyrus, or King David, at 1600 Pennsylvania Avenue, with Supreme Court justices ready to abate the tragedy of *Roe* and a cabinet official focused on allowing Catholic education—vouchers—instead of continuance of the terrible system of education that had tainted so many young minds (and souls)! Would the trend toward persecuting American Christians—making the Bible seem like the work of a criminal, and morality hateful—be stopped? The apple cart needed to be overturned; there needed to be a bull in the china shop. America needed a radical transformation, and perhaps—only perhaps—would get it. One could only pray. The tide of globalism might be halted, for a season. There were more Christians on board. As former House Speaker Newt Gingrich (a convert to Catholicism), in speaking about Trump and the resistance to him, even in his own party, said, "They cannot imagine—he's an outsider, he's not part of them, he's not part of the club, he's uncontrollable, he hasn't been through the initiation rites, he's not part of the secret society. They have no idea how to relate to him." There will be the opportunity for a sea change—and to halt the "secular totalitarianism" that sought to replace America's Judeo-Christian morality with atheistic "values." There would perhaps be more law and order and less terrorism—less oppression of regular Christian Americans.

Merry Christmas.

Perhaps you could now choose to bake or not bake a cake for gay weddings (in this "free" country). Perhaps the Little Sisters of the Poor would no longer have to sue the federal government to avoid funding health plans that covered birth control.

Perhaps.

Yet, no elected official controlled what was in the souls of the people. There was free will. And always—always—the issue of materialism. As Mary phrased it at Medjugorje on December 2, 2016, nearly a month after the incredible election, looking unusually sad, but never referring to a specific nation (always addressing the entire world, which had *not* gone through an election):

"Dear children, my motherly heart is crying as I am looking at what my children are doing. Sins are multiplying, the purity of souls is all the less important; my Son is being forgotten—honored all the less; and my children are being persecuted. That is why, you my children, apostles of my love, with soul and heart invoke the Name of my Son. He will have the words of light for you. He manifests Himself to you, He breaks the bread with you and gives you the words of love so that you may transform them into merciful acts and, thus, be witnesses of truth. That is why, my children, do not be afraid. Permit my Son to be in you. He will make use of you to care for the wounded and to convert lost souls. Therefore, my children, return to the prayer of the Rosary. Pray it with feelings of goodness, sacrifice, and mercy. Pray, not only with words, but with merciful acts. Pray with love for all people. My Son, by His sacrifice, exalted love. Therefore, live with Him so that you may have strength and hope; that you may have the love which is life and which leads to eternal life. Through God's Love, I am also with you, and will lead you with motherly love."

It was not just a laundry list of formulaic sins. Anything that argued against compassion tended toward evil, which was hate itself; division itself; strife itself; pride itself—the prince of that.

When we had pride, we were in touch with him.

He had a claim to the territory of our souls in proportion to what darkness was there.

So here was the real goal, the chore, the test of life: purifying the soul in concert with Jesus.

We were called to interior perfection.

And whether or not we could reach that, what God wanted—what He took into deep consideration—was how hard we tried.

It was something that had to be on our minds every second.

We could conjoin with Jesus only as much as we had purified inside and only in Him was true protection and solace no matter what swirled around us—no matter a tornado, no matter the heat of a comet. If the societies of men were rent by hatred, so too would the very earth on which those societies stood be rent.

The earth was going to be renewed, was going to be purged, with or without us.

This was true mercy: chastising here so we wouldn't have to be chastised in eternity. (What conceivably was more important than direct entry into paradise—or at least the full-hearted attempt?)

If consumerism became as frenzied, as turbo-charged, as now threatened—if it wasn't already around the bend—one recalled that "in those days before the Flood they were eating and drinking, marrying and giving in marriage, until the day that Noah entered the ark" (*Matthew* 24:38).

Only if we forsook greed and materialism—Our Lady's prime concern—could we reclaim the United States.

Could Harvard, Yale, or Princeton return anything close to the Christian institutions they had been founded (Harvard going back to 1636) to be?

As for the Church, were we beginning to see a materialization of the prophecy from Akita of "bishops against bishops, and cardinals against cardinals," as little fracases erupted at the Vatican over matters such as Communion for the divorced and civilly remarried—between "traditional" and "progressive" factions, as a Pope with a far less systematic approach, and a penchant for freelance (some said ambiguity), set the Church on a less theological, academic route, emphasizing the spirit of the law instead of the letter?

When Chauncey saw Mary—impressive because he was Baptist—he "didn't turn on the lights, but I could see her through the sheet [covering him on his 'deathbed'] because the glow from the corridor lights partially illuminated the room. I couldn't take my eyes off of her as she came up to my bed and pulled the sheet from my face. She was the most beautiful woman I had ever seen. My eyes must have been as big as saucers. There was something about this woman that was breathtaking. It was as though I had known her all my life and had just been reunited. Her skin was glowing with a hue that can only be described as a burnt golden color. Her hair was black as coal. Her voice was soothing and musical.

"She told me not to be afraid."

Chapter 48

In 2004 had come an additional "word of knowledge" to the same presumed recipient, this one stating, on December 22 (days before the Asian tsunami), *"The angels have their instruction from east to west, and now a timetable has been set in motion,"* adding, *"When the huge light is seen, I will act in a way I have not acted before."* The angels had their orders. Then and finally a few years later:

"The trials of your time now head to the crescendo of meaning, whereby to each will be shown the imperfection of the past and the need for purification of the future. In these transgressions is found the enemy of Creation, and the one who seeks to install his spirit as the spirit that conquers for all time.

"It is a final battle in which the trials of the future will serve as engagements complete unto themselves . . .

"While love prevails, so does courage, and so does the uncovering of those spirits which now install themselves as guardians for those who have invited falsity into their hearts.

"The angels stand ready to assist those who unleash power with humility and belief. Only those in union with God will be able to see in the darkness which so many expected and that already is upon the earth.

"New Mexico I have ordained as a beacon of light and also the place near the water where the cross stands.

"In this time, expect the error of premature expectation, but not [error in] the truth of the expectation itself. For these times, you have the Rosary, and even more so, praise. In union with God comes all protection, as the dark spirits are now allowed to materialize in full due to the pretense and aspirations of man. Not until the initial event will the curtain be drawn that reveals the entirety of the plan, and even then, it will be parted only slowly, in the woes of purification."

New Mexico a beacon of light "and also the place near the water where the cross stands"?

This brought us back to Columbus, to DeLeon, to Menendez.

It brought us out west, where Catholics arrived after Florida.

It had started in 1598 in Las Cruces, New Mexico ("city of the crosses") and through the 1600s, with the same Spanish Catholic missionaries, this time with names like Junipero Serra and Fermín Francisco de Lasuén, with Serra, as if for force and guidance, stopping at Tepeyac at the spot of Guadalupe before venturing to what became New Mexico and California. "In the 28th chapter of the Gospel of Matthew, the Risen Savior gives His disciples the great commission: 'Go, make disciples of all nations, baptizing them in the name of the Father, and of the Son, and of the Holy Spirit,'" noted the Archdiocese of Santa Fe. "All those that are true followers of Jesus, not merely His admirers, have sought to obey that command. Thus it was with those who sought to bring the Gospel to the deserts, mountains, and valleys of our beloved New Mexico four hundred years ago. Reigning over this humble kingdom of the Lord is our Blessed Mother who has always had a special place in the hearts of the people of New Mexico. Whether under her title as Queen of Peace conquering the divisions among her children, or as Our Lady of Guadalupe championing the poor and forgotten, the Virgin Mary continues to intercede for her children."

There was Santa Fe (with the oldest still-standing church). There was Santa Cruz ("Holy Cross"). There was Chimayó—where a miraculous Crucifix had been unearthed. "Sometime around 1810, a Chimayó friar was performing penances when he saw a light bursting from a hillside," noted an online source. "Digging, he found a Crucifix, quickly dubbed the miraculous Crucifix of Our Lord of Esquipulas. A local priest brought the Crucifix to Santa Cruz, but three times it disappeared and was later found back in its hole. By the third time, everyone understood that El Senor de Esquipulas wanted to remain in Chimayó, and so a small chapel was built on the site."

There was Saint Fráncìsco de Asís Church in Rancos de Taos, where a painting of Christ showed Him at the Sea of Galilee, a phenomenon that evoked wonder when the lights went out and (as one report noted) "the life-size image of Jesus standing on the shore of the Sea of Galilee fades to a shadow as the wispy white clouds in pale blue sky and green water begin to glow around Him, as if all were bathed in moonlight. Soon the silhouette of Jesus grows three-dimensional and appears more like a dark statue than flat image. His robes seem to billow in a breeze."

During daylight, the boat and Cross are not seen.

A "beacon of light"?

It was called "The Shadow of the Cross"—with no scientists able to explain it.

Reported the newspaper for the Archdiocese of Denver: "According to a host who presents the painting to visitors, scientists have examined the chemical properties of the paint and have confirmed that no radium or other luminescent chemicals or materials are present to produce the eerie glow. In plain light the painting is a life-size portrait of Jesus Christ standing on a rock near some water. One Hand lies close to His heart and the other by His side. However, in the darkness the painting emits a glow and becomes luminescent with the Lord appearing in silhouette. According to one observer, the figure of Christ seems to move or flicker slowly as if the figure is walking or moving. A black band or shadow in the shape of a Cross appears over his right shoulder and the dark outline of what appears to be the bow of a boat also appears. A very faint, nearly imperceptible halo appears above his head and, according to some, faint white letters can be found near the top of the painting, near the head."

There was thus New Mexico and also the "place near the water where the Cross stands."

This brought us back—I believe—to St. Augustine.

Where else was there a Cross so fitting of the description—a Cross as tall, as beckoning, by a mightier shore, at the site of the first official Mass?

In Texas, a nineteen-story cross towered over a roadside near Pampas, with an arm span of a hundred and ten feet (but no significant water nearby). An even taller Protestant Cross stood at land-locked Effingham, Illinois, at one hundred and ninety-eight feet.

But one turned back to where it began: Florida and specifically the inlet at St. Augustine—ironically the only city older than Santa Fe.

As we've seen, in 1965 the diocese of St. Augustine, with an inspired sense of history, and perhaps the future, erected the gigantic stainless-steel Cross at the site where Father Lopez had planted a makeshift one precisely four hundred years before, and where Menendez made his official landing, on September 8, a few days later. It was also near what some believed was the earlier point of landing for Ponce de Leon.

The point was that a Cross—the world's tallest, as far as anyone knew—stood along the inlet, and the inlet was not only a substantial body of water in and of itself, but part of one of the world's *greatest* bodies of water: the Atlantic Ocean, beckoning to the same sea once traversed by explorers!

As I said I'd had no clue of all this when I first moved to Florida, nor had I put it together when first I heard the alleged prophecy. But in fact, coincidentally, the diocese even *described* it, in its literature, as a beacon. "This massive structure, made of stainless steel and rising two hundred and eight feet above the marshes of the Matanzas River, stands as a sentinel over the Mission and a 'Beacon of Faith' for all who pass this way," said its website. "The plaque at the base of the world's tallest cross, which is 208 feet high, says that it 'marks the approximate site where in 1565 the Cross of Christianity was first permanently planted in what is now the United States.' That's right—Jesus arrived in America here first, over a half-century before the Pilgrims even touched their toes to Plymouth Rock (and forty-two years before Jamestown). 'The Great Cross' (as it's known) was erected to mark the 400th anniversary of that momentous day. It's built of seventy tons of stainless steel plates, packed with concrete in its lower third to prevent toppling by hurricanes. It's part of the Shrine of Our Lady of La Leche, and its height was designed so that everyone near St. Augustine could see it, and be reminded 'of the religious beginning of our nation.'"

Close by was a famous lighthouse—another beacon.

And of course there was the shrine of Nombre de Dios with the chapel housing Our Lady of La Leche, a place of purported miracles. Our Lady was fashioned after a statue back in Spain that was said to have survived the blasphemy of a drunken sailor and was credited with saving the pregnant and desperately ill wife of a man who rescued the image, as today her image is implored by women who are pregnant or wish to be. She is shown nursing a Child the same way she nursed the birth of America right from this place.

Would Our Lady of La Leche too—despite its precarious location in the hurricane belt—serve as a special spot in coming times? One needed not fear storms. In the early 1800s—two and a half centuries after Father Lopez recorded that comet—a cargo ship sailing from Spain had suddenly been engulfed in a storm as it neared the treacherous port there.

"The captain, fearing the loss of his vessel and the lives of his crew, ordered the men to throw everything overboard," wrote Nancy H. Murray (in The Madonnas of St. Augustine). "A lighter load would better the chances for survival. In a corner of the ship's hold, among motley contents, the men discovered a statue of striking beauty. No one knew where it came from nor to whom it was going. When the captain saw the statue, he immediately bade the men kneel down and pray for safety to the Virgin Mary. As the salty spray washed over the deck, they heard the imploring voice of their captain: 'Oh, Hurricane Lady, if this storm may pass and we arrive safely in port, we will give your beautiful statue to be enshrined permanently in the port of St. Augustine . . . Almost immediately, the wind calmed, the waves subsided and the cargo ship limped into port."

More to the point: might Catholicism, and with it Christianity, somehow, one day—soon—be brought back to full original life—revived—in this area, if not at this spot, after major events occurred, after purification?

Perhaps! But for now: I knew where things were headed. It was daunting. Not only were gays marrying each other (Vice President Joseph Biden, a Catholic, would even officiate at one), but religious institutions of whatever stripe were being forced in Europe to hire openly homosexual applicants. Meanwhile there was that eruption of vandalism against Catholic statues that was reminiscent of the statue destruction across Rwanda just before Kibeho, which of course had been followed by the great genocide.

Signs of the times.

Never mind the shattered Clearwater glass! She was painted black, was Mary, covered with satanic graffiti, beheaded, as were statues of Jesus; she was smashed to pieces.

Every week brought a new article about a desecrated statue, usually the Virgin, somewhere in North America. Would Trump stop this—could he?

He was a last hope, if a hope he was. For the spiritual war was breaking forth in many ways and very blatantly:

• In Switzerland, a pagan show replete with horned man, an all-seeing eye, and new-world sexual imagery served as ceremony for the world's longest tunnel (Gotthard).

• In that same nation a statue of the Hindu "god" Shiva, also known as "The Destroyer" (his duty was to "destroy worlds at the end of creation and dissolve them into nothingness") was placed in front of the European Organization for Nuclear Research (CERN) and its controversial Hadron Collider (which some feared would spark a tremendous subatomic chain reaction). In 2016, an occult ritual—some said as a staged hoax by scientists—was held before it, in front of a camera.

• During Super Bowl half-times, similar Shiva-like, horned costumes were part of the entertainment.

Skull tattoos, nose piercings, "Buffy the Vampire Slayer," "Lucifer," Harry Potter, Pokémon ("pocket monster"): it was breaking out everywhere.

Was there really evil in things like abortion and euthanasia (in Canada there was a proposal to legalize bestiality)?

I interviewed a Christian activist whose group forced an abortion clinic to vacate a building in Michigan. "Before we took over the building, when we would come through, we would find bats in here—hanging on the doorways of some of the rooms where abortions were performed," he said. "You could feel the heaviest and darkness. You could feel the oppression. The day we took possession we had a meeting and opened the doors up and brought in folks—one hundred and forty came to the building that night and we had a local pastor who was a worship leader and another elderly Godly man who had worked in a theological seminary and he did a teaching on cleansing and re-dedication and we all recited a prayer they wrote out dedicating it to life and the Lord. And then we released those people to pray through the building, every floor, and they anointed in rooms where the abortions occurred. There were a lot of tears and repentance and cleansing prayers to re-dedicate and to reclaim this place for God's glory."

The following Sunday the organization's board had decided to walk through the building. They retraced the daily steps of an abortionist who entered through a back alley because the sidewalk counselors were out front. Ten members prayed for about fifteen minutes in the hallway "where death entered." One prayer: "I ask you Lord God, in the name of Jesus, to fill this place. Death, you may no longer enter through this door!"

The moment the prayer leader said "Amen," according to the activist, "this doorway—a heavy steel one—blew open from the inside and slammed against the outside wall, and this gust of cool wind came gushing in the building. A pastor said, 'Something just left here in a hurry.' It was like death exited and the Holy Spirit blew in."

There was "an exchange of authority and power," and the building was "sealed" in Christ.

Where some had initially reported a pungent smell ("like strong sulfur"), that was also now gone.

It was what now had to be done in America, from sea to shining sea, and in every community, in every home, in every bedroom, if the amber fields of grain, if the battlefields of the Revolution, if New York and Los Angeles and Washington were to be reclaimed. It was a war that had to be fought and won. This was a war Mary said could be won with the Rosary, the sacraments. *"Gather the children in this wild country and teach them what they should know for salvation,"* she'd told Adele near Green Bay. *"Teach them, their catechism, how to sign themselves with the Sign of the Cross, and how to approach the sacraments; that is what I wish you to do. Go and fear nothing, I will help you."* But the warning remained. It had not been mitigated by politics—not yet. We were a long way from that. There were still bends—and pitfalls—on the road. Alongside it, ravines. There was the chance of great deception—deceiving ourselves that all was now well (while remaining in personal sin). Would there be enough souls—the figurative ten or twenty as at Sodom? It was dangerous—highly so—to allow an election to lull one into complacency. In fact, if instead of inspiring holiness, society was flown to new reaches of materialism and carnality it might be in worse shape than before November 2016. *"What happens to the world depends on those who live in it,"* we recall yet one last time from the American apparitions. *"There must be much more good than evil prevailing in order to prevent the holocaust that is so near approaching."*

Preach it from the pulpits!

This land of the free, "home of the brave"? Where were the courageous, the masses who in their outrage should have staged a revolt against the revolting: stormed the clinics, stormed legislatures, stormed courts and Congress, stormed blasphemous gay parades? Where had they been for Terri Schiavo? Would they now be emboldened under Trump? Was it not time to take America back—in this small window of opportunity, to mitigate what was coming: the disturbances, in society and nature?

That was the "prophecy" here: that a time was upon us that would bring about a complete overhaul or else a time of chaos.

Epidemics. Riots. Seismic shifts. Volcanic eruptions somewhere, perhaps at Yellowstone, perhaps more than one, perhaps under the ocean; the threat of an asteroid or comet—perhaps more than a threat; and great economic gyrations: Tremendous shortages and runs on banks. It could all seem fine, stock markets skyrocketing, consumer confidence at post-9/11 highs, employment steadily ticking upward, with jobs coming back from overseas, and then, like a house of cards—like a sand castle—suddenly all collapse.

Was this why, at Medjugorje, Mary appeared to Mirjana on the second of each month and also March 18 each year, the seer's birthday—not because it was a birthday but a date when an event would occur? (Mirjana had said when secrets unfolded, she would warn in advance and that date of the 18th would make more sense.) Did it mean a window of two weeks, from the second to the 18th, for preparation?

America!

Be ready.

Prepare with morality.

How could not the entire country, the courts, the legislators, the governor, the president, the Church, seeing this spectacle—Schiavo, her slow day-to-day descent into unnecessary death, with a terrified look on her face—not have shut down that facility?

How could we have gone so long without forcing lewd magazine covers out of supermarkets?

Did we really just sit back (with our cell phones, with our six packs) as they glorified a former Olympic decathlon superstar whose name had been Bruce but now, to media acclaim, was "Caitlyn"?

No wonder Vladimir Putin of the Soviet Union, who some accused of terminating political foes, could nonetheless find the nerve to castigate us for losing our Christian way—America!—and for putting good and evil on equal footing and even reversing them. At least his nation allowed public crosses and he was even photographed lighting candles at an Orthodox church (for what it was worth, kissing an image of Mary).

Russia was now the "Christian" superpower!

Or at least, for the time being.

Russia!

Noted a publication called *American Thinker*: "For those of us who grew up in America being told that the godless communist atheists in Russia were our enemies, the idea that America might give up on God and Christianity while Russia embraces religion might once have been difficult to accept. But by 2015, the everyday signs in America show a growing contempt for Christianity, under the first president whose very claims of being a Christian are questionable. The exact opposite trend is happening in Russia and its leaders—a return to Christian roots."

While the U.S. Navy was allowing witches to conduct rituals at its chapels—and welcoming transgenders (naming a new ship after a homosexual activist), Russia was naming ships after Orthodox saints.

What we were allowing in the U.S. was incredible. What a long way since Fatima! The experiments on embryos, the creation of genetically modified plants, the "GMO" seeds dispersed on fields and raising havoc with natural plants (animals wanted little to do with synthetic trees).

Nature was being meddled with at its smallest level, or at least the smallest that we could detect. Would Trump or anyone address this? Would his successor? There was manipulation of nano-particles. There were aerosols dispersed in the atmosphere. I figured we had a decade or two before the climax. No wonder another of those messages that sprung from the 1990 prophecy said, *"The world is now seriously out of conformance with the Will of God and what He created and intended. There are those who would reconfigure the very creatures He has formed, and who meddle with the texture of life. For this reason, the Lord will allow a huge reorientation. If not for the action of Heaven, what God has created on earth will soon be damaged beyond recovery.*

"A very dramatic effect already is in progress as regards the support structures of what man calls nature. Such cannot be allowed to take the final realization of total realignment when it comes to the very way elements and life forces interact. The event to come will surprise everyone who has offered a prognostication, and will show even recalcitrant scientists, though not all, that there is a fundamental alarm in Heaven over their arrogant and wayward course. Nothing that is artificial in a way that disrupts what God intended will be allowed to stand."

We were hearing *"strange loud rumblings"* around the world, but especially North America, as that prophecy also foresaw, reports of booms, bangs, strange subterranean echoes. They were frequently in the news, along with a torrent of UFO reports—more than ever. A loud boom disturbed residents of Colorado Springs while that same month dozens of people in Fairfield, Ohio, reported a stunning, inexplicable, and explosive noise. "Officials stumped by reports of rumbling," said the Lewiston, Maine *Sun Journal.*

Far below the surface, was something afoot, a shift in mass of the earth's crust, a deep grind of tectonic plates, or much further down, an imbalance in the hot core? Was a change in the axis coming? Might it one day cause a phenomenon science had never before encountered? Or might it be an electromagnetic phenomenon related to spectacular shows of the aurora borealis? Was it the forerunner of a solar flare or electromagnetic weapon that would take down the nation's electrical grid? Edison would roll over! "In our opinion, the source of such powerful and immense manifestation of acoustic-gravity waves must be very large-scale energy processes," said a group of scientists. "These processes include powerful solar flares and huge energy flows generated by them, rushing towards earth's surface and destabilizing the magnetosphere, ionosphere and upper atmosphere. Thus, the effects of powerful solar flares: the impact of shock waves in the solar wind, streams of corpuscles and bursts of electromagnetic radiation are the main causes of generation of acoustic-gravitation waves following increased solar activity."

Oh solar flare! Oh fear of "fire."

Were such dangers discussed at Bilderberg meetings or at Bohemian Grove?

Perhaps a better place to search was Scripture.

There one was struck by the number of times the word "rumbling" appeared. In *Revelation* Chapter 4 it came with lightning from the Throne; in Chapter 8 it arrived with flashes of lightning; in Chapter 11, rumblings accompanied hail.

"Then there came flashes of lightning, rumblings, peals of thunder and a severe earthquake," said *Revelation* Chapter 16, verses 17-19. "No earthquake like it has ever occurred since man has been on earth, so tremendous was the quake."

Or did rumblings recall the blast of a trumpet—like the wail of the shofar emanating from the thick cloud on Mount Sinai that made the Israelites tremble (*Exodus* 19, 16)?

Yes, something above; something in the wind; something underfoot.

Did everyone really think it was pure happenstance that there were "historic wildfires in one place such as California, even up in Canada, or down in Arizona, at the high reaches of mountains; and across to Tennessee—at the same time as "historic" floods in West Virginia and Texas and Louisiana (coffins floating there!) and Maryland or New Jersey; or that all the quakes from Japan to Oklahoma, but especially along the Pacific "Rim of Fire," did not portend something; did we think the Asian tsunami could not be exceeded; that the smoldering volcanoes (I saw hot lava flow from one into the ocean in Hawaii from a helicopter and then by car; so very eerie), could not become a Vesuvius or Krakatau tenfold, or a thousand fold, and not only at Yellowstone National Park (where there was a known "mega-volcano") but in other places not yet excavated or as I said beneath the waves, where but a fraction of volcanic sites had been studied; that hurricanes Andrew or Katrina could not one day arrive as a far wider swath (for example, stretching from Palm Beach to Daytona); or that the flares seen thus far from the sun (including one that took out a large electrical grid in Quebec) could not come with much greater effect; that a mega-drought could not once more engulf massive parts of America not for years (as during the "Dust Bowl") but centuries (they had through pre-history); or that all the little glimmerings in the way of Zika, HIV, swine flu, chicken viruses, and fearsome ebola might not one day come as an unexpected plague like Justinian against which there was absolutely no defense ("super"-bugs already were defying antibiotics in many hospitals); or that a breakdown in infrastructure could not cause catastrophic food shortages (the average American pantry had enough only for a few days, not to mention what would happen without electricity to pump water and gas); that the discord whether among blacks or Mexicans or embedded Muslim troublemakers or disaffected whites might not one day cause what amounted to the chastisement in Lincoln's time (civil war, or at least very severe uprisings; and perhaps a splintering of the nation into a handful of republics, with enclaves according to ethnicity, race, or religion), roaming, looting, violent gangs? I knew a devout Catholic evangelist from Pittsburgh (respected by his bishop) who'd had such a vivid vision of planes firing down—foreign planes—that at great expense he'd excavated a gigantic root cellar, really a warehouse, for the storage of food in such an eventuality (and built a house over it). Politics may even become irrelevant, in a certain way, as far as major change. For when it came to the presidency, there were candidates whose election might be more likely to bring civil discord—uprisings, as in Venezuela, as too with the crime in places like Brazil—while others, if elected to office, might, as proponents of such things as Planned Parenthood, be more likely to tempt unprecedented natural disasters.

I didn't know. I felt that 2020 to 2040 would be the critical time period. During the wildfires in Tennessee a man raking through debris spotted a piece of paper that somehow had survived in a puddle and saw that it was from verses thirteen to twenty in Chapter One of the Book of Joel (*"Gird yourselves with sackcloth and lament, O priests; wait, O ministers of the altar! Come, spend the night in sackcloth O ministers of my God . . . To You, O Lord, I cry; for fire has devoured the pastures of the wilderness and the flame has burned up all the trees of the field"*). There was still time. There was still mercy. It is why God had sent a Pope named Francis to speak of it so often: mercy, mercy, mercy. We needed to be merciful—to love, for sure; simplicity—and at the same time, through the devotions of Faustina, through Catholic prayer, through First Saturdays—ourselves seek Divine mercy. Could we not look at the laundry list of possible calamities and pray at least a decade of the Rosary each day that a certain type of disaster not be sent (depending on region)? Did it not make sense to schedule prayers in an effort to stave off earthquakes one day, war the next, riots, plague another time, and down the list. Did anyone really want to see an epidemic take out nearly a third of the populace, as occurred in Europe, Asia, and the Mideast in the century before Columbus?

When seismologists studied that strange and powerful quake near Richmond, Virginia, they found evidence of a new major movement far beneath our feet—the movement of a continent. No one knew! But we did know that it wasn't just California to which, seismically, we needed to pay heed. Had not a quake once caused portions of the Mississippi ("River of the Immaculate Conception") to flow backwards? And signs? The Virginia quake had shaken Washington to such an extent that cracks in the Washington Monument led to that national symbol's closure for more than a year. Closed! So too, after Hurricane Sandy washed over Liberty Island, and so much of New Jersey, did they have to shutter the Statue of Liberty for an extensive time. (Meanwhile colonies of a microscopic organism were leaving black powdery taints to the Lincoln and Jefferson memorials and the Washington Monument.) If that still seemed in the realm of coincidence, one perhaps could look at September 11 and note that the seismic effect of those collapsing towers had caused a network of cracks in the foundation of Federal Hall on Wall Street where the Bill of Rights had been etched and where Washington was sworn in—a building that once was the nation's capitol! The Trade Center was on land once owned by the historic chapel of Saint Paul in lower Manhattan, which miraculously survived the mayhem in 2001 and which was where Washington and the first cabinet and Congress held a prayer service consecrating the nation of God and imploring His protection. Now, "Ground Zero"!

Here was joy, here was optimism, here was hope: praying bad things away instead of excitedly anticipating them. Lord, make me just a false prophet, a worrywart, like Jonah was initially.

Have mercy, Lord. Let there be no earthquakes as I warn, no terrifying, taunting winds, no comets or meteors, no ocean rise, no volcano. No fire! Oh Lord, spare us from societal breakdown, from economic collapse, from famine, from terrorism, from epidemic.

If we entered a new period of materialism, we approached doom.

There was the account of a fellow who was given glimpses of the afterlife and on the way to hell found himself falling feet first into a damp, musty tunnel where he saw a huge, glowing, terrifying red ball "almost like the light on the front of a train," he wrote. "Visions of wealth appeared before my eyes, like a three-dimensional movie. Diamonds, money, cars, gold, beautiful women, everything." It was the way of the devil. Mystical encounters had been claimed from Toowomba, Australia, to Aleppo, Syria—Aleppo!—and in Ontario, Canada, and Ohio (many there!), and Kentucky and Denver and Arizona and California (still more), nearly all with the same message we have seen and the large majority meeting with no formal ecclesiastic acknowledgement, making them tender territory that therefore was to be considered but not accepted at face value. The devil was active! There were two quakes in Norcia, Italy, the second destroying the basilica of the great Saint Benedict, famous for his battles with Satan. Also in Italy, dire warnings—scientific and mystical—about Mount Vesuvius and Campi Flegrei, that massive volcano field west of Naples (one of the craters named for Vulcan, the "god of fire"). As Hurricane Matthew headed for the Southeast—as it churned and slashed its way over voodoo-plagued Haiti—a distinct demonic skull could be seen on one frame of radar, as many also considered the New Testament Book of Matthew wherein Christ spoke of perturbations.

There were "secrets," they alleged.

In 2016, Mirjana Dragicevic Soldo of Medjugorje released a book called *My Heart Will Triumph* that shed light on rumors about her confidential prophecies (one of which, in some way, she confirmed, will one year allegedly involve March 18. "The significance of the date will be clear," she wrote.) At her last daily apparition (a traumatic event for this young woman who had seen the Blessed Mother for a year and a half: hundreds of times), Mirjana claimed that upon finalizing a discussion of the secrets—which would start with the warnings to the world and end with massive chastisement, affecting the entire globe, eventually changing it for the better (and allowing that triumph)—the Blessed Mother "then held out a rolled-up scroll, explaining that all ten secrets were written on it, and that I should show it to the priest I choose when the time came to reveal them." She took it from the Virgin's hand without looking at it. *"Now you will have to turn to God in faith like any other person,"*

Mary intoned. *"Mirjana, I have chosen you; I have confided in you everything that is essential. I have also shown you many terrible things. You must now bear it all with courage. Think of me and think of the tears I must shed for that. You must remain brave. You have quickly grasped the messages. You must also understand now that I have to go away. Be courageous."*

Ironic it was that soon after release of her book, Italy experienced a quake killing nearly three hundred—ironic because when asked about her first secret, and whether people would want to go to see the site of the secret, she had replied, to her spiritual director: "Surely no one wishes to watch disasters, distress, and misfortune. I don't think that this sort of thing attracts people at all. Why would people go to see something of that sort? It is one thing to go and see a sign, quite another to go and see suffering or a disaster. Who would, for example, *go to Italy to see a dam collapse?*" She said the first secret needed nothing to precede it and would "abundantly speak for itself."

The Blessed Mother still appears daily to three of the six, who, allegedly (and I always await final Church judgment), have not yet been given their final secrets.

"When Our Lady first entrusted the secrets to me, they caused me a great amount of stress and anxiety," said this visionary. "In time, however, God helped me comprehend and accept everything. Contrary to what many people think, the secrets are hardly on my mind. If I was not always asked about them, days and months could pass without me thinking of the secrets. The people who are concerned about the secrets have not seen Our Lady and do not know about God's complete project—why Our Lady comes here at all, or what she's preparing us for. But if your life is in her hands, and God is in your heart, what can harm you? If everyone knew me and could see how much I laugh and joke, no one would be afraid of the secrets. Those who truly know God's love should be full of joy."

In a recent message to another reputed seer (August 25, 2016), Mary said, *"Dear children! Today I desire to share Heavenly joy with you. You, little children, open the door of your heart so that hope, peace and love, which only God gives, may grow in your hearts. Little children, you are too bound to the earth and earthly things; that is why, Satan is rolling you like the wind rolls the waves of the sea. Therefore, may the chain of your life be prayer with the heart and Adoration of my Son Jesus."*

In the earliest days, when Blessed Mother had said, *"Tell them to convert before it's too late"* (referring to everyone), was this in relation to impending events or simply an admonition to each to purify interiorly because we never know when we will die? Were we as concerned with what we knew was going to happen—our own eventual passing—as the more exotic prophecies pertaining to the physical world? Was not Heaven the important point? And might it be the case that chastisement occurred in a region when more people in that region were headed for hell than Heaven?

God allows what is beneficial in drawing us closer to Him.

Divine Mercy!

"My child," Mary had told Mirjana, *"your life is only a blink in contrast to eternal life."*

What hope!

Eternity.

One only had to read near-death experiences to get a sense of the overwhelming beauty and bliss available to those faithful to the Church, to the Commandments, to love, to the pursuit of inward perfection, to Jesus. ("Lord, fill me with purity and love, purity and love, oh Lord": there was no more important prayer than this.)

The Blessed Mother personifies the beauty of paradise. One day we will see this. We all will be visionaries—and so much more. The flowers and landscape, the waters, crystalline, the aromas of sanctity, will be like none on earth. "I took out my drawing supplies and sketched her outline, her dress, her outstretched arms, and even the locks of long, dark hair that peek out from behind her veil," said Mirjana. "But when I tried to draw her face, it looked nothing like her. I tried repeatedly but my disappointment grew with each unsuccessful attempt. Eventually I understood that hers is another kind of beauty altogether. Just as words cannot describe how she looks, neither can art. Great artists have attempted likenesses of Our Lady according to our descriptions, but none came close. Even the world's finest paintings, icons, and sculptures of the Blessed Mother are only shadows of her splendor."

"I cannot divulge more about the secrets," added this seer—who, as I knew from personal interaction, was fantastically able to elude questions about them.

"But I can say this," she wrote. "Our Lady is planning to change the world. She did not come to announce our destruction; she came to save us, and with her Son, she will triumph over evil.

"If our mother has promised to defeat evil, then what do we have to fear?"

Indeed.

But does it not behoove us to work with her and Jesus in purging the evil?

Where love is planted there will flourish a place of reconciliation, after purification, between God and this lower realm. Only through love is the truth seen, and in truth will come all beauty and knowledge. Those who seek to claim truth as exclusively their own have neither knowledge nor wisdom, both of which come only from the truth of love. Thus is love the essence of life and the creator of life, for God is love. Only in Him are known the secrets of the mysteries of life everlasting.

I am kayaking in the inlet beneath the Cross at *Nombre de Dios* in St. Augustine, in the very same place where Father Lopez and Admiral Menendez approached the reeds, the oaks, the sabal palms, some brush, tolerant of the brackishness, spotting Timucuan huts fashioned with palm trunks and palmetto and perhaps smoke from outdoor hearths. It is awesome to imagine them and to feel His Presence here—and you do. This must become America's refuge. This must become a major place of pilgrimage. It is where the first documented Mass was celebrated—where the Cross was planted, as we must now march across our land and plant crosses again where once they stood and replace the gremlins of culture with the Crucifix. Jesus was "hung on a tree" in the form of a Cross that replaced the Tree of the Knowledge of Good and Evil. All wisdom is in Him. Where holiness is, there will be your refuge! That will be your oasis! I know a Carmelite priest who believes St. Augustine will be the epicenter of America's return to true Christianity. It will come full circle, he believes he was shown, in his own kind of "revelation," for there is a special quality here, whether kayaking here or praying on land in the little chapel or walking near the archeological site where they have found remnants of America's first parish.

Come back, America!

Pray goodness back!

At Guadalupe in Mexico the Virgin appears pregnant. She is the Virgin of the Americas. Her image is seen in so many places—ardently revered whether by Americans or Mexicans; a common ground; a binding thread. In many places the image is seen miraculously. Who can doubt it? Who can doubt that something is not up, that something is not in the air?

Salt air—here at St. Augustine inlet. Many prayers to pray and thoughts to think. If she was pregnant at Guadalupe, here she is Our Lady of La Leche. Will this spot one day be similar to Guadalupe, but instead of pregnancy, representing, as the nursing mother, a new birth?

This I ponder, beneath the Cross that towers unfathomably above, that is a beacon. This I mull, as my boat rolls and I listen to the same soughing surf that Father Lopez and Admiral Menendez heard.

Notes:

The information on Columbus comes from a number of sources, most particularly George Barton's *Columbus the Catholic—A Comprehensive Story of the Discovery.* Some of the information on Extremadura is drawn from the Center for the Study of Material and Visual Cultures of Religion (an article by Jeanette Favrot Peterson). The historians I refer to as far as expectations of the Second Coming are Timothy J. Johnson and Gert Melville in *From La Florida to La California: Franciscan Evangelization in the Spanish Borderlands.* Other information on Florida comes from diocesan records I perused and books such as *Cross & Crozier: The History of the Diocese of Saint Augustine* by Dr. Charles Gallagher and *Fides*, published by the Society for the Propagation of the Faith, Diocese of Saint Augustine. See also the book I mention, *The Madonnas of St. Augustine,* by Nancy H. Murray. I thank Bishop Filipe J. Estévez for the spark (in discussions about the history of St. Augustine) that set this work in motion. The accounts of Masonry in Washington come from a website www.theforbiddenknowledge.com, as well as sources as varied as Masonic websites and the book, *Freemasons For Dummies* by Christopher Hodapp. While President Donald J. Trump is not a Mason, it might be noted that his pastor, the famed Norman Vincent Peale, was. Some of the information on Guadalupe is from articles written by Frank Denke, while other facts are from the Jody Brant Smith's splendid work, *The Image of Guadalupe.* The information on Elizabeth Cady Stanton and her occult involvement is from *Deliver Us From Evil* by Cindy Jacobs. The official rendition of the Champion, Wisconsin, apparitions is from the Diocese of Green Bay (where in 2010 the apparition was deemed authentic and supernatural) and a personal visit to the shrine. The website quoted in the Peshtigo fire explosion is called "Exploring Off the Beaten Path." Lincoln's declaration of chastisement and call for fasting is from the "American Presidency Project," University of California at Santa Barbara. The *Smithsonian* account, by Terry Alford, was in the March 2015 edition of that magazine. Father Penin's book on the Wisconsin disaster was *The Great Peshtigo Fire: An Eyewitness Account.* For spiritists in Chicago I used *History of Chicago,* by Alfred Theodore Andreas (A. T. Andreas, 1884, pp. 353-354). The quote on Freud comes from a Catholic website called "Theotokos" (in the United Kingdom) while much of the information on Pope Leo and the St. Michael Prayer comes from *Pope Leo XIII and the Prayer to St. Michael* by Kevin J. Symonds. The exorcist's quote on the Enlightenment is from in *Mary Crushes the Serpent* by Father Theodore Geiger. Some of the information on Robert Johnson came from Wikipedia. William Shafer's book, cited in the text, was *Rock Music.* Much of the information about rock stars and UFOs comes from the book *Alien Rock: The Rock 'n' Roll Extraterrestrial Connection* by Michael C. Luckman. Father Laurentin's book of messages, co-authored with René LeJeune, was *Messages and Teachings of Mary at Medjugorje: Chronological Corpus of the Messages.* Dr. Howard Storm's book was *My Descent into Death* (currently in the works as a major movie; I did an all-day retreat in New Orleans with Reverend Storm in the late 1990s and draw too from personal conversations.) The chronology on disasters for the Soviet nuclear program were outlined in *The Final Hour*; the website I quote is that of the Eternal Word Television Network. The book by Christian Ravaz is *The Apparitions In Damascus.* The Chimayó quote is from *Roadside America.* For the places in New Mexico see *Shrines and Wonders: the Pilgrim's Guide To Santa Fe and Northern New Mexico* by Marion Amberg. The websites for information on Katka in Litmanova: www.magnificat.sk, www.carpatho-rusyn.org, and www.tccweb.org, along with a personal interview. In general I also draw from travels to more than thirty sites (and alleged sires) of apparitions around the world, and visits since 1990 to more than two hundred U.S. cities. Messages from Medjugorje are from *Words From Heaven* (Saint James Publishing, Birmingham,, Alabama). A number of items and message quotes are also from Peter Heinz's excellent *A Guide to Apparitions of the Blessed Virgin Mary* (Gabriel Press, Sacramento, California).

As always, I'd like to thank my dear wife Lisa for her most capable and dedicated editing (my deep love always!); Judy Berlinski for her most capable work in formatting this book; Peter Massari for the cover (excellent as usual); and Ray Dominey for the great photograph on the front (and special thanks for his generosity in allowing its use). Visit the shrine there for a memorable experience!).